pie favourites

THE AUSTRALIAN Women's Weekly

pie favourites

contents

about pastry	6
chicken	8
seafood	26
meat	50
vegetable and egg	92
sweet pies and tarts	126
glossary	170
conversion chart	173
index	174

about pastry

Pies, both sweet and savoury, have been around for centuries and just keep evolving. It's well-worth mastering the art of making pastry – especially the ever-popular shortcrust pastry. The key to perfect pastry is to allow yourself time and to follow the rules carefully. Don't panic if it doesn't work the first time, it takes practice and experience to get it just right.

Kneading and Rolling

When kneading and rolling pastry, the golden rules are to handle it quickly, lightly and as little as possible. Heavy handling develops the gluten (protein) in the flour, which can make the pastry tough. Also, if the butter gets too soft, the pastry will be tough and leathery. Roll in short light strokes from the centre out to the edge of the pastry – it will make the edge too thin; never roll over the edge of the pastry. Food processors make good pastry too, providing the ingredients are "pulsed" together using short bursts of power and processed until the ingredients just cling together.

Resting

Always rest pastry, wrapped in plastic, in the refrigerator for up to 30 minutes before rolling and after lining the dish and covering the pie. This allows the gluten (protein) in the flour to relax and prevents the pastry from shrinking too much during baking.

Storing

Pastry can be stored, wrapped securely in plastic wrap or a plastic bag in the refrigerator for one or two days, or frozen for up to two months. To defrost, place overnight in the refrigerator and return to room temperature before rolling.

Blind Baking

This is the process of baking a pastry case before putting in the filling – this ensure the pastry stays crisp. Line the pastry case with a piece of baking paper, or unwaxed greaseproof paper, then fill with dried beans, uncooked rice, lentils or purpose-made ceramic pastry weights to stop the pastry from rising during cooking. Bake in a moderately hot oven for 10 minutes or as the recipe specifies. Remove the paper and beans carefully then bake a further 5 minutes or as the recipe specifies.

Fillo Pastry

Fillo is a particularly tricky pastry to master, unless you're totally committed. Frozen fillo saves time and works just as well. Keep fillo covered while you are working with it as the thin sheets tend to dry out quickly and crumble or break. It's best to cover the pastry completely with a piece of plastic wrap or greaseproof paper, then a well wrung-out damp tea towel.

Frozen Pastry

These days, ready-rolled frozen pastry sheets make the job a lot easier. Frozen sheets of various types of pastry – including sweet and savoury shortcrust – are readily available in supermarkets so it's worthwhile keeping your home freezer fully-stocked.

BASIC SHORTCRUST PASTRY

1½ cups (225g) plain (all-purpose) flour
125g (4 ounces) cold butter, chopped coarsely
1 egg yolk
2 tablespoons iced water, approximately

HAND-MADE METHOD
1 Sift flour into large bowl, rub in butter with fingertips until mixture is crumbly.
2 Add egg yolk and enough of the water to make ingredients just cling together.
3 Knead pastry on floured surface until smooth; press into a disc shape.
4 Enclose pastry in plastic wrap, refrigerate 30 minutes.

note This recipe makes the equivalent of two sheets of store-bought shortcrust pastry.

FOOD PROCESSOR METHOD
1 Sift flour into processor bowl, add butter, pulse, until mixture is crumbly.
2 Add egg yolk and most of the water, pulse until ingredients just cling together – add more water if necessary.
3 Knead pastry on floured surface until smooth; press into a disc shape.
4 Enclose pastry in plastic wrap, refrigerate 30 minutes.

sweet shortcrust pastry variation Sift 2 tablespoons icing (confectioners') sugar with the flour.

chicken

chicken and leek pie

2 cups (500ml) chicken stock
600g (1¼ pounds) chicken breast fillets
1 tablespoon olive oil
40g (1½ ounces) butter
1 large leek (500g), sliced thinly
2 stalks celery (300g), trimmed, chopped finely
1 tablespoon plain (all-purpose) flour
2 teaspoons fresh thyme leaves
½ cup (125ml) milk
1 cup (250ml) pouring cream
2 teaspoons wholegrain mustard
2 sheets shortcrust pastry
1 sheet puff pastry
1 egg yolk

1 Bring stock to the boil in medium saucepan. Add chicken; return to the boil. Reduce heat; simmer, covered, about 10 minutes or until chicken is cooked. Cool chicken in poaching liquid 10 minutes. Remove chicken; reserve ⅓ cup of the poaching liquid (keep remainder for another use, or discard). Chop chicken coarsely.
2 Heat oil and butter in medium saucepan; cook leek and celery, stirring, until leek softens. Add flour and thyme; cook, stirring, 1 minute. Gradually stir in reserved poaching liquid, milk and cream; cook, stirring, until mixture boils and thickens. Stir in chicken and mustard. Cool 10 minutes.
3 Preheat oven to 200°C/400°F. Oil 1.5-litre (6-cup) ovenproof dish.
4 Line base and side of dish with shortcrust pastry, trim to fit; prick all over with fork. Bake 10 minutes. Cool 5 minutes.
5 Spoon chicken mixture into pastry case; place puff pastry over filling, trim to fit dish. Brush pastry with egg yolk; cut two small slits, or one circle, in top of pastry.
6 Bake pie about 20 minutes or until browned lightly.

prep + cook time 1 hour 35 minutes **serves** 6
nutritional count per serving 52g total fat (26g saturated fat); 3181kJ (761 cal); 41.3g carbohydrate; 31.8g protein; 3.5g fibre

chicken pie with parsnip mash

2 teaspoons vegetable oil
1 medium brown onion (150g), chopped finely
750g (1½ pounds) minced (ground) chicken
1 medium carrot (120g), chopped finely
2 stalks celery (300g), trimmed, chopped finely
¼ cup (35g) plain (all-purpose) flour
1 cup (250ml) chicken stock
2 tablespoons worcestershire sauce
155g (5 ounces) button mushrooms, quartered
¾ cup (120g) frozen peas
parsnip mash
4 medium potatoes (800g), chopped coarsely
2 medium parsnips (500g), chopped coarsely
¼ cup (60ml) milk
45g (1½ ounces) butter
½ cup (40g) finely grated parmesan cheese

1 Make parsnip mash.
2 Preheat oven to 200°C/400°F.
3 Meanwhile, heat oil in large saucepan; cook onion and chicken, stirring, until browned. Add carrot and celery; cook, stirring, until soft. Stir in flour then gradually add stock, sauce and mushrooms; cook, stirring, until mixture boils and thickens. Stir in peas; season to taste.
4 Spoon mixture into 2.5-litre (10-cup) ovenproof dish; top with parsnip mash.
5 Bake pie about 30 minutes or until browned and heated through.

parsnip mash Boil, steam or microwave potatoes and parsnip, separately, until tender; drain. Mash potato and parsnip with milk and butter in bowl until smooth. Stir in cheese; season to taste.

prep + cook time 1 hour 10 minutes **serves** 6
nutritional count per serving 31.7g total fat (13.5g saturated fat); 2976kJ (712 cal); 49g carbohydrate; 52.4g protein; 10.6g fibre

chicken and fennel pies

1 tablespoon olive oil
1 medium brown onion (150g), sliced thinly
1 baby fennel bulb (130g), sliced thinly
500g (1 pound) minced (ground) chicken
¼ cup (35g) plain (all-purpose) flour
1½ cups (375ml) chicken stock
1 medium potato (200g), cut into 1cm (½-inch) cubes
2 tablespoons finely chopped fresh flat-leaf parsley
2 sheets shortcrust pastry, halved diagonally
1 sheet puff pastry, quartered
1 egg yolk
½ teaspoon fennel seeds

1 Heat oil in large saucepan; cook onion and fennel, stirring, until soft. Add chicken; cook, stirring, until chicken is cooked through. Add flour; stir until bubbling. Gradually stir in stock. Add potato; cook, stirring occasionally, about 10 minutes or until potato is tender and mixture thickens. Remove from heat. Stir in parsley; season to taste. Cool 30 minutes.
2 Preheat oven to 200°C/400°F.
3 Grease four 1-cup (250ml) pie dishes. Line base and side of each dish with shortcrust pastry; trim edges. Divide chicken mixture into pastry cases; top with puff pastry, trim edges. Brush with egg yolk and sprinkle with seeds. Place dishes on oven tray.
4 Bake pies about 45 minutes or until browned. Stand 10 minutes before serving.

prep + cook time 1 hour 20 minutes (+ cooling)
makes 4
nutritional count per pie 28.1g total fat (10.3g saturated fat); 2161kJ (517 cal); 33.6g carbohydrate; 31.2g protein; 2.9g fibre

thai chicken curry pies

2 tablespoons peanut oil
1 medium brown onion (150g), sliced thinly
1 clove garlic, crushed
10cm (4-inch) stick fresh lemon grass (20g), chopped finely
2cm (¾-inch) piece fresh ginger (10g), grated
600g (1¼ pounds) chicken thigh fillets, cut into 2.5cm (1-inch) pieces
1 teaspoon ground cumin
½ teaspoon ground turmeric
⅔ cup (160ml) coconut milk
1 tablespoon cornflour (cornstarch)
¼ cup (60ml) chicken stock
1 tablespoon fish sauce
1 fresh kaffir lime leaf, shredded finely
1 fresh long red chilli, sliced thinly
¼ cup coarsely chopped fresh coriander (cilantro)
2 sheets shortcrust pastry
1 egg, beaten lightly
2 sheets puff pastry

1 Heat oil in large saucepan; cook onion, garlic, lemon grass and ginger, stirring, until onion softens. Add chicken; cook, stirring, until browned. Add spices; cook, stirring, until fragrant. Add coconut milk; bring to the boil. Reduce heat; simmer, uncovered, 10 minutes. Add blended cornflour and stock; cook, stirring, until mixture boils and thickens; cool. Stir in sauce, lime leaf, chilli and coriander.
2 Preheat oven to 200°C/400°F. Oil 6-hole (¾-cup/180ml) texas muffin pan.
3 Using 12cm (5-inch) cutter, cut six rounds from shortcrust pastry; press rounds into pan holes. Brush pastry edges with a little of the egg. Divide chicken mixture among pastry cases.
4 Using 9cm (3½-inch) cutter, cut six rounds from puff pastry; top chicken mixture with puff pastry rounds. Press edges firmly to seal. Brush tops with remaining egg. Cut a small slit in top of each pie.
5 Bake pies about 25 minutes. Stand in pan 5 minutes before serving, top-side up.

prep + cook time 1 hour 15 minutes **serves** 6
nutritional count per pie 45.4g total fat (21.4g saturated fat); 3005kJ (719 cal); 49.6g carbohydrate; 27.7g protein; 2.3g fibre

chicken

chicken and vegetable pie

60g (2 ounces) butter
1 medium leek (350g), sliced thinly
⅓ cup (50g) plain (all-purpose) flour
¾ cup (180ml) milk
1 cup (250ml) chicken stock
4 cups (480g) shredded cooked chicken
2½ cups (350g) frozen peas, corn and capsicum (bell pepper) mix
¼ cup coarsely chopped fresh flat-leaf parsley
4 sheets fillo pastry
cooking-oil spray

1 Preheat oven to 220°C/425°F.
2 Melt butter in large saucepan; cook leek, stirring, until softened. Add flour; cook, stirring, until mixture bubbles and thickens. Gradually stir in milk and stock; cook, stirring, until mixture boils and thickens. Add chicken, vegetables and parsley; stir until heated through.
3 Spoon chicken filling into a shallow 1.5-litre (6-cup) ovenproof dish. Place one sheet of pastry over filling; spray with cooking-oil spray. Repeat process with remaining pastry sheets, overlapping pastry around dish. Roll and fold pastry around edge of dish. Spray top of pastry with cooking-oil spray.
4 Bake pie about 10 minutes or until browned lightly.

prep + cook time 35 minutes **serves** 4
nutritional count per serving 26g total fat (12.2g saturated fat); 2203kJ (527 cal); 30.2g carbohydrate; 39.8g protein; 6.6g fibre

serving suggestion Serve with a garden salad.

chicken

chicken and olive empanadas

2 cups (500ml) chicken stock
1 bay leaf
3 chicken thigh fillets (330g)
1 tablespoon olive oil
1 small brown onion (80g), chopped finely
2 cloves garlic, crushed
2 teaspoons ground cumin
½ cup (80g) sultanas
⅓ cup (40g) seeded green olives, chopped coarsely
5 sheets shortcrust pastry
1 egg, beaten lightly

1 Bring stock and bay leaf to the boil in medium saucepan. Add chicken; return to the boil. Reduce heat; simmer, covered, about 10 minutes or until chicken is cooked. Cool chicken in poaching liquid 10 minutes. Remove chicken; reserve 1 cup of poaching liquid. Shred chicken finely.
2 Meanwhile, heat oil in large frying pan; cook onion, stirring, until softened. Add garlic and cumin; cook, stirring, until fragrant. Add sultanas and reserved poaching liquid; bring to the boil. Reduce heat; simmer, uncovered, about 15 minutes or until liquid is almost evaporated. Stir in chicken and olives.
3 Preheat oven to 200°C/400°F. Oil two oven trays.
4 Using 9cm (3½-inch) cutter, cut 24 rounds from pastry. Place 1 level tablespoon of the filling in centre of each round; fold in half to enclose filling, pinching edges to seal. Press around edges of empanadas with a fork.
5 Place empanadas on oven trays; brush tops with egg. Bake about 25 minutes or until browned lightly.

prep + cook time 1 hour 10 minutes **makes** 24
nutritional count per empanada 11.1g total fat (5.3g saturated fat); 794kJ (190 cal); 17.4g carbohydrate; 5.4g protein; 0.9g fibre

chicken, spinach and cheese gözleme

2 cups (300g) plain (all-purpose) flour
½ teaspoon salt
¾ cup (180ml) warm water
2 tablespoons olive oil
1 medium brown onion (150g), chopped finely
2 cloves garlic, crushed
2 teaspoons ground cumin
1 teaspoon ground cinnamon
200g (6½ ounces) spinach, trimmed
1 cup (160g) finely shredded cooked chicken
100g (3 ounces) fetta cheese, crumbled
½ teaspoon finely grated lemon rind
2 tablespoons lemon juice

1 Combine flour and salt in medium bowl. Gradually stir in the water; mix to a soft dough. Knead dough on floured surface about 5 minutes or until smooth and elastic. Return to bowl; cover, while preparing filling.
2 Heat half the oil in medium frying pan; cook onion and garlic, stirring, until onion softens. Add spices; cook, stirring, until fragrant. Transfer mixture to medium heatproof bowl; cool.
3 Meanwhile, boil, steam or microwave spinach until wilted; rinse under cold water. Drain; squeeze out excess water. Shred spinach finely. Stir spinach, chicken, cheese, rind and juice into onion mixture; season to taste.
4 Divide dough in half; roll each piece on floured surface into 25cm x 35cm (10-inch x 14-inch) rectangle. Divide spinach filling across centre of each rectangle. Fold top and bottom edges of dough over filling; tuck in ends to enclose.
5 Cook gözleme, both sides, on heated oiled grill plate (or grill or barbecue), over low heat, brushing with remaining oil until browned lightly and heated through. Stand 5 minutes before cutting each gözleme into 8 slices; serve with lemon wedges.

prep + cook time 1 hour 30 minutes **makes** 16
nutritional count per slice 4.7g total fat (1.5g saturated fat); 531kJ (127 cal); 14.2g carbohydrate; 6.1g protein; 1.2g fibre

chicken, raisin and pine nut empanadas

1 litre (4 cups) water
1 chicken breast fillet (200g)
2 teaspoons olive oil
1 small brown onion (80g), chopped finely
2 cloves garlic, crushed
200g (6½ ounces) canned crushed tomatoes
1 bay leaf
¼ teaspoon dried chilli flakes
2 tablespoons raisins, chopped coarsely
2 tablespoons pine nuts, roasted
½ teaspoon ground cinnamon
2 tablespoons finely chopped fresh flat-leaf parsley
1 egg, beaten lightly
pastry
1⅔ cups (250g) plain (all-purpose) flour
150g (4½ ounces) cold butter, chopped
1 egg
1 tablespoon cold water

1 Bring the water to the boil in medium saucepan. Add chicken; return to the boil. Reduce heat; simmer, covered, about 10 minutes or until chicken is cooked. Cool chicken in poaching liquid 10 minutes. Remove chicken; discard poaching liquid. Shred chicken finely.
2 Heat oil in medium frying pan; cook onion and garlic, stirring, until onion softens. Add undrained tomatoes, bay leaf and chilli; cook, stirring occasionally, about 5 minutes or until mixture thickens.
3 Add chicken, raisins, nuts and cinnamon to tomato mixture; stir until heated through. Discard bay leaf; stir in parsley. Cool mixture, covered, in the refrigerator.
4 Meanwhile, make pastry.
5 Preheat oven to 200°C/400°F. Line oven trays with baking paper.
6 Divide pastry in half. Roll one half between sheets of baking paper until 3mm (⅛-inch) thick. Using 10cm (4-inch) cutter, cut 10 rounds from pastry.
7 Place 1 level tablespoon of chicken mixture in centre of each round; fold in half to enclose filling, pinching edges to seal. Press around edges of empanadas with a fork. Repeat with remaining pastry half and chicken mixture to make a total of 20 empanadas, re-rolling pastry scraps as required.
8 Place empanadas on oven trays; brush with egg. Bake about 20 minutes or until browned lightly.

pastry Process flour and butter until crumbly. Add egg and the water and process until ingredients come together. Knead dough on floured surface until smooth, enclose with plastic wrap; refrigerate 30 minutes.

prep + cook time 2 hours (+ refrigeration) **makes** 20
nutritional count per empanada 8.9g total fat (4.5g saturated fat); 594kJ (142 cal); 10.6g carbohydrate; 4.6g protein; 0.9g fibre

chicken

chicken, leek and mushroom pies

1 tablespoon vegetable oil
1 medium leek (350g), sliced thinly
2 rindless bacon slices (130g), sliced thinly
200g (6½ ounces) mushrooms, halved
1 tablespoon plain (all-purpose) flour
1 cup (250ml) chicken stock
⅓ cup (80ml) pouring cream
1 tablespoon dijon mustard
3 cups (480g) coarsely chopped barbecued chicken
1 sheet puff pastry, quartered
1 egg, beaten lightly

1 Preheat oven to 200°C/400°F.
2 Heat oil in medium saucepan; cook leek, bacon and mushrooms, stirring, until leek softens. Stir in flour; cook, stirring, until mixture thickens and bubbles. Gradually add stock; cook, stirring, until mixture boils and thickens. Stir in cream, mustard and chicken.
3 Divide chicken mixture into four 1-cup (250ml) ovenproof dishes; top each with a pastry quarter, brush with egg.
4 Bake pies about 20 minutes or until browned.

prep + cook time 1 hour **makes** 4
nutritional count per pie 38.3g total fat (11.6g saturated fat); 2625kJ (628 cal); 21.1g carbohydrate; 48g protein; 4.9g fibre

chicken

chicken and vegetable pasties

2 teaspoons vegetable oil
1 medium brown onion (150g), chopped finely
2 cloves garlic, crushed
1½ cups (240g) coarsely chopped cooked chicken
2 cups (240g) frozen pea, corn and carrot mixture
2 teaspoons dijon mustard
½ cup (120g) sour cream
¼ cup (30g) coarsely grated cheddar cheese
4 sheets puff pastry
1 egg, beaten lightly

1 Preheat oven to 220°C/425°F. Oil oven tray.
2 Heat oil in large frying pan; cook onion and garlic, stirring, until onion softens. Add chicken, frozen vegetables, mustard, sour cream and cheese; stir until heated through.
3 Cut one 22cm (9-inch) round from each pastry sheet. Spoon a quarter of the filling in centre of each round. Brush edge of pastry with a little of the egg; fold pastry over to enclose filling, pinching edges together to seal. Place pasties on tray; brush with remaining egg.
4 Bake pasties about 30 minutes or until browned.

prep + cook time 45 minutes **makes** 4
nutritional count per pasty 62.5g total fat (32.3g saturated fat); 4063kJ (972 cal); 69.1g carbohydrate; 31.4g protein; 5.9g fibre

mini chicken, celery and thyme pies

1 cup (250ml) chicken stock
1 chicken breast fillet (170g)
1 tablespoon olive oil
1 small leek (200g), sliced thinly
½ stalk celery (75g), trimmed, chopped finely
2 teaspoons plain (all-purpose) flour
2 teaspoons fresh thyme leaves
¼ cup (60ml) pouring cream
1 teaspoon wholegrain mustard
2 sheets shortcrust pastry
1 sheet puff pastry
1 egg yolk
2 teaspoons sesame seeds

1 Bring stock to the boil in small saucepan. Add chicken; return to the boil. Reduce heat; simmer, covered, about 10 minutes or until chicken is just cooked. Cool chicken in poaching liquid 10 minutes. Remove chicken; reserve ¼ cup of the poaching liquid (keep remainder for another use, or discard). Chop chicken finely.
2 Heat oil in medium saucepan; cook leek and celery, stirring, until leek softens. Add flour and half the thyme; cook, stirring, 1 minute. Gradually stir in reserved poaching liquid and cream; cook, stirring, until mixture boils and thickens. Stir in chicken and mustard. Cool 10 minutes.
3 Preheat oven to 220°C/425°F. Oil eight holes in each of two 12-hole patty pans.
4 Using 7.5cm (3-inch) cutter, cut 16 rounds from shortcrust pastry; press one round into each pan hole. Spoon 1 tablespoon of the chicken mixture into each pastry case.
5 Using 6cm (2½-inch) cutter, cut 16 rounds from puff pastry; top with puff pastry rounds. Brush with yolk; sprinkle with sesame seeds and remaining thyme. Cut two small slits in top of each pie.
6 Bake pies 20 minutes or until browned lightly.

prep + cook time 1 hour 20 minutes **makes** 16
nutritional count per pie 11.5g total fat (5.6g saturated fat); 740kJ (177 cal); 13.5g carbohydrate; 5.1g protein; 1g fibre

seafood

individual fish pies

1½ cups (375ml) fish stock
1 cup (250ml) water
2 sprigs fresh thyme
1 bay leaf
6 black peppercorns
300g (9½ ounces) salmon fillets, cut into 3cm (1¼-inch) pieces
300g (9½ ounces) smoked cod fillets, cut into 3cm (1¼-inch) pieces
300g (9½ ounces) snapper fillets, cut into 3cm (1¼-inch) pieces
4 large potatoes (1.2kg), chopped coarsely
¼ cup (60ml) milk
60g (2 ounces) butter
¼ cup (35g) plain (all-purpose) flour
2 tablespoons each coarsely chopped fresh chervil and chives

1 Bring stock, the water, thyme, bay leaf and peppercorns to the boil in large saucepan. Add fish, reduce heat; simmer gently, uncovered, about 1 minute or until cooked through. Using a slotted spoon, remove fish from pan; divide fish among four 1½-cup (375ml) ovenproof dishes. Strain liquid through sieve into large heatproof jug. Discard solids; reserve stock.
2 Boil, steam or microwave potato until tender; drain. Push potato through sieve into large bowl; add milk and half the butter, stir until smooth. Cover to keep warm.
3 Preheat oven to 220°C/425°F.
4 Melt remaining butter in medium saucepan, add flour; cook, stirring, until mixture bubbles and thickens slightly. Gradually stir in reserved stock; cook, stirring, until mixture boils and thickens. Stir in herbs; season.
5 Divide sauce among dishes; cover each with potato mixture. Place dishes on oven tray.
6 Bake pies 15 minutes or until browned lightly.

prep + cook time 45 minutes **makes** 4
nutritional count per pie 20.7g total fat (10.5g saturated fat); 2353kJ (563 cal); 39.2g carbohydrate; 52.4g protein; 4.3g fibre

creamy fish pie

10g (½ ounce) butter
2 teaspoons olive oil
1 small brown onion (80g), chopped finely
1 medium carrot (120g), chopped finely
1 stalk celery (150g), chopped finely
1 tablespoon plain (all-purpose) flour
1 cup (250ml) fish stock
500g (1 pound) firm white fish fillets, chopped coarsely
½ cup (125ml) pouring cream
1 tablespoon english mustard
1 cup (120g) frozen peas
½ cup (40g) finely grated parmesan cheese
1 sheet puff pastry
1 egg, beaten lightly

1 Preheat oven to 220°C/425°F.
2 Melt butter with oil in large saucepan; cook onion, carrot and celery, stirring, until carrot softens. Stir in flour; cook, stirring, 2 minutes. Add stock and fish; cook, stirring, until fish is cooked through and mixture boils and thickens. Remove from heat; stir in cream, mustard, peas and cheese.
3 Spoon fish mixture into shallow small 1.5-litre (6-cup) baking dish; place pastry over filling, trim to fit dish. Brush pastry with egg.
4 Bake pie about 20 minutes or until browned.

prep + cook time 1 hour **serves** 4
nutritional count per serving 35.1g total fat (19.1g saturated fat); 2366kJ (566 cal); 23.5g carbohydrate; 37.5g protein; 4.1g fibre

seafood

smoked trout tarts

cooking-oil spray
6 sheets fillo pastry
1 whole smoked trout (240g), skinned, flaked
½ cup (60g) frozen peas
3 eggs
¼ cup (60ml) skim milk
2 tablespoons light sour cream
1 tablespoon coarsely chopped fresh dill

1 Preheat oven to 200°C/400°F. Oil six 10cm (4-inch) round loose-based fluted flan tins.
2 Spray one pastry sheet with cooking-oil spray; fold into a square, then fold into quarters to form a smaller square. Repeat with remaining pastry. Line tins with pastry, ease into base and side.
3 Divide trout and peas among pastry cases.
4 Whisk eggs, milk, cream and dill in medium jug. Pour equal amounts into pastry cases.
5 Bake tarts about 20 minutes or until filling sets. Cool 10 minutes before serving.

prep + cook time 40 minutes **makes** 6
nutritional count per tart 8.7g total fat (3.2g saturated fat); 748kJ (179 cal); 9g carbohydrate; 15.9g protein; 1g fibre

salmon and herb quiche

3 eggs
2 egg whites
1½ cups (375ml) skim milk
½ cup (80g) wholemeal self-raising flour
1 medium brown onion (150g), chopped finely
20g (¾ ounce) butter, melted
2 tablespoons finely chopped fresh flat-leaf parsley
1 tablespoon finely chopped fresh chervil
¼ cup (20g) finely grated parmesan cheese
415g (13 ounces) canned pink salmon, drained, flaked

1 Preheat oven to 180°C/350°F. Oil deep 24cm (9½-inch) round fluted pie dish.
2 Whisk eggs, egg whites, milk, flour, onion, butter, herbs and cheese in large bowl until combined. Add salmon; mix gently. Pour mixture into dish.
3 Bake quiche about 50 minutes. Stand 10 minutes before serving.

prep + cook time 1 hour 10 minutes **serves** 6
nutritional count per serving 11.4g total fat (4.8g saturated fat); 1049kJ (251 cal); 14.1g carbohydrate; 22.3g protein; 1g fibre

Coulibiac is basically a layered fish pie. You can prepare and refrigerate the individual layers the day before cooking, then simply assemble and bake when required. If the ocean trout fillet is too long, tuck the tail under to make the fillet a similar thickness all the way through. This recipe is delicious with a rocket (arugula) salad.

coulibiac

1 tablespoon olive oil
1 small brown onion (80g), chopped finely
1 clove garlic, crushed
1 cup (200g) jasmine rice
1 cup (250ml) fish stock
1 cup (250ml) water
500g (1 pound) spinach, trimmed
200g (6½ ounces) swiss brown mushrooms, sliced thinly
2 shallots (50g), sliced thinly
9 sheets fillo pastry
cooking-oil spray
1 egg white
650g (1¼ pounds) ocean trout fillet, skin removed

1 Heat half the oil in medium saucepan; cook onion and garlic until soft. Stir in rice, then add stock and the water; bring to the boil. Reduce heat; simmer, covered, 15 minutes. Stand, covered, 5 minutes.
2 Boil, steam or microwave spinach until wilted. Drain; squeeze out excess liquid. Chop coarsely.
3 Heat remaining oil in large frying pan; cook mushrooms and shallot until browned lightly.
4 Preheat oven to 220°C/425°F.
5 Spray pastry sheets with cooking-oil spray; fold into 25cm (10-inch) square. Stack three squares, spraying each layer with oil. Place one stack on baking-paper-lined oven tray, brush with a little egg white. Layer rice mixture, mushroom mixture, spinach then trout, leaving 2.5cm (1-inch) border all around. Overlap remaining squares over trout; fold pastry to seal. Cut slits in top; brush with egg white.
6 Bake coulibiac about 30 minutes. Stand 20 minutes before serving.

prep + cook time 1 hour 20 minutes (+ standing)
serves 6
nutritional count per serving 8.4g total fat (1.3g saturated fat); 1492kJ (357 cal); 39.4g carbohydrate; 28.7g protein; 3.1g fibre

seafood

macaroni tuna bake

375g (12 ounces) macaroni pasta
40g (1½ ounces) butter
¼ cup (35g) plain (all-purpose) flour
2½ cups (625ml) skim milk, warmed
425g (12½ ounces) canned tuna in spring water, drained, flaked
1 cup (120g) frozen peas
3 shallots (75g), chopped finely
1 tablespoon finely chopped fresh flat-leaf parsley
2 teaspoons finely grated lemon rind
2 tablespoons lemon juice
1 cup (120g) coarsely grated cheddar cheese
1 cup (70g) stale breadcrumbs
40g (1½ ounces) butter, chopped finely, extra

1 Preheat oven to 180°C/325°F. Grease six 1½-cup (375ml) ovenproof dishes.
2 Cook pasta in large saucepan of boiling water until tender; drain.
3 Meanwhile, melt butter in medium saucepan, add flour; cook, stirring, until mixture bubbles and thickens slightly. Gradually stir in milk; cook, stirring, until sauce boils and thickens. Combine sauce, tuna, peas, shallot, parsley, rind, juice and pasta in large bowl.
4 Spoon mixture evenly into dishes; sprinkle with combined cheese and breadcrumbs, then extra butter.
5 Bake about 30 minutes or until browned lightly. Stand 5 minutes before serving.

prep + cook time 45 minutes **makes** 6
nutritional count per bake 20.6g total fat (12.4g saturated fat); 2424kJ (580 cal); 62g carbohydrate; 33.9g protein; 4.1g fibre

prawn fillo tarts

6 sheets fillo pastry
cooking-oil spray
¼ cup (60g) light sour cream
1 tablespoon lemon juice
1 tablespoon water
1 tablespoon mayonnaise
1 medium avocado (250g), chopped coarsely
150g (4½ ounces) grape tomatoes, quartered
18 cooked medium king prawns (shrimp) (810g), shelled, deveined
1 baby cos lettuce (180g), shredded finely

1 Preheat oven to 200°C/400°F. Oil oven tray; line with baking paper.
2 Spray one pastry sheet with oil; fold in half lengthways and in half again so you have a strip of pastry about 7cm (3 inches) wide. Using an 8cm (3¼-inch) cutter, wrap one long edge of pastry around outside of cutter; gather pastry together under cutter to make a tart case. Lower pastry, still wrapped around cutter, onto oven tray; gently ease cutter from pastry leaving a tart case. Repeat with remaining pastry sheets.
3 Bake cases about 10 minutes or until browned lightly. Press centre of cases down with the back of a spoon; lift onto wire rack to cool.
4 Meanwhile, combine sour cream, juice, the water and mayonnaise in medium bowl. Add avocado, tomato and prawns; stir to combine.
5 Divide lettuce among tart cases, top with prawn mixture.

prep + cook time 30 minutes **makes** 6
nutritional count per tart 12.5g total fat (3.1g saturated fat); 928kJ (222 cal); 10g carbohydrate; 16.7g protein; 1.8g fibre

tuna spinach potato pie

50g (1½ ounces) butter
1 medium brown onion (150g), sliced thinly
¼ cup (35g) plain (all-purpose) flour
2 cups (500ml) milk, warmed
150g (4½ ounces) baby spinach leaves
425g (12½ ounces) canned tuna in springwater, drained
2 tablespoons lemon juice

potato and celeriac mash
400g (12½ ounces) potatoes, chopped coarsely
300g (9½ ounces) celeriac (celery root), chopped coarsely
2 tablespoons milk
30g (1 ounce) butter
¼ cup (20g) finely grated parmesan cheese

1 Make potato and celeriac mash.
2 Melt butter in medium saucepan; cook onion, stirring, about 5 minutes or until softened. Add flour; cook, stirring, until mixture thickens and bubbles. Gradually add milk; stir until mixture boils and thickens. Remove from heat; stir in spinach, tuna and juice. Season to taste.
3 Preheat grill (broiler).
4 Spoon tuna mixture into shallow flameproof 1.5-litre (6-cup) dish; top with mash. Place under grill until browned lightly.

potato and celeriac mash Boil, steam or microwave potato and celeriac, separately, until tender; drain. Place potato and celeriac in large bowl; mash with milk and butter until smooth. Stir in cheese; season to taste. Cover to keep warm.

prep + cook time 50 minutes **serves** 4
nutritional count per serving 25.8g total fat (12.1g saturated fat); 2040kJ (488 cal); 29.7g carbohydrate; 31.7g protein; 5.8g fibre

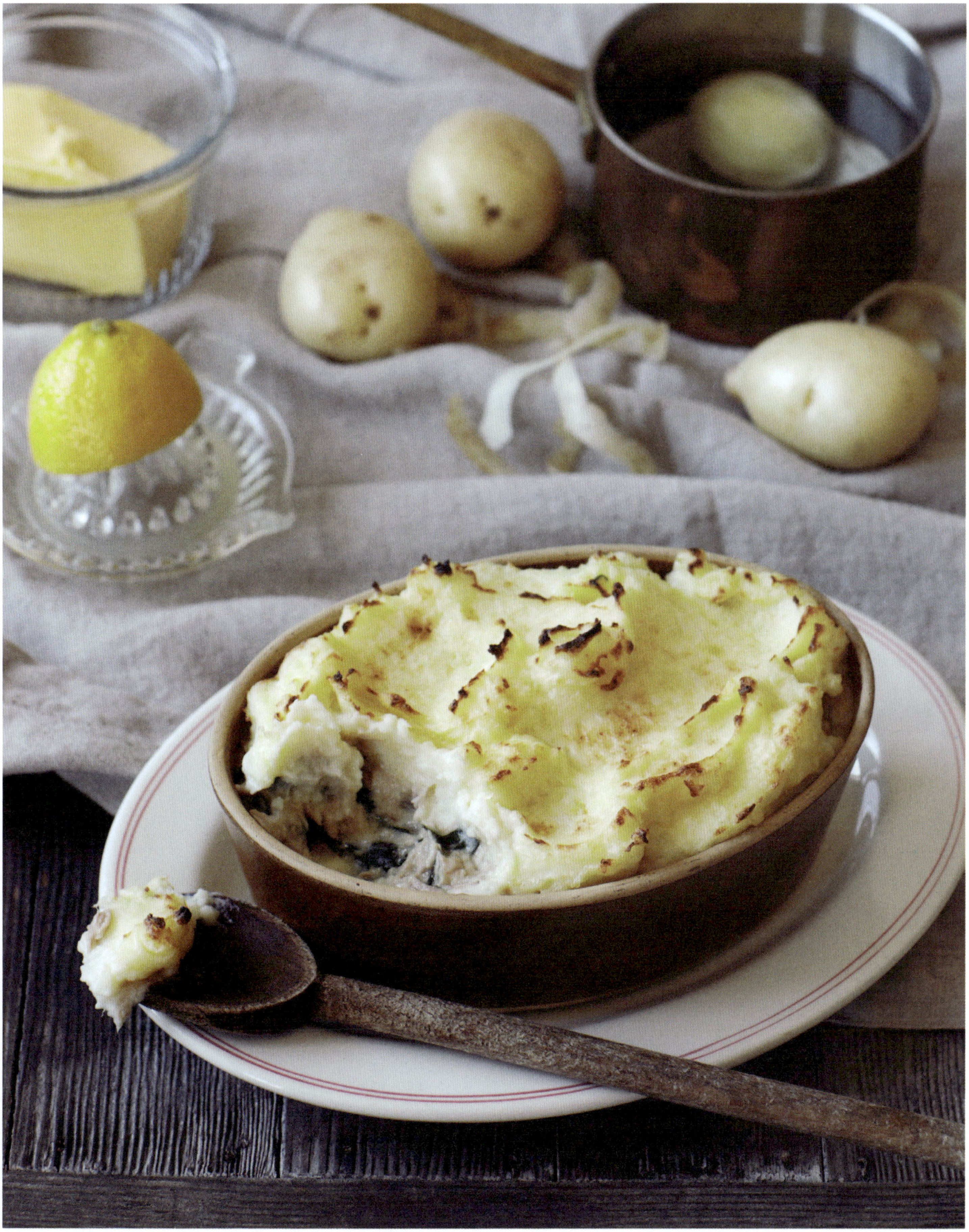

potato and tuna bake

3 medium potatoes (600g), cut into 1cm (½-inch) cubes
20g (¾ ounce) butter
1 tablespoon olive oil
3 shallots (75g), chopped coarsely
425g (12½ ounces) canned tuna in oil, drained
250g (8 ounces) frozen spinach, thawed, drained
½ cup (125ml) milk
1½ cups (180g) coarsely grated cheddar cheese
½ cup drained semi-dried tomatoes, chopped coarsely

1 Preheat oven to 220°C/425°F. Oil four 1-cup (250ml) shallow baking dishes.
2 Boil, steam or microwave potato until almost tender; drain.
3 Heat butter and oil in large frying pan, add potato; cook, stirring occasionally, about 10 minutes or until browned lightly. Add shallot; cook, stirring, until shallot softens. Transfer mixture to medium bowl; coarsely crush potato mixture with fork.
4 Stir tuna, spinach, milk, ½ cup of the cheese and tomatoes into potato mixture. Divide mixture among dishes; sprinkle with remaining cheese.
5 Bake about 10 minutes or until browned lightly.

prep + cook time 40 minutes **makes** 4
nutritional count per bake 38.8g total fat (15.9g saturated fat); 2696kJ (645 cal); 28.6g carbohydrate; 41.5g protein; 8.8g fibre

You could also make this recipe in a 1-litre (4-cup) baking dish.

smoked salmon pie

1kg (2 pounds) pink-eye potatoes, peeled, chopped coarsely
40g (1½ ounces) butter, softened
¼ cup (60g) sour cream
200g (6½ ounces) smoked salmon, chopped coarsely
2 eggs, separated
2 green onions (scallions), chopped finely

1 Preheat oven to 200°C/400°F. Oil deep 22cm (9-inch) round ovenproof dish.
2 Boil, steam or microwave potato until tender; drain. Mash potato in large bowl with butter and sour cream. Stir in salmon, one egg yolk, the egg whites and onion.
3 Spoon mixture into dish; smooth top with spatula, brush with remaining egg yolk.
4 Bake pie about 25 minutes or until heated through and browned lightly.

prep + cook time 45 minutes **serves** 6
nutritional count per serving 12.9g total fat (7g saturated fat); 1120kJ (268 cal); 22.4g carbohydrate; 14.2g protein; 2.7g fibre

You could also use a 22cm (9-inch) round loose-based fluted flan tin for this recipe. You can also use lasoda or sebago potatoes in this recipe.

crab and celeriac remoulade cups

40 wonton wrappers (320g)
cooking-oil spray
¼ cup (60g) sour cream
¼ cup (75g) whole-egg mayonnaise
¼ small celeriac (celery root) (80g), grated coarsely
1 small green apple (130g), grated coarsely
2 tablespoons finely chopped fresh flat-leaf parsley
1 tablespoon wholegrain mustard
1 tablespoon lemon juice
¾ cup (150g) fresh cooked crab meat, shredded finely

1 Preheat oven to 200°C/400°F. Oil two 12-hole (1 tablespoon/20ml) mini muffin pans.
2 Using 7.5cm (3-inch) cutter, cut one round from 24 wonton wrappers. Push rounds carefully into pan holes; spray each lightly with oil. Bake about 7 minutes or until wonton cases are golden brown. Stand in pans 2 minutes; turn onto wire racks to cool. Repeat process with remaining wonton wrappers.
3 Combine sour cream, mayonnaise, celeriac, apple, parsley, mustard and juice in medium bowl; gently fold in crab meat, season to taste.
4 Place one rounded teaspoon of remoulade in each wonton cup.

prep + cook time 50 minutes makes 40
nutritional count per cup 1.7g total fat (0.5g saturated fat); 180kJ (43 cal); 5.3g carbohydrate; 1.5g protein; 0.2g fibre

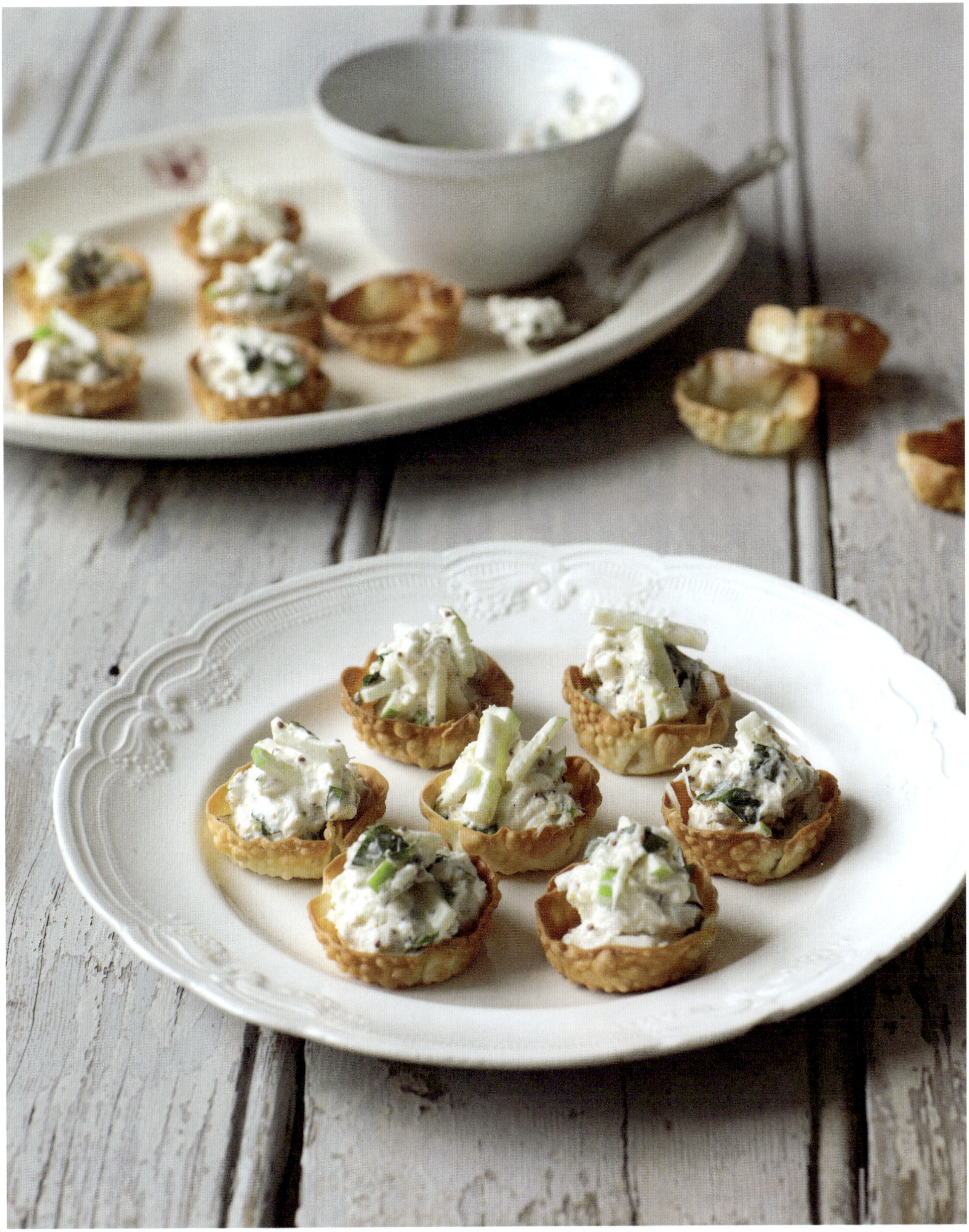

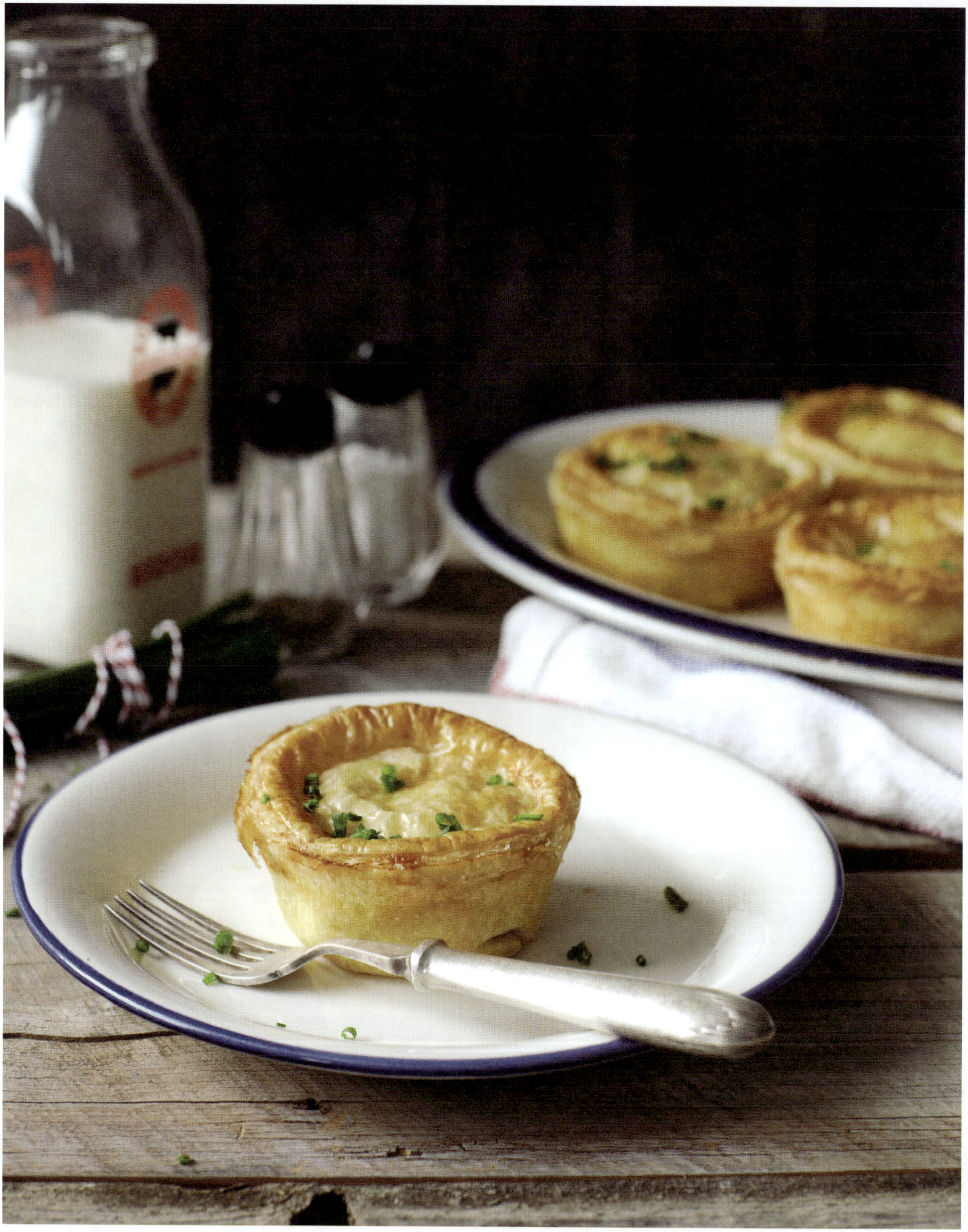

fish chowder pies

40g (1½ ounces) butter
1 medium brown onion (150g), chopped coarsely
1 clove garlic, crushed
3 rindless bacon slices (120g), chopped coarsely
2 tablespoons plain (all-purpose) flour
1 cup (250ml) milk
½ cup (125ml) pouring cream
2 small potatoes (240g), cut into 1cm (½-inch) cubes
600g (1¼ pounds) firm white fish fillets, cut into 2cm (¾-inch) pieces
¼ cup finely chopped fresh chives
2 sheets shortcrust pastry
1 egg, beaten lightly
2 sheets puff pastry

1 Melt butter in large saucepan; cook onion, garlic and bacon, stirring, until onion softens.
2 Add flour; cook, stirring, 1 minute. Gradually stir in combined milk and cream; bring to the boil. Add potato; simmer, covered, stirring occasionally, 8 minutes. Add fish; simmer, uncovered, 2 minutes; cool. Stir in chives.
3 Preheat oven to 200°C/400°F. Oil 6-hole (¾-cup/180ml) texas muffin pan.
4 Using 12cm (5-inch) cutter, cut six rounds from shortcrust pastry; press into pan holes. Brush edges with a little of the egg. Divide fish chowder among pastry cases.
5 Using 9cm (3½-inch) cutter, cut six rounds from puff pastry; top pies with puff pastry rounds. Press edges firmly to seal; brush tops with remaining egg.
6 Bake pies about 25 minutes. Stand pies in pan 5 minutes before serving, top-side up, sprinkled with chopped fresh chives.

prep + cook time 1 hour 10 minutes **makes** 6
nutritional count per pie 49.8g total fat (27.4g saturated fat); 3415kJ (817 cal); 55.9g carbohydrate; 35.5g protein; 2.9g fibre

fish pie with potato and celeriac mash

1 medium celeriac (celery root) (750g), peeled, chopped coarsely
4 medium potatoes (800g), peeled, chopped coarsely
25g (¾ ounce) butter
¼ cup (60ml) milk, warmed
90g (3 ounces) butter, extra
3 small leeks (600g), sliced thickly
¼ cup (35g) plain (all-purpose) flour
1½ cups (375ml) milk, extra
1kg (2 pounds) boneless white fish fillets, chopped coarsely
2 teaspoons lemon juice
¼ cup coarsely chopped fresh chives

1 Boil, steam or microwave celeriac and potato, separately, until soft; drain. Mash celeriac and potato with butter and warmed milk until smooth.
2 Meanwhile, heat 60g (2 ounces) of the extra butter in large saucepan; cook leeks, covered, until soft. Add flour; cook, stirring, about 2 minutes. Gradually stir in extra milk; bring to the boil, stirring constantly.
3 Add fish to pan; simmer, covered, 3 minutes. Gently stir in juice and chives without breaking up fish.
4 Preheat oven to 220°C/425°F.
5 Spoon fish mixture into 2.5-litre (10-cup) ovenproof dish. Melt remaining butter. Top fish mixture with potato and celeriac mash; brush top liberally with melted butter. Place dish on oven tray; bake about 25 minutes or until golden brown.

prep + cook time 1 hour 10 minutes **serves** 6
nutritional count per serving 22.9g total fat (13.4g saturated fat); 2387kJ (518 cal); 30.5g carbohydrate; 43.3g protein; 0.6g fibre

crab, fennel and herb quiche

3 sheets shortcrust pastry
1 tablespoon olive oil
1 medium fennel bulb (300g), sliced thinly
250g (8 ounces) crab meat
2 tablespoons finely chopped fennel fronds
2 tablespoons finely chopped fresh flat-leaf parsley
½ cup (60g) coarsely grated cheddar cheese
1¼ cups (310ml) pouring cream
¼ cup (60ml) milk
3 eggs

1 Preheat oven to 200°C/400°F. Oil 12-hole (⅓-cup/80ml) muffin pan.
2 Using 9cm (3½-inch) cutter, cut 12 rounds from pastry; press rounds into pan holes.
3 Heat oil in large frying pan; cook fennel, stirring, about 5 minutes or until fennel softens and browns slightly. Divide fennel among pastry cases; top with combined crab, fronds, parsley and cheese.
4 Whisk cream, milk and eggs in large jug; pour into pastry cases.
5 Bake quiches about 25 minutes. Stand in pan 5 minutes before serving.

prep + cook time 50 minutes **makes** 12
nutritional count per quiche 27.1g total fat (15g saturated fat); 1509kJ (361 cal); 20.3g carbohydrate; 9g protein; 1.3g fibre

It is fine to use just one 300ml carton of cream for this recipe.

fish pies with cheesy mash

2½ cups (625ml) milk
½ small brown onion (40g)
1 bay leaf
6 black peppercorns
4 x 170g (5½-ounce) trevally fillets, skinned
3 large potatoes (900g), chopped coarsely
600g (1¼ pounds) celeriac (celery root), chopped coarsely
1 egg yolk
½ cup (40g) finely grated parmesan cheese
¾ cup (180ml) pouring cream
60g (2 ounces) butter
¼ cup (35g) plain (all-purpose) flour
2 tablespoons coarsely chopped fresh flat-leaf parsley

1 Bring milk, onion, bay leaf and peppercorns to the boil in large saucepan. Add fish, reduce heat; simmer, covered, about 5 minutes or until cooked through. Remove fish; divide among four 1½-cup (375ml) ovenproof dishes. Strain milk through sieve into medium jug. Discard solids; reserve milk.
2 Boil, steam or microwave potato and celeriac, separately, until tender; drain. Push potato and celeriac through sieve into large bowl; stir in yolk, cheese, ¼ cup of the cream and half the butter until smooth. Cover to keep warm.
3 Preheat grill (broiler).
4 Meanwhile, melt remaining butter in medium saucepan, add flour; cook, stirring, about 3 minutes or until mixture bubbles and thickens slightly. Gradually stir in reserved milk and remaining cream; cook, stirring, until mixture boils and thickens. Stir in parsley.
5 Divide sauce among dishes; cover each with potato mixture. Place dishes on oven tray under grill until tops are browned lightly.

prep + cook time 50 minutes **makes** 4
nutritional count per pie 47.8g total fat (28.9g saturated fat); 3511kJ (840 cal); 45g carbohydrate; 53.8g protein; 9.5g fibre

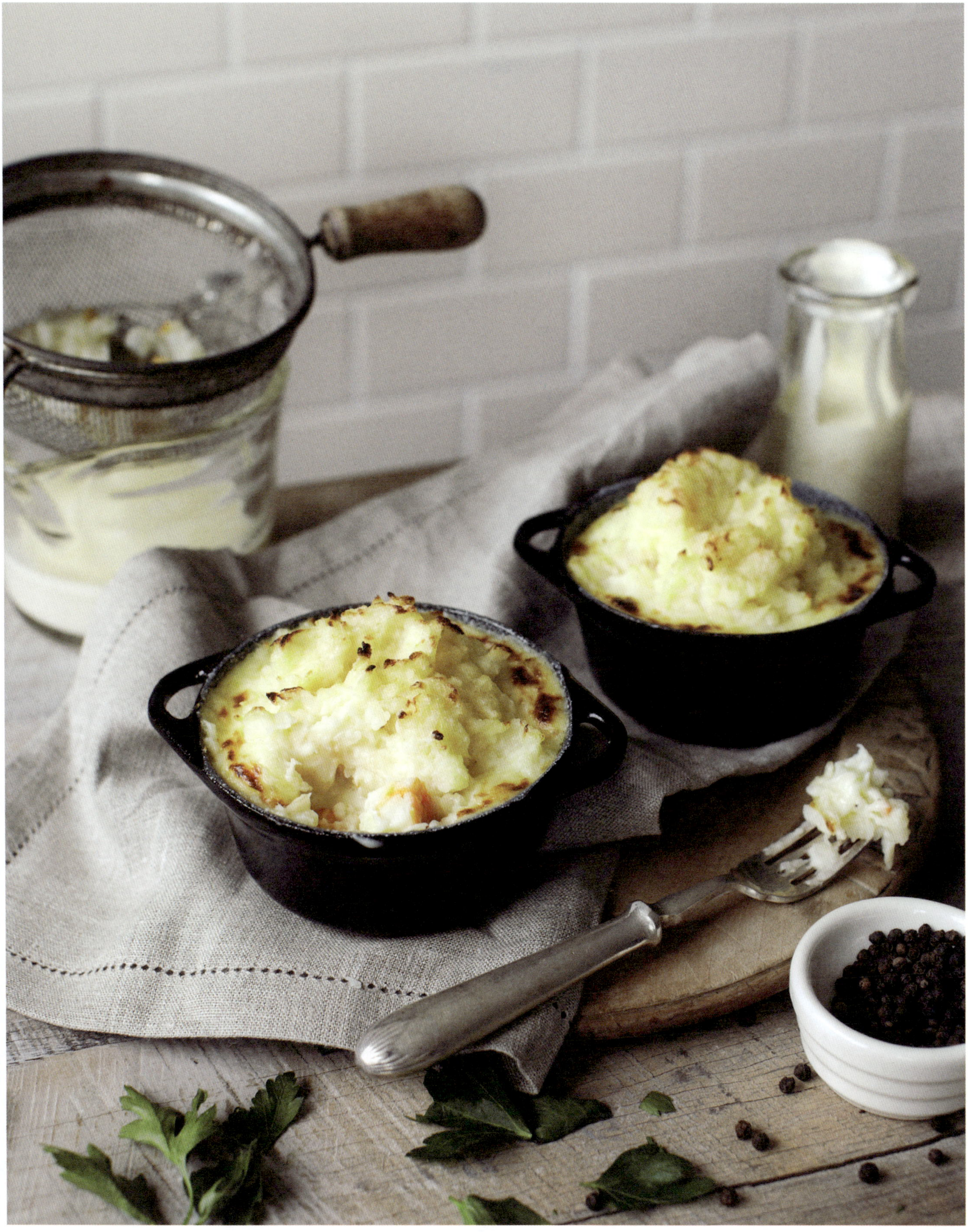

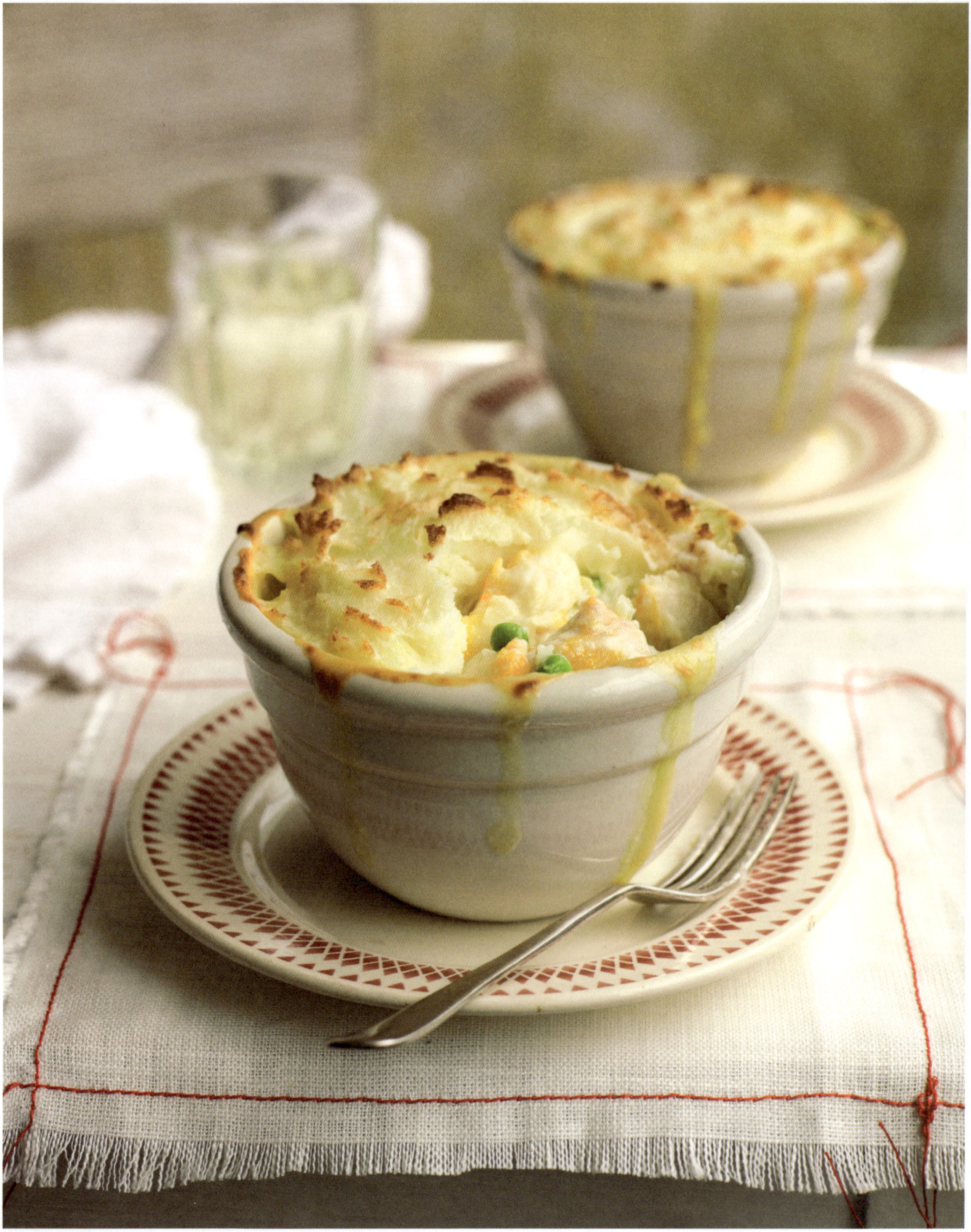

smoked fish pot pies

750g (1½ pounds) smoked cod fillets
2 cups (500ml) milk
1 bay leaf
6 black peppercorns
1kg (2 pounds) coliban potatoes, peeled, chopped coarsely
50g (1½ ounces) butter, softened
20g (¾ ounce) butter, extra
1 large brown onion (200g), chopped finely
1 clove garlic, crushed
¼ cup (35g) plain (all-purpose) flour
2½ cups (625ml) milk, extra
1 cup (120g) frozen peas
1 teaspoon finely grated lemon rind
2 tablespoons lemon juice
2 hard-boiled eggs, quartered

1 Place fish, milk, bay leaf and peppercorns in medium saucepan; bring to the boil. Reduce heat; simmer, uncovered, 10 minutes. Drain; discard liquid and spices. Remove and discard skin from fish; flake flesh into large chunks in medium bowl.
2 Meanwhile, boil, steam or microwave potato until tender; drain. Mash potato with softened butter in large bowl; cover to keep warm.
3 Melt extra butter in medium saucepan; cook onion and garlic, stirring, until onion softens. Add flour; cook, stirring, until mixture thickens and bubbles. Gradually add extra milk; stir until mixture boils and thickens. Add peas, rind and juice; remove from heat. Stir in fish.
4 Preheat grill (broiler).
5 Divide egg, fish mixture and potato mixture among four 2-cup (500ml) flameproof dishes. Place dishes on oven tray under grill until tops are browned lightly.

prep + cook time 1 hour **makes** 4
nutritional count per pie 30.4g total fat (18.1g saturated fat); 3160kJ (756 cal); 58.8g carbohydrate; 57.7g protein; 6.8g fibre

meat

pork pie

375g (12 ounces) minced (ground) pork
315g (10 ounces) lean boneless pork, chopped coarsely
4 rindless bacon slices (260g), chopped finely
2 tablespoons finely chopped fresh sage
1 tablespoon finely chopped fresh flat-leaf parsley
½ teaspoon each ground nutmeg, allspice and black pepper
1 drained anchovy fillet, chopped finely
1 egg, beaten lightly

hot water pastry
¾ cup (180ml) water
90g (3 ounces) unsalted butter, chopped coarsely
2⅔ cups (400g) plain (all-purpose) flour

jelly
½ cup (125ml) chicken stock
½ cup (125ml) water
2½ teaspoons powdered gelatine

1 Make hot water pastry and jelly.
2 Preheat oven to 220°C/425°F. Oil 20cm (8-inch) round springform tin.
3 Combine pork, bacon, herbs, spices and anchovy in large bowl. Season.
4 Roll two-thirds of the pastry on floured surface until large enough to line base and side of tin. Lift pastry into tin; press into base and side, trim edge, make sure there are no cracks in the pastry. Place on oven tray. Fill with pork mixture then pour over ⅓ cup jelly; brush edge of pastry with egg. Roll remaining pastry to cover filling; pinch edge to seal. Cut 2.5cm (1-inch) circle from top of pie, discard circle; brush top with egg.
5 Bake pie 30 minutes. Reduce oven to 200°C/400°F; bake a further 1¼ hours. Cool.
6 Using a funnel, pour remaining slightly warmed jelly slowly into hole in pie. Cover; refrigerate overnight. Cut pie into wedges to serve.

hot water pastry Bring water and butter to the boil in small saucepan, add to processor with the flour; process until ingredients come together. Knead dough on floured surface until smooth, enclose with plastic wrap; refrigerate 45 minutes.

jelly Bring stock and the water to the boil in small saucepan. Remove from heat; stir in gelatine until dissolved.

prep + cook time 2 hours 20 minutes (+ refrigeration)
serves 10
nutritional count per serving 13.7g total fat (7.1g saturated fat); 1450kJ (347 cal); 29.1g carbohydrate; 25.8g protein; 1.5g fibre

Use as much of the jelly mixture as the pie will hold – keep topping it up slowly to allow time for the jelly to settle through the meat mixture.

shepherd's pie

30g (1 ounce) butter
1 medium brown onion (150g), chopped finely
1 medium carrot (120g), chopped finely
½ teaspoon dried mixed herbs
4 cups (750g) finely chopped cooked lamb
¼ cup (70g) tomato paste
¼ cup (60ml) tomato sauce (ketchup)
2 tablespoons worcestershire sauce
2 cups (500ml) beef stock
2 tablespoons plain (all-purpose) flour
⅓ cup (80ml) water

potato topping
5 medium potatoes (1kg), chopped coarsely
60g (2 ounces) butter
¼ cup (60ml) milk

1 Preheat oven to 200°C/400°F. Oil shallow 2.5-litre (10-cup) ovenproof dish.
2 Make potato topping.
3 Meanwhile, heat butter in large saucepan; cook onion and carrot, stirring, until tender. Add mixed herbs and lamb; cook, stirring, 2 minutes. Stir in paste, sauces and stock, then blended flour and water; stir over heat until mixture boils and thickens. Season to taste. Pour mixture into dish.
4 Drop heaped tablespoons of potato topping onto lamb mixture. Bake pie about 20 minutes or until browned and heated through.

potato topping Boil, steam or microwave potato until tender; drain. Mash with butter and milk until smooth. Season to taste.

prep + cook time 1 hour **serves** 4
nutritional count per serving 36.2g total fat (20.2g saturated fat); 2976kJ (712 cal); 44.7g carbohydrate; 48.8g protein; 6g fibre

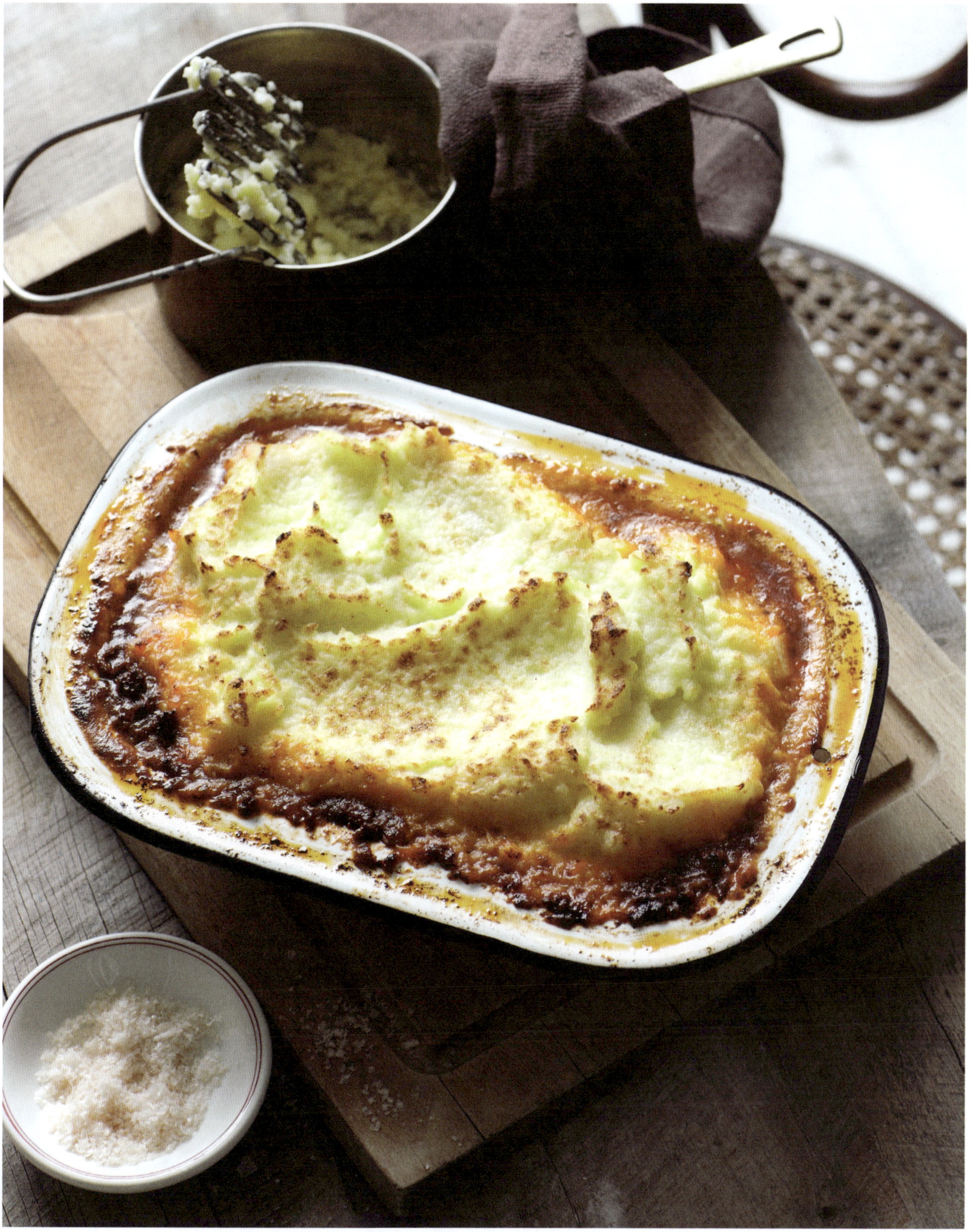

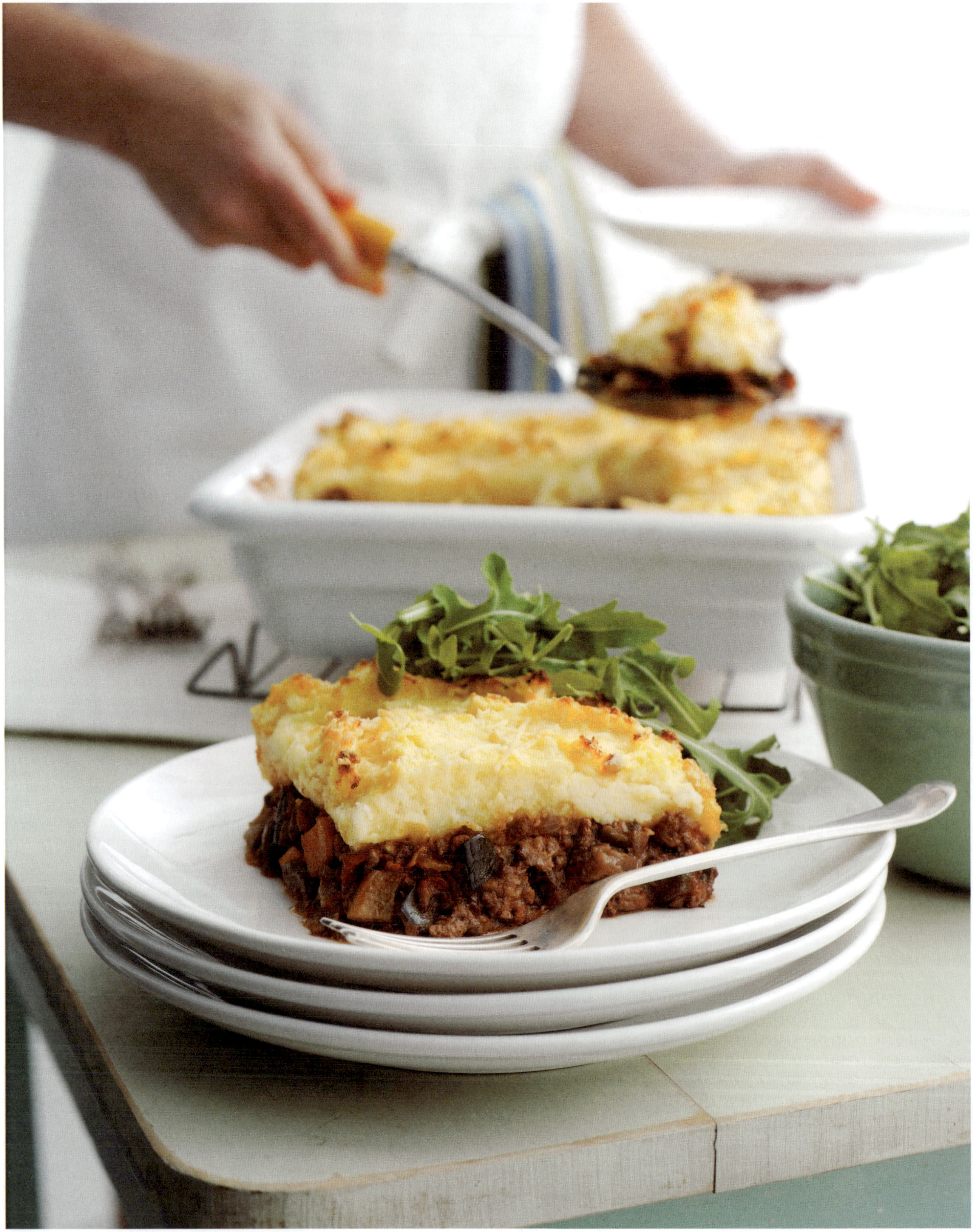

italian cottage pie

1 tablespoon olive oil
1 medium brown onion (150g), chopped finely
2 cloves garlic, crushed
200g (6½ ounces) mushrooms, sliced thinly
1 large carrot (180g), cut into 1cm (½-inch) pieces
1 medium eggplant (300g), cut into 1cm (½-inch) pieces
750g (1½ pounds) minced (ground) lamb
1 tablespoon plain (all-purpose) flour
½ cup (125ml) dry red wine
425g (12½ ounces) canned crushed tomatoes
2 tablespoons tomato paste
1 tablespoon worcestershire sauce
2 tablespoons finely chopped fresh oregano
800g (1½ pounds) potatoes, chopped coarsely
20g (¾ ounce) butter
⅓ cup (80ml) milk
¼ cup (20g) finely grated parmesan cheese
soft polenta
1¼ cups (310ml) chicken stock
¾ cup (180ml) milk
½ cup (85g) polenta
¼ cup (20g) finely grated parmesan cheese

1 Preheat oven to 200°C/400°F. Oil deep 2.5-litre (10-cup) casserole dish.
2 Heat oil in large frying pan; cook onion, garlic, mushrooms, carrot and eggplant, stirring, until onion softens. Add lamb; cook, stirring, until browned. Add flour; cook, stirring, 1 minute. Add wine; bring to the boil, stirring. Stir in undrained tomatoes, paste, sauce and oregano. Reduce heat; simmer, uncovered, about 10 minutes or until mixture thickens slightly.
3 Meanwhile, make soft polenta.
4 Boil, steam or microwave potato until tender; drain. Mash potatoes with butter and milk in large bowl until smooth. Using wooden spoon, gently swirl hot polenta mixture into potato mixture.
5 Spoon lamb mixture into dish; top with potato polenta mixture, sprinkle with cheese.
6 Bake pie about 25 minutes or until cheese browns lightly. Serve with baby rocket (arugula) leaves in balsamic vinaigrette.

soft polenta Bring stock and milk to the boil in large saucepan. Gradually add polenta to stock mixture, stirring constantly. Reduce heat; cook, stirring, about 10 minutes or until polenta thickens. Stir in cheese.

prep + cook time 1 hour 25 minutes **serves** 6
nutritional count per serving 19.4g total fat (8.8g saturated fat); 2040kJ (488 cal); 37.1g carbohydrate; 37.5g protein; 6.7g fibre

liver, mushroom and bacon pies

500g (1 pound) lamb liver
2 tablespoons olive oil
1 clove garlic, crushed
1 medium brown onion (150g), chopped finely
4 rindless bacon slices (240g), chopped coarsely
200g (6½ ounces) button mushrooms, quartered
2 tablespoons plain (all-purpose) flour
½ cup (125ml) dry red wine
1½ cups (375ml) beef stock
1 sheet butter puff pastry
1 egg yolk
1 tablespoon milk

1 Preheat oven to 220°C/425°F. Line oven tray with baking paper.
2 Discard membrane and any fat from liver; chop coarsely. Heat half of the oil in large non-stick frying pan; cook liver, in batches, over high heat until browned and cooked as desired.
3 Heat remaining oil in same pan; cook garlic, onion, bacon and mushrooms, stirring, until onion softens. Add flour; cook, stirring, until mixture thickens and bubbles. Gradually add wine and stock; stir until mixture boils and thickens. Return liver to pan.
4 Using 9.5cm (3½-inch) cutter, cut four rounds from pastry sheet; place on oven tray, brush with combined egg and milk.
5 Bake pastry about 5 minutes or until rounds are browned lightly.
6 Divide liver mixture among four 1¼-cup (310ml) ramekins; top with pastry rounds.

prep + cook time 45 minutes **serves** 4
nutritional count per serving 35.3g total fat (11.8g saturated fat); 2638kJ (631 cal); 25.8g carbohydrate; 46.5g protein; 2.6g fibre

serving suggestion Shoestring chips.

Turn a ramekin upside down on one corner of the pastry sheet and cut around it to make each pie "cap". You'll easily get four from the one sheet, with enough left over to make tiny leaves or stars to decorate each pie's cover, if you desire.

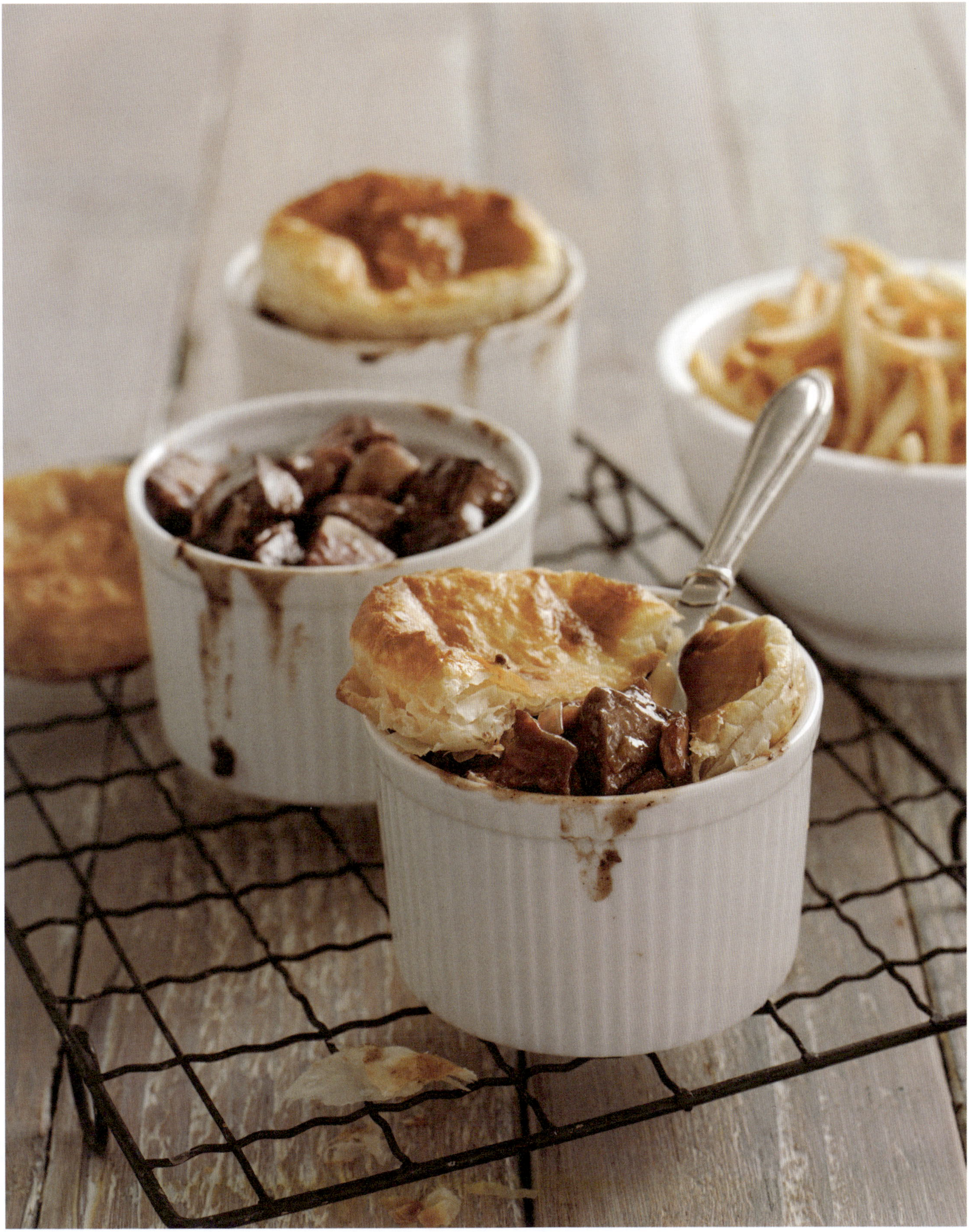

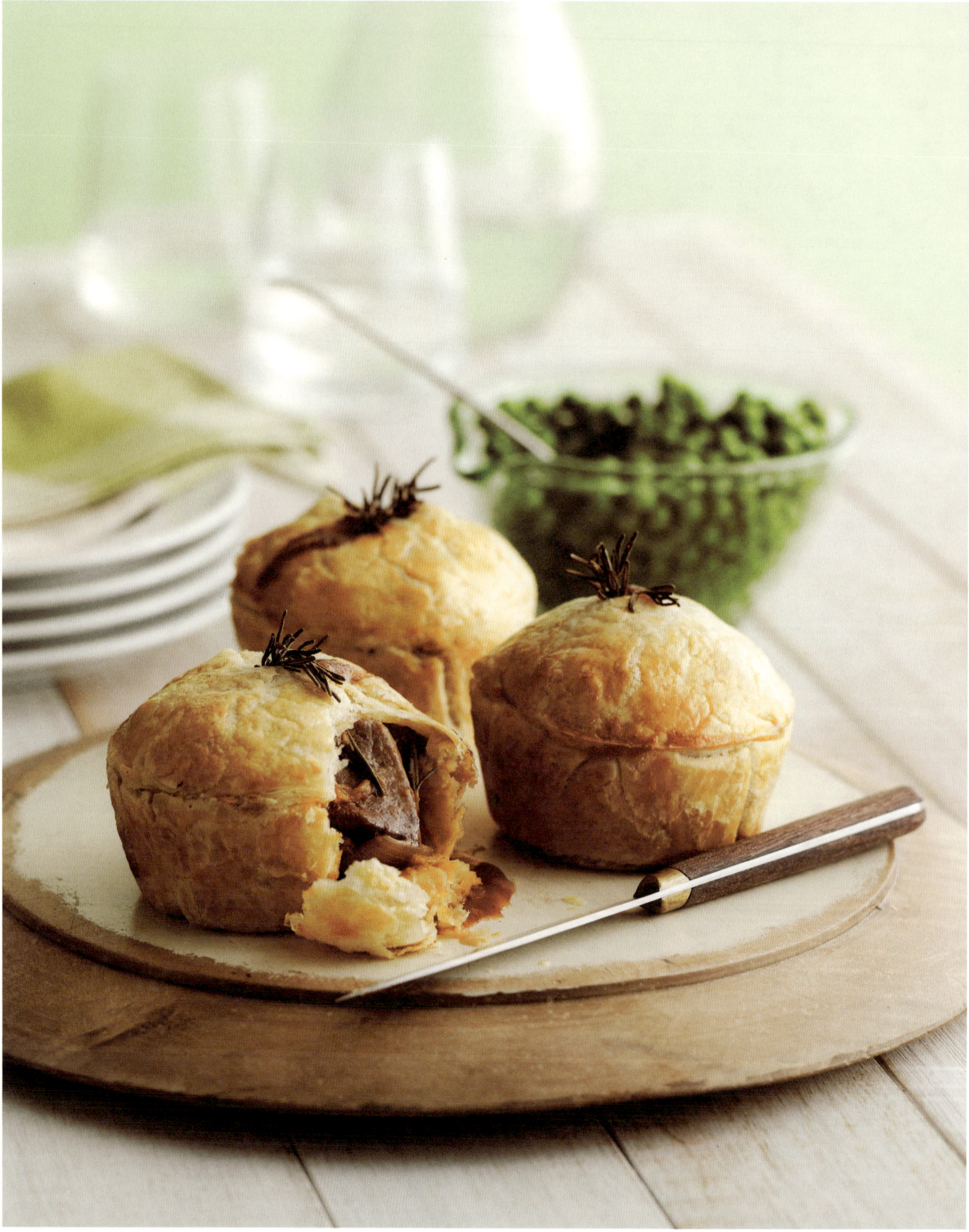

lamb and rosemary pies

2 tablespoons olive oil
400g (12½ ounces) diced lamb
4 baby onions (100g), quartered
1 tablespoon plain (all-purpose) flour
¼ cup (60ml) dry red wine
¾ cup (180ml) beef stock
1 tablespoon tomato paste
1 tablespoon fresh rosemary leaves
2 sheets puff pastry
1 egg, beaten lightly
4 fresh rosemary sprigs
20g (¾ ounce) butter
2½ cups (300g) frozen peas
1 tablespoon lemon juice
½ cup (125ml) water

1 Heat half the oil in large saucepan; cook lamb, in batches, uncovered, until browned all over. Remove from pan.
2 Heat remaining oil in same pan; cook onions, stirring, until soft. Add flour; cook, stirring, until mixture bubbles and thickens. Gradually add wine, stock, paste and rosemary leaves; stir until mixture boils and thickens. Stir in lamb; cool 10 minutes.
3 Preheat oven to 200°C/400°F. Oil four holes of 6-hole (¾-cup/180ml) texas muffin pan.
4 Using 13cm (5¼-inch) cutter, cut two rounds from opposite corners of each pastry sheet. Using 9cm (3½-inch) cutter, cut two rounds from remaining corners of each sheet. Place larger rounds in pan holes to cover bases and sides; trim any excess pastry, prick bases with fork.
5 Spoon lamb mixture into pastry cases; brush around edges with a little egg. Top pies with smaller rounds; gently press around edges to seal. Brush tops with remaining egg; press one rosemary sprig into top of each pie.
6 Bake pies about 15 minutes or until browned lightly. Stand 5 minutes in pan before serving.

prep + cook time 45 minutes **makes** 4
nutritional count per pie 38.3g total fat (7.1g saturated fat); 2537kJ (607 cal); 34.1g carbohydrate; 28.6g protein; 1.7g fibre

chunky beef and vegetable pie

1 tablespoon olive oil
1.5kg (3 pounds) gravy beef, cut into 2cm (¾-inch) pieces
60g (2 ounces) butter
1 medium brown onion (150g), chopped finely
1 clove garlic, crushed
¼ cup (35g) plain (all-purpose) flour
1 cup (250ml) dry white wine
3 cups (750ml) hot beef stock
2 tablespoons tomato paste
2 medium potatoes (400g), cut into 2cm (¾-inch) pieces
1 large carrot (180g), cut into 2cm (¾-inch) pieces
2 stalks celery (300g), trimmed, cut into 2cm (¾-inch) pieces
1 large zucchini (150g), cut into 2cm (¾-inch) pieces
150g (4½ ounces) mushrooms, quartered
1 cup (120g) frozen peas
½ cup finely chopped fresh flat-leaf parsley
1 egg, beaten lightly
pastry
1½ cups (225g) plain (all-purpose) flour
125g (4 ounces) cold butter, chopped coarsely
1 egg yolk
2 tablespoons iced water, approximately

1 Heat oil in large saucepan; cook beef, in batches, until browned all over. Remove from pan.
2 Melt butter in same pan; cook onion and garlic, stirring, until onion softens. Add flour; cook, stirring, until mixture thickens and bubbles. Gradually stir in wine and stock; continue stirring until mixture boils and thickens slightly.
3 Return beef to pan with paste, potato and carrot; bring to the boil. Reduce heat; simmer, covered, 1 hour.
4 Meanwhile, make pastry.
5 Add celery, zucchini and mushrooms to beef mixture; simmer, uncovered, about 30 minutes or until beef is tender. Remove from heat; stir in peas and parsley.
6 Preheat oven to 220°C/425°F.
7 Spoon beef mixture into deep 3-litre (12-cup) ovenproof dish; brush outside edge of dish with a little egg. Roll pastry between sheets of baking paper until large enough to cover dish. Lift pastry over dish, pressing edges with a fork to seal. Trim edge; brush pastry with egg.
8 Bake pie about 20 minutes or until browned.

pastry Process flour and butter until crumbly. Add egg yolk and enough of the water until ingredients come together. Knead dough onto floured surface until smooth, enclose with plastic wrap; refrigerate 30 minutes.

prep + cook time 2 hours 40 minutes **serves** 8
nutritional count per serving 34.7g total fat (18.1g saturated fat); 2788kJ (667 cal); 34.1g carbohydrate; 46.9g protein; 5.6g fibre

To save time, you can join two sheets of frozen shortcrust pastry together to cover the pie; roll edges together with a rolling pin.

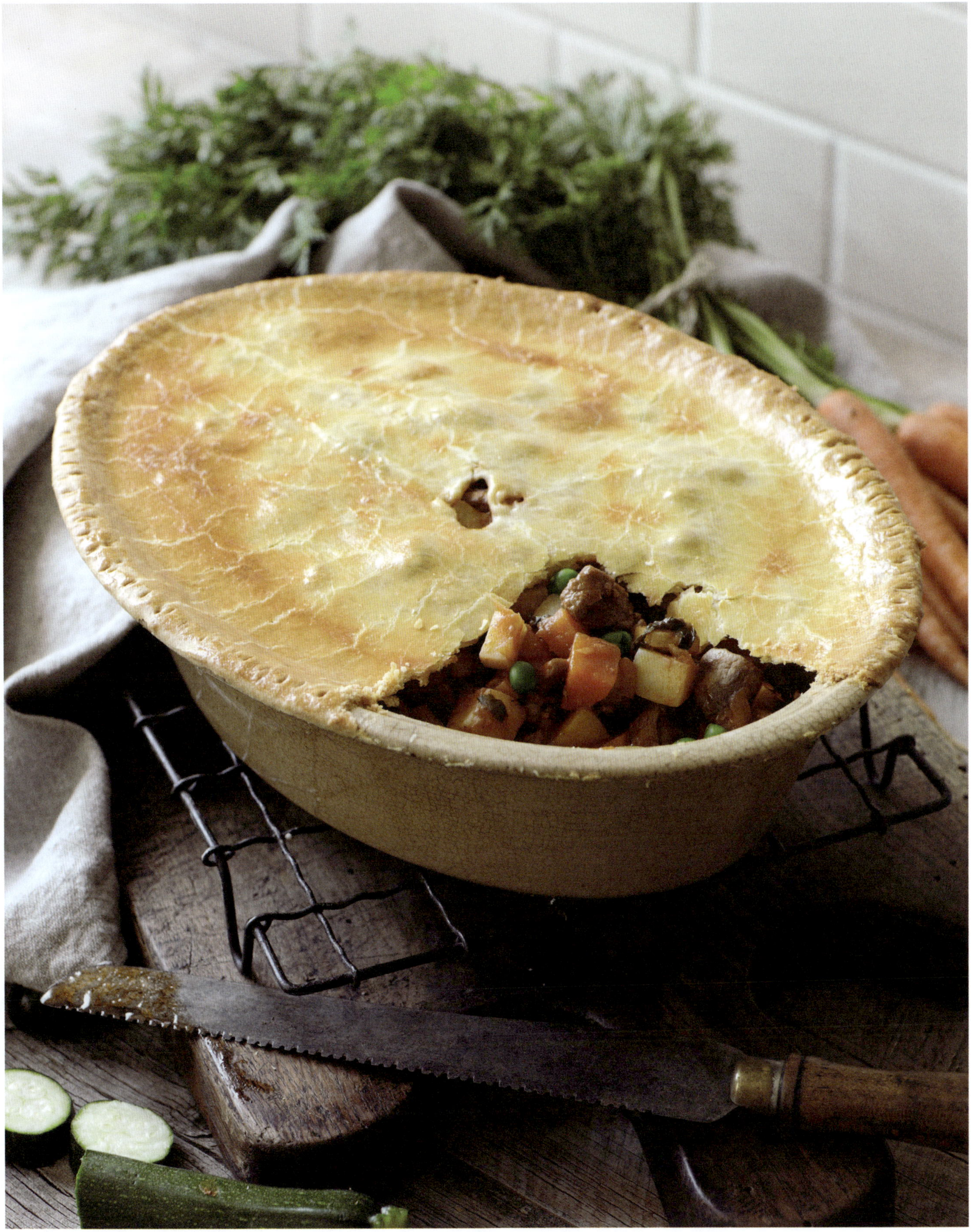

This recipe can be made in a 2-litre (8-cup) ovenproof dish, rather than individual dishes, if you prefer.

veal goulash and potato pies

¼ cup (60ml) olive oil
1kg (2 pounds) boneless veal shoulder,
    cut into 2cm (¾-inch) pieces
1 large brown onion (200g), chopped coarsely
1 large red capsicum (bell pepper) (350g),
    chopped coarsely
1 clove garlic, crushed
1 tablespoon plain (all-purpose) flour
2 teaspoons each hot paprika and sweet paprika
2 teaspoons caraway seeds
2 cups (500ml) beef stock
400g (12½ ounces) canned diced tomatoes
1 tablespoon tomato paste
4 medium potatoes (800g), chopped coarsely
1 cup (120g) coarsely grated cheddar cheese

1 Heat 1 tablespoon of the oil in large saucepan; cook veal, in batches, until browned. Remove from pan.
2 Heat remaining oil in same pan; cook onion, capsicum and garlic, stirring, until onion softens. Add flour, spices and seeds; cook, stirring, 2 minutes.
3 Return veal to pan with stock, undrained tomatoes and paste; bring to the boil. Reduce heat; simmer, covered, 1 hour. Uncover; simmer about 30 minutes or until veal is tender and sauce thickens slightly.
4 Meanwhile, boil, steam or microwave potato until tender; drain. Mash potato in medium bowl until smooth.
5 Preheat grill (broiler). Divide goulash mixture among six oiled 1¼-cup (310ml) ovenproof dishes; top with potato, sprinkle with cheese. Grill until browned.

prep + cook time 2 hours 25 minutes **makes** 6
nutritional count per pie 20.6g total fat (6.8g saturated fat); 2011kJ (481 cal); 23g carbohydrate; 48.8g protein; 3.9g fibre

meat

You can top this tart with finely chopped fresh flat-leaf parsley or mint leaves and serve with a salad of baby spinach and orange segments.

moroccan tart

1 sheet shortcrust pastry
1 tablespoon olive oil
300g (9½ ounces) minced (ground) lamb
1 teaspoon ground coriander
½ teaspoon ground cinnamon
400g (12½ ounces) canned chickpeas (garbanzo beans), rinsed, drained
1 clove garlic, crushed
2 tablespoons lemon juice
1 piece preserved lemon (35g), trimmed, chopped finely
2 tablespoons roasted pine nuts
125g (4 ounces) fetta cheese, crumbled

1 Preheat oven to 200°C/400°F. Oil oven tray.
2 Roll pastry out to 28cm x 30cm (11¼-inch x 12-inch) rectangle; place on oven tray. Fold edges of pastry over to make a 1cm (½-inch) border all the way around. Prick pastry base with fork; bake 10 minutes.
3 Meanwhile, heat half the oil in medium frying pan; cook lamb, coriander and cinnamon, stirring, 5 minutes. Drain away excess oil.
4 Combine chickpeas, garlic, juice and remaining oil in medium bowl. Using fork, coarsely mash mixture; stir in preserved lemon. Spread over pastry base. Top with lamb mixture; sprinkle with nuts and cheese.
5 Bake tart about 10 minutes.

prep + cook time 45 minutes **serves** 4
nutritional count per serving 34.8g total fat (14.3g saturated fat); 2274kJ (544 cal); 27.7g carbohydrate; 28.4g protein; 4.4g fibre

moroccan lamb party pies

1 tablespoon vegetable oil
1 small brown onion (80g), chopped finely
1 clove garlic, crushed
400g (12½ ounces) minced (ground) lamb
2 teaspoons ground cumin
1 cup (280g) undrained canned crushed tomatoes
¼ cup (40g) roasted pine nuts
2 tablespoons finely chopped raisins
2 tablespoons finely chopped fresh coriander (cilantro)
3 sheets shortcrust pastry
1 egg, beaten lightly
2 sheets puff pastry

1 Heat oil in medium frying pan; cook onion and garlic, stirring, until onion softens. Add lamb; cook, stirring, until lamb changes colour. Add cumin; cook, stirring, until fragrant. Add tomatoes; bring to the boil. Reduce heat; simmer, uncovered, about 5 minutes or until thickened slightly. Stir in nuts, raisins and coriander. Cool.
2 Preheat oven to 200°C/400°F. Oil two 12-hole (2-tablespoons/40ml) deep flat-based patty pans.
3 Using 7cm (3-inch) cutter, cut 24 rounds from shortcrust pastry; press into pan holes. Brush edges with a little of the egg. Spoon lamb mixture into pastry cases.
4 Using 6cm (2¼-inch) cutter, cut 24 rounds from puff pastry; top pies with puff pastry lids. Press edges firmly to seal; brush lids with egg. Cut a small slit in top of each pie.
5 Bake pies about 20 minutes or until browned lightly. Stand in pan 5 minutes before serving.

prep + cook time 1 hour **makes** 24
nutritional count per pie 12.2g total fat (5.5g saturated fat); 828kJ (198 cal); 15.6g carbohydrate; 6.2g protein; 0.9g fibre

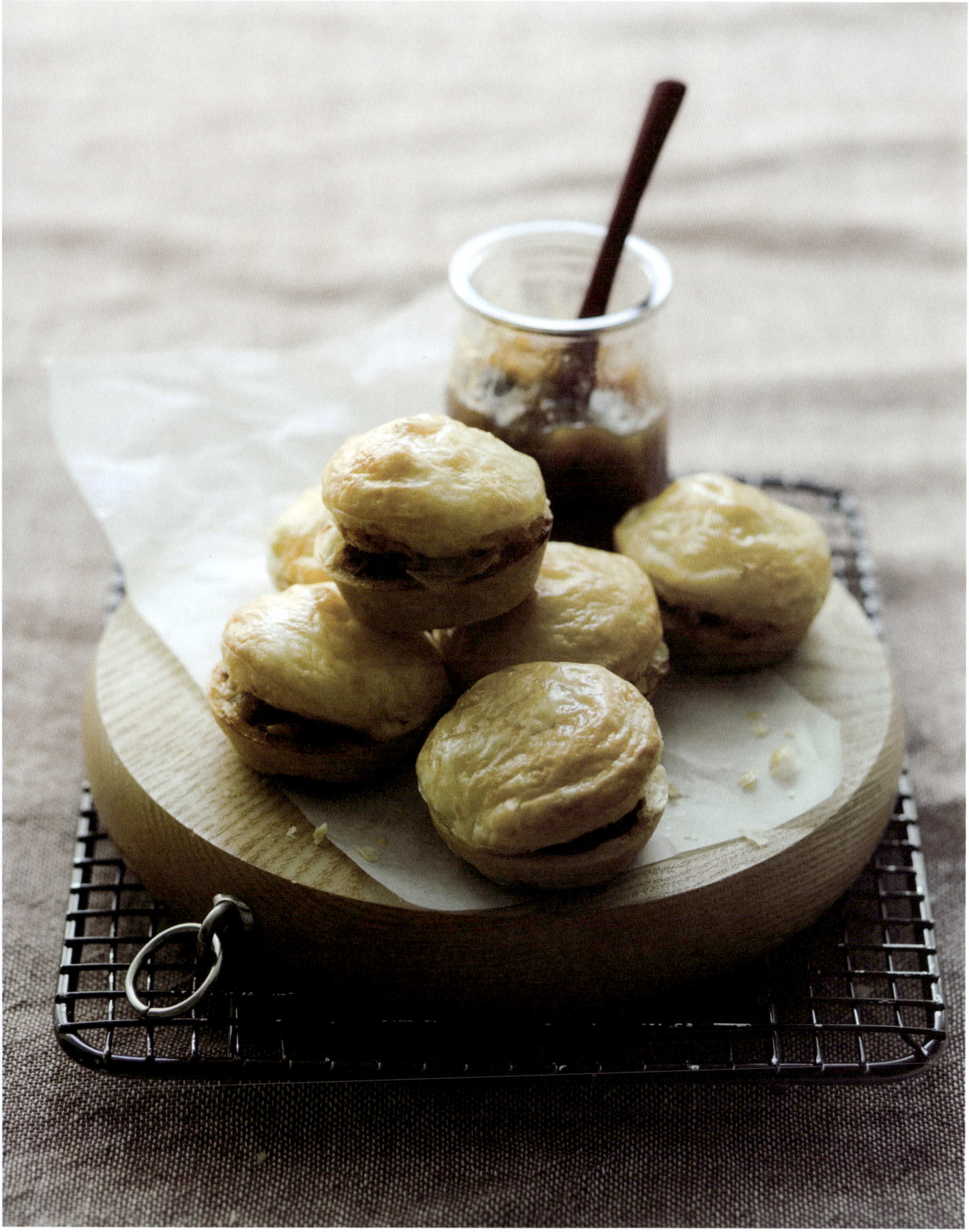

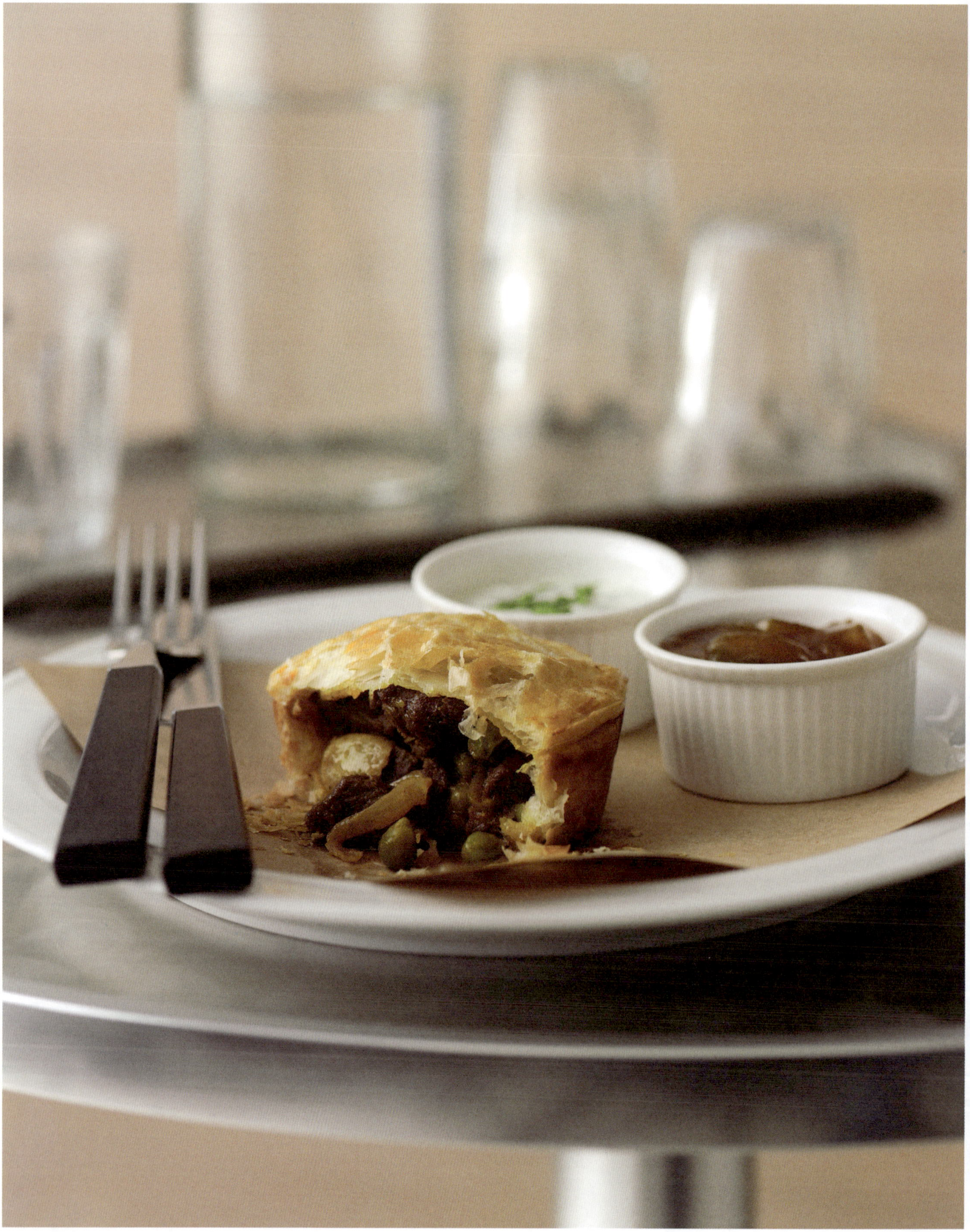

lamb korma pies

20g (¾ ounce) butter
2 tablespoons olive oil
600g (1¼ pounds) lamb fillets, chopped coarsely
1 medium brown onion (150g), sliced thinly
1 clove garlic, crushed
2cm (¾-inch) piece fresh ginger (10g), grated
¼ cup (20g) roasted flaked almonds
⅓ cup (100g) korma paste
⅓ cup (80ml) chicken stock
½ cup (140g) yogurt
1 cup (120g) frozen peas
1 tablespoon lemon juice
⅓ cup firmly packed fresh coriander (cilantro) leaves
6 sheets puff pastry
1 egg, beaten lightly

1 Heat half the butter with half the oil in large saucepan; cook lamb, in batches, until browned. Remove from pan.
2 Heat remaining butter and oil in same pan; cook onion, garlic and ginger, stirring, until onion softens. Add nuts and paste; cook, stirring, until fragrant.
3 Return lamb to pan with stock and yogurt; simmer, uncovered, about 20 minutes or until sauce thickens. Stir in peas, juice and coriander. Cool.
4 Oil two 6-hole (¾-cup/180ml) texas muffin pans. Using 13cm (5¼-inch) cutter, cut two rounds from opposite corners of each pastry sheet. Using 9cm (3½-inch) cutter, cut two rounds from remaining corners of each sheet. Press large rounds in pan holes; prick bases with fork. Refrigerate 30 minutes. Cover small rounds with damp cloth; refrigerate.
5 Preheat oven to 200°C/400°F.
6 Line each pastry case with baking paper; fill with dried beans or rice. Bake 10 minutes. Remove paper and beans; cool pastry cases.
7 Fill pastry cases with lamb mixture. Brush pastry edges with egg; top pies with small pastry rounds, pressing edges to seal. Brush top with remaining egg.
8 Bake pies about 15 minutes. Stand 5 minutes before serving.

prep + cook time 1 hour 25 minutes (+ refrigeration)
makes 12
nutritional count per pie 29.6g total fat (13.1g saturated fat); 1977kJ (473 cal); 32.9g carbohydrate; 17.7g protein; 3g fibre

serving suggestion Mango chutney and raita.

beef pies with polenta tops

500g (1 pound) beef chuck steak, cut into 4cm (1½-inch) pieces
1 tablespoon plain (all-purpose) flour
2 tablespoons olive oil
1 small brown onion (80g), chopped finely
2 cloves garlic, crushed
100g (3 ounces) button mushrooms, halved
½ cup (125ml) dry red wine
½ cup (125ml) beef stock
1 cup (280g) canned crushed tomatoes
1 small red capsicum (bell pepper) (150g), chopped coarsely
¼ cup (40g) seeded black olives
¼ cup (35g) coarsely chopped, drained sun-dried tomatoes in oil
⅓ cup coarsely chopped fresh basil
2 sheets shortcrust pastry
1 large potato (300g), chopped coarsely
20g (¾ ounce) butter
1 tablespoon milk
¼ cup (20g) finely grated parmesan cheese
soft polenta
¼ cup (60ml) chicken stock
¾ cup (180ml) milk
¼ cup (40g) polenta
¼ cup (20g) finely grated parmesan cheese

1 Coat beef in flour; shake off excess. Heat half the oil in large saucepan; cook beef, in batches, until browned. Remove from pan.
2 Heat remaining oil in same pan; cook onion, garlic and mushrooms, stirring, until vegetables soften. Add wine; bring to the boil. Return beef to pan with stock and crushed tomatoes; bring to the boil. Reduce heat; simmer, covered, 1 hour. Uncover, stir in capsicum, olives and sun-dried tomato; simmer 15 minutes or until sauce thickens; cool. Stir in basil.
3 Preheat oven to 180°C/350°F. Oil 6-hole (¾-cup/180ml) texas muffin pan.
4 Make soft polenta.
5 Meanwhile, boil, steam or microwave potato until tender; drain. Mash potato with butter and milk in medium bowl until smooth.
6 Gently swirl hot polenta mixture into hot potato mixture.
7 Using 12cm (5-inch) cutter, cut six rounds from shortcrust pastry; press into pan holes. Divide beef mixture among pastry cases; top with potato and polenta mixture, sprinkle with cheese.
8 Bake pies about 30 minutes. Stand pies in pan 5 minutes; use a palette knife to loosen pies from side of tin and ease out.

soft polenta Bring stock and milk to the boil in small saucepan; gradually stir in polenta. Reduce heat; cook, stirring, about 5 minutes or until polenta thickens. Stir in cheese.

prep + cook time 2 hours 35 minutes **makes** 6
nutritional count per pie 32.3g total fat (14.6g saturated fat); 2533kJ (606 cal); 44.8g carbohydrate; 28.6g protein; 4.5g fibre

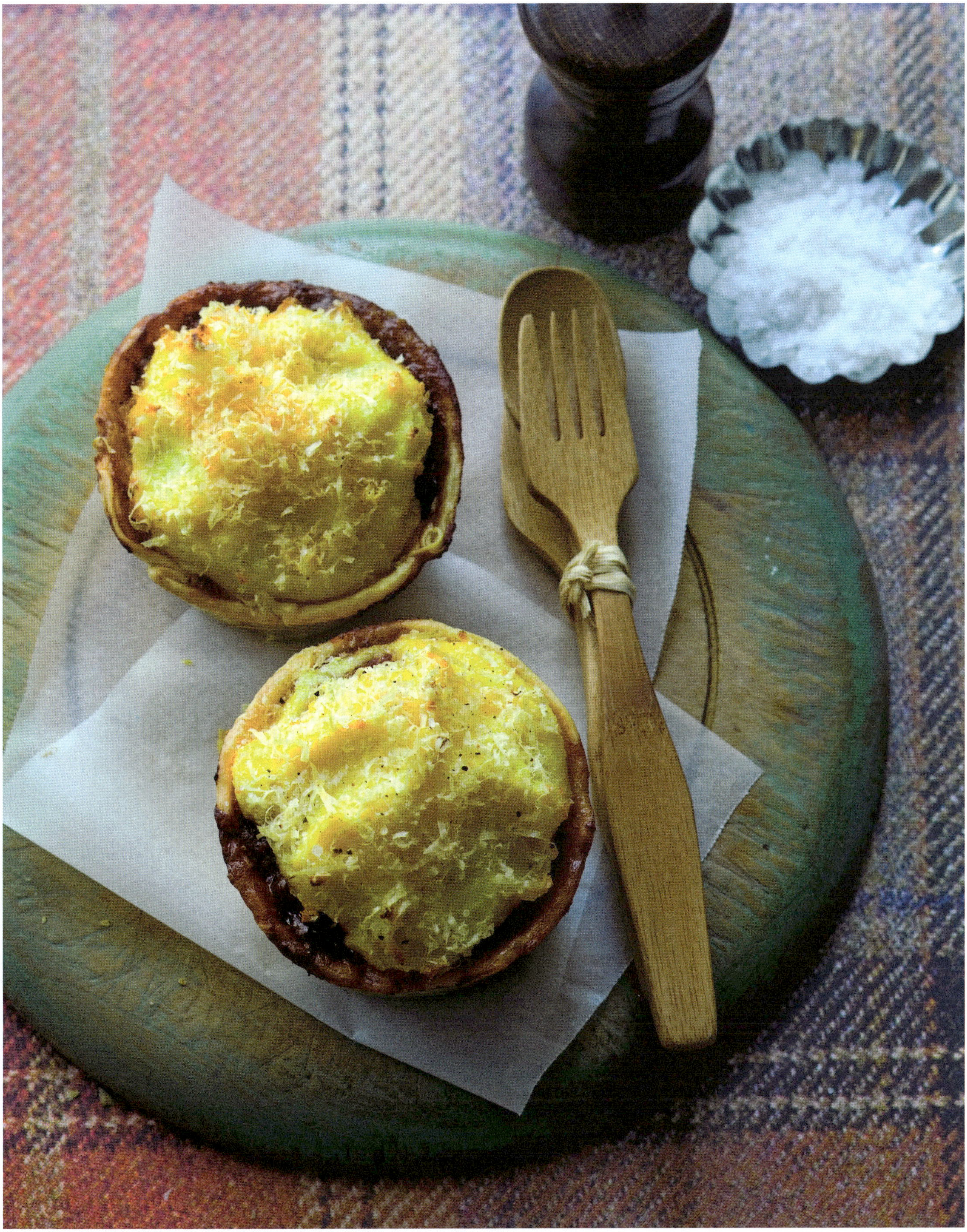

prosciutto and roasted capsicum quiches

6 slices prosciutto (90g)
3 sheets shortcrust pastry
4 slices (170g) bottled roasted red capsicum (bell pepper), chopped coarsely
⅓ cup coarsely chopped fresh basil
¾ cup (75g) pizza cheese
1¼ cups (310ml) pouring cream
¼ cup (60ml) milk
3 eggs

1 Preheat oven to 200°C/400°F. Oil 12-hole (⅓-cup/80ml) muffin pan.
2 Cook prosciutto in heated oiled large frying pan until crisp. Cool; chop coarsely.
3 Using 9cm (3½-inch) cutter, cut 12 rounds from pastry; press into pan holes. Divide combined prosciutto, capsicum, basil and cheese among pastry cases.
4 Whisk cream, milk and eggs in large jug; pour into pastry cases.
5 Bake quiches about 25 minutes. Stand in pan 5 minutes before serving.

prep + cook time 50 minutes **makes** 12
nutritional count per quiche 26.5g total fat (14.8g saturated fat); 1462kJ (350 cal); 19.7g carbohydrate; 8.3g protein; 0.8g fibre

It is fine to use just one 300ml carton of cream for this recipe.

pork and olive empanadas

1 tablespoon olive oil
1 medium brown onion (150g), chopped finely
½ teaspoon each ground cumin, cinnamon and smoked paprika
¼ teaspoon each ground nutmeg and cloves
375g (12 ounces) minced (ground) pork
2 hard-boiled eggs, coarsely grated
⅓ cup (40g) seeded black olives, chopped finely
6 sheets shortcrust pastry
1 egg, beaten lightly

1 Heat oil in large frying pan, add onion; cook, stirring, until soft. Add spices and pork; cook, stirring, until browned. Cool.
2 Stir hard-boiled eggs and olives into pork mixture, season to taste.
3 Preheat oven to 200°C/400°F. Oil two oven trays.
4 Using 12cm (5-inch) cutter, cut 24 rounds from pastry sheets. Drop heaped tablespoons of filling onto rounds; brush edges with beaten egg. Fold rounds in half to enclose filling; pinch edges to seal. Place on oven trays; brush with egg.
5 Bake empanadas about 25 minutes or until browned lightly. Serve with lemon wedges.

prep + cook time 1 hour **makes** 24
nutritional count per empanada 14g total fat (6.7g saturated fat); 961kJ (230 cal); 19.2g carbohydrate; 6.7g protein; 0.9g fibre

mini beef and guinness pies

2 teaspoons vegetable oil
250g (8 ounces) beef skirt steak, chopped finely
1 small brown onion (80g), chopped finely
1 tablespoon plain (all-purpose) flour
1 cup (250ml) guinness stout
½ cup (125ml) beef stock
3 sheets shortcrust pastry
1 egg, beaten lightly

1 Heat oil in large saucepan; cook beef, stirring, until browned all over. Add onion; cook, stirring, until softened. Add flour; cook, stirring, until mixture bubbles and is well browned.
2 Gradually stir in stout and stock, stirring, until gravy boils and thickens slightly. Cover, reduce heat; simmer, stirring occasionally, 1 hour. Uncover; simmer, stirring occasionally, 30 minutes. Cool filling 10 minutes then refrigerate until cold.
3 Preheat oven to 220°C/425°F. Oil two 12-hole (1-tablespoon/20ml) mini muffin pans.
4 Using 6cm (2¼-inch) cutter, cut 24 rounds from pastry sheets; place one round in each pan hole. Using 5cm (2-inch) cutter, cut 24 rounds from remaining pastry sheets.
5 Spoon one heaped teaspoon of the cold filling into each pastry case; brush around edges of pastry with egg. Top each pie with smaller pastry round; press gently around edge to seal, brush with remaining egg. Cut two small slits in top of each pie.
6 Bake pies about 15 minutes or until browned lightly. Stand 5 minutes in pan before serving.

prep + cook time 2 hours 20 minutes (+ refrigeration)
makes 24
nutritional count per pie 6.2g total fat (2.5g saturated fat); 477kJ (114 cal); 10g carbohydrate; 4.1g protein; 0.2g fibre

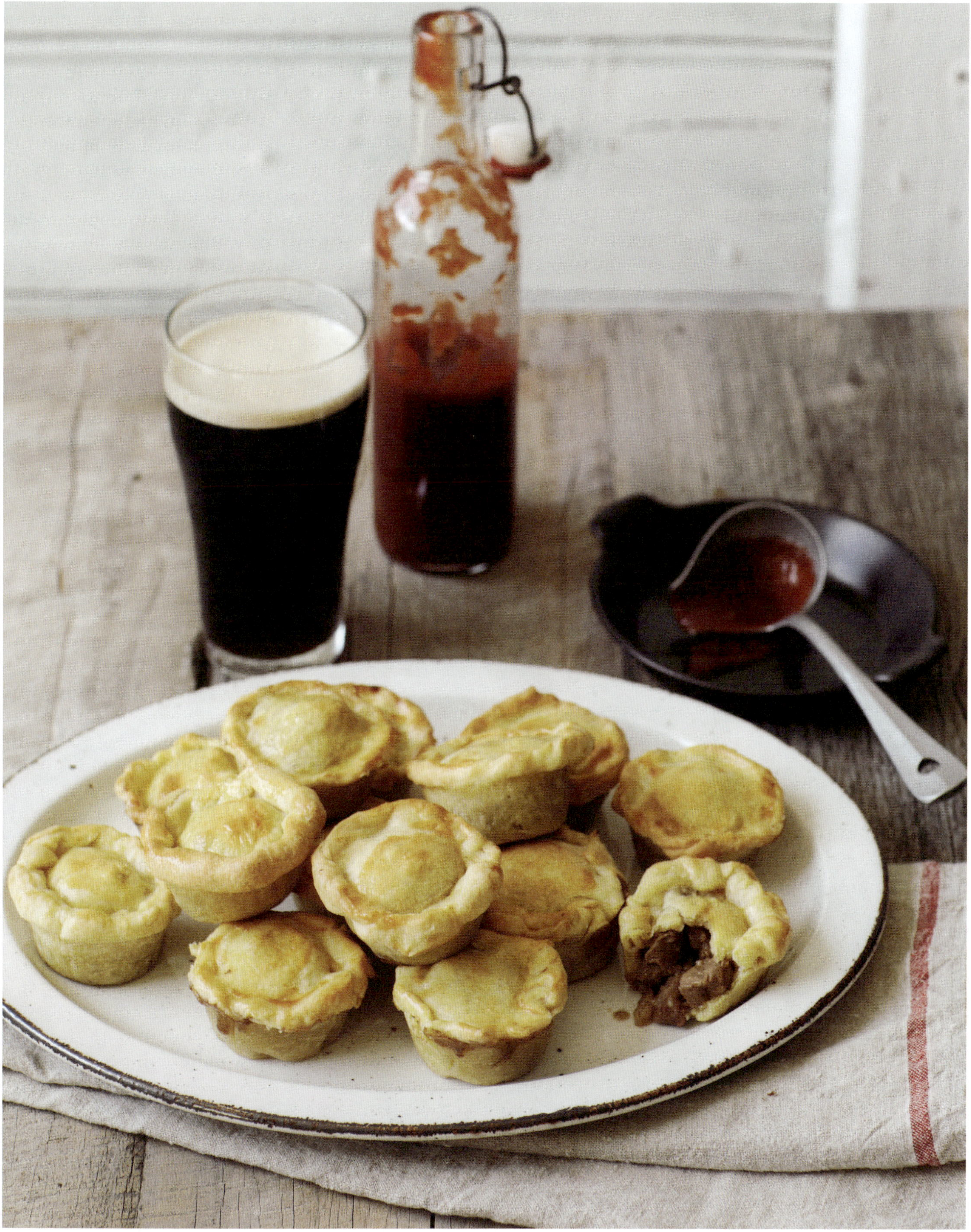

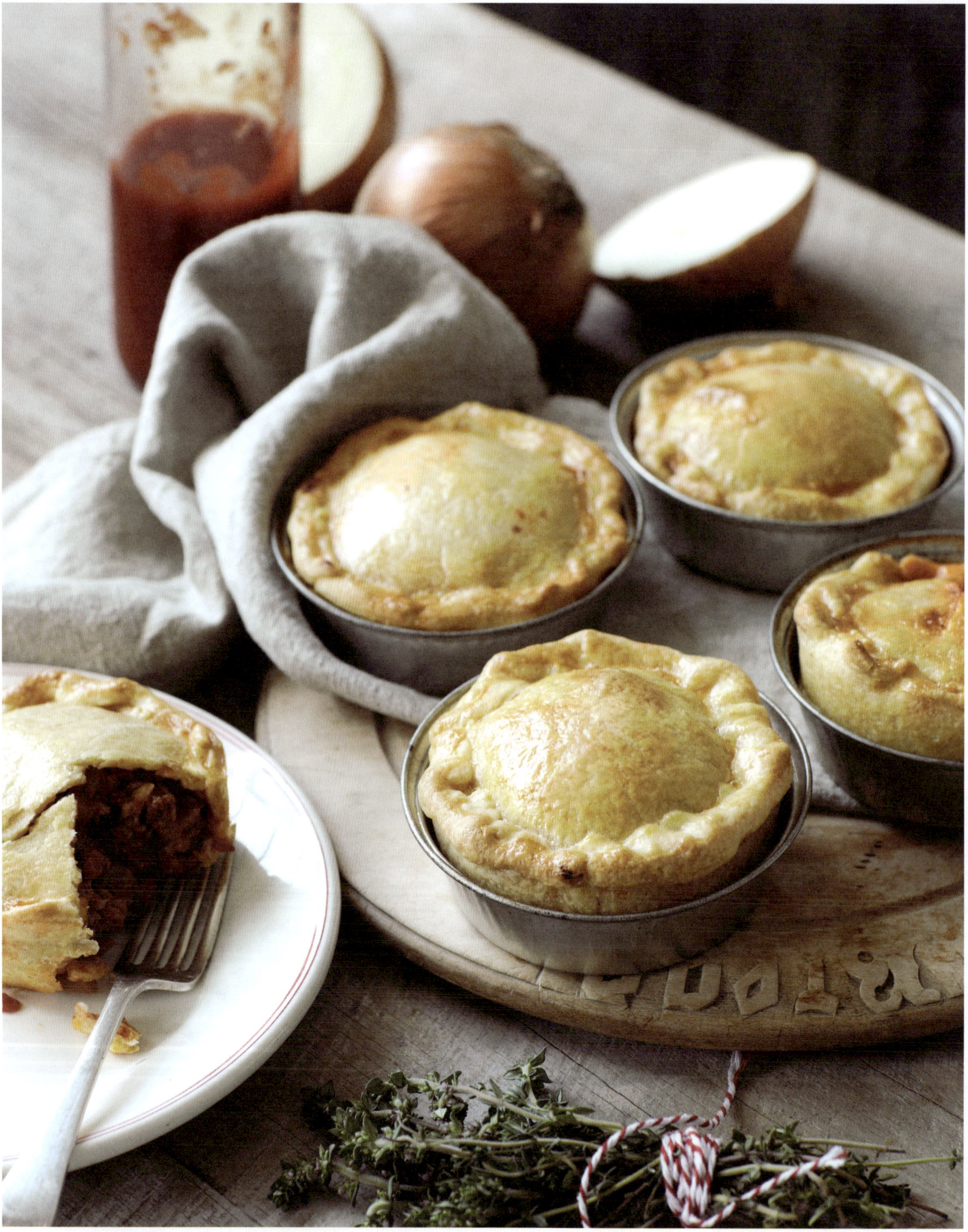

meat pies

1½ cups (225g) plain (all-purpose) flour
100g (3 ounces) cold butter, chopped coarsely
1 egg
1 tablespoon iced water, approximately
2 sheets puff pastry
1 egg, extra
beef filling
1 tablespoon vegetable oil
1 small brown onion (80g), chopped finely
600g (1¼ pounds) minced (ground) beef
415g (13 ounces) canned crushed tomatoes
2 tablespoons tomato paste
2 tablespoons worcestershire sauce
¾ cup (180ml) beef stock
1 teaspoon finely chopped fresh thyme

1 Process flour and butter until crumbly. Add egg and enough of the water to make ingredients come together. Knead pastry on floured surface until smooth, enclose with plastic wrap; refrigerate 30 minutes.
2 Meanwhile, make beef filling.
3 Oil six ⅔-cup (160ml) pie tins. Divide pastry into six portions; roll each between sheets of baking paper until large enough to line tins. Lift pastry into tins; gently press over base and sides, trim edge. Cover; refrigerate 30 minutes.
4 Using 11cm (4½-inch) cutter, cut six rounds from puff pastry. Refrigerate until required.
5 Preheat oven to 200°C/400°F.
6 Place pie tins on oven tray; line pastry cases with baking paper, fill with dried beans or rice. Bake 10 minutes. Remove paper and beans; bake further 5 minutes. Cool.
7 Fill pastry cases with beef filling; brush edges of pastry with extra egg. Top with puff pastry rounds; press edges to seal. Brush tops with egg. Cut a slit in top of pies.
8 Bake pies about 20 minutes or until pastry is golden. Serve pies with tomato sauce (ketchup).

beef filling Heat oil in large saucepan; cook onion and beef, stirring, until beef is well browned. Stir in undrained tomatoes, paste, sauce and stock; bring to the boil. Reduce heat; simmer, uncovered, about 20 minutes or until thick. Stir in thyme; season to taste. Cool.

prep + cook time 1 hour 35 minutes (+ refrigeration)
makes 6
nutritional count per pie 39.3g total fat (14.6g saturated fat); 2893kJ (692 cal); 52.4g carbohydrate; 30.8g protein; 3.5g fibre

lamb spanakopita

1 tablespoon olive oil
1 medium brown onion (150g), chopped coarsely
2 cloves garlic, chopped finely
625g (1¼ pounds) minced (ground) lamb
2 teaspoons dried oregano
60g (2 ounces) butter, melted
8 sheets fillo pastry
silver beet and cheese filling
½ bunch (500g) silver beet (swiss chard)
1 tablespoon olive oil
1¼ cups (300g) ricotta cheese
185g (6 ounces) fetta cheese, crumbled
2 teaspoons finely grated lemon rind
¼ cup finely shredded fresh mint

1 Heat oil in large frying pan; cook onion and garlic, stirring, until soft. Add lamb and oregano; stir until cooked through.
2 Make silver beet and cheese filling.
3 Preheat oven to 220°C/425°F. Brush 20cm (8-inch) loose-based square cake pan with a little of the butter.
4 Layer three pastry sheets, brushing each sheet with butter. Place in cake pan to cover base and two opposite sides with edges overhanging. Brush top pastry sheet with butter. Repeat with three more sheets, placing crossways over sheets in pan.
5 Spread half the lamb mixture over pastry base then half the filling; repeat with remaining lamb mixture and filling. Fold overhanging pastry over filling. Layer remaining sheets of pastry, brushing each with butter, fold to fit top of pie. Brush with butter.
6 Bake pie about 25 minutes or until pastry is browned lightly. Serve hot or at room temperature.

silver beet and cheese filling Finely slice silver beet stems and leaves separately. Heat oil in large frying pan; cook stems, stirring, until tender. Add leaves; cook, stirring, until soft. Remove from heat; stir in cheeses, rind and mint. Season to taste.

prep + cook time 1 hour 10 minutes **serves** 6
nutritional count per serving 38.1g total fat (19.5g saturated fat); 2324kJ (556 cal); 16.4g carbohydrate; 36.2g protein; 3.3g fibre

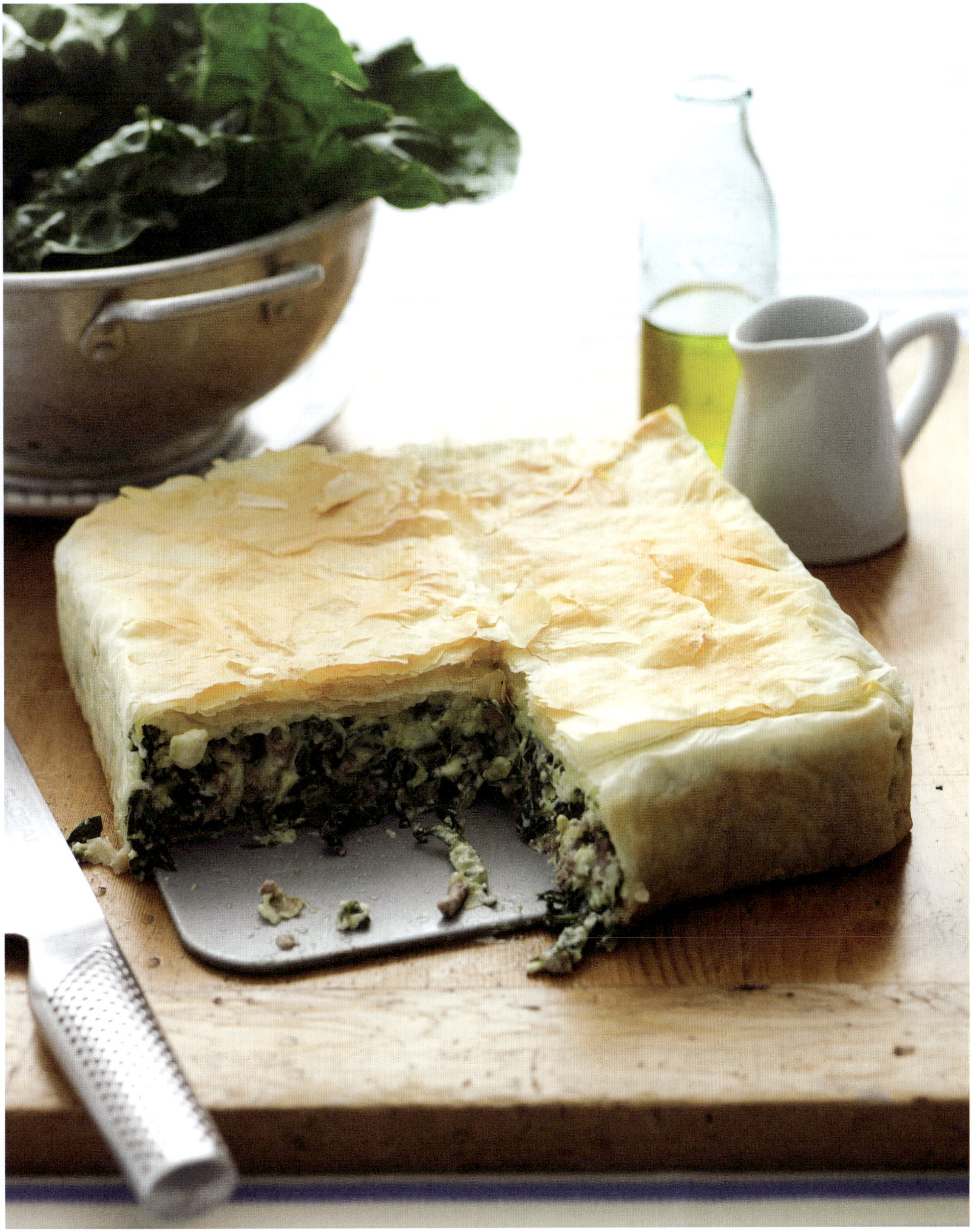

beef bourguignon and potato pie

500g (1 pound) minced (ground) beef
30g (1 ounce) butter
1 medium brown onion (150g), chopped finely
2 cloves garlic, crushed
4 rindless bacon slices (260g), chopped finely
155g (5 ounces) button mushrooms, sliced thinly
2 tablespoons plain (all-purpose) flour
1 cup (250ml) dry red wine
1 cup (250ml) beef stock
2 tablespoons tomato paste
2 fresh bay leaves
1kg (2 pounds) potatoes, chopped coarsely
30g (1 ounce) butter, extra
⅓ cup (80ml) pouring cream, heated

1 Heat oiled large saucepan; cook beef, stirring, until browned. Remove from pan.
2 Melt butter in same pan; cook onion, garlic, bacon and mushrooms; cook, stirring, until vegetables soften.
3 Return beef to pan with flour; cook, stirring, 2 minutes. Stir in wine, stock, paste and bay leaves; bring to the boil, stirring. Reduce heat; simmer, uncovered, about 45 minutes or until thickened. Discard bay leaves.
4 Meanwhile, boil, steam or microwave potatoes until tender; drain. Push potato through fine sieve into large bowl; stir in butter and cream until smooth.
5 Preheat grill (broiler).
6 Spoon beef mixture into oiled 1.5-litre (6-cup) ovenproof dish; top with potato. Grill 5 minutes or until browned.

prep + cook time 1 hour 20 minutes **serves** 4
nutritional count per serving 41.7g total fat (22.1g saturated fat); 3148kJ (753 cal); 36.6g carbohydrate; 45.1g protein; 5.8g fibre

sumac beef and pine nut tarts

1 tablespoon olive oil
1 medium brown onion (150g), chopped finely
1 clove garlic, crushed
375g (12 ounces) minced (ground) beef
1 tablespoon sumac
2 teaspoons finely grated lemon rind
2 tablespoons pine nuts
2 sheets puff pastry
1 egg, beaten lightly
125g (4 ounces) grape tomatoes, quartered
¼ cup each coarsely chopped fresh mint and flat-leaf parsley
¼ cup (70g) yogurt
2 tablespoons lemon juice

1 Preheat oven to 200°C/400°F. Oil two oven trays.
2 Heat oil in large frying pan; cook onion and garlic, stirring, until onion softens. Add beef and sumac; stir until browned. Remove from heat; stir in rind and nuts.
3 Cut pastry sheets in half; place on trays. Spoon beef mixture into centre of pastry, brush edges with a little egg; fold edges over to make 2cm (¾-inch) border, press firmly. Brush pastry with remaining egg.
4 Bake tarts about 25 minutes or until browned lightly.
5 Meanwhile, combine tomato and herbs in small bowl; season to taste. Combine yogurt and juice in another small bowl.
6 Serve tarts drizzled with yogurt mixture and topped with tomato mixture.

prep + cook time 50 minutes **makes** 4
nutritional count per tart 39.3g total fat (6.9g saturated fat); 2508kJ (600 cal); 34.4g carbohydrate; 26.4g protein; 3.1g fibre

gluten-free mini meat pies

2 teaspoons vegetable oil
1 medium brown onion (150g), chopped finely
2 rindless bacon slices (130g), chopped finely
350g (11 ounces) minced (ground) beef
2 tablespoons tomato paste
¼ cup (35g) arrowroot
2 cups (500ml) gluten-free beef stock
1 egg, beaten lightly
pastry
1¾ cups (315g) rice flour
⅓ cup (50g) (corn) cornflour (cornstarch)
⅓ cup (40g) soya flour
200g (6½ ounces) cold butter, chopped
¼ cup (60ml) cold water, approximately

1 Heat oil in medium saucepan; cook onion and bacon, stirring, until onion softens and bacon is browned. Add beef; cook, stirring, until browned. Add paste and blended arrowroot and stock; bring to the boil, stirring. Reduce heat; simmer, uncovered, until thickened. Cool.
2 Meanwhile, make pastry.
3 Preheat oven to 220°C/425°F. Oil 12 x ¼-cup (60ml) foil pie cases (7cm/3-inch top diameter, 5cm/2-inch base diameter); place on oven tray.
4 Roll pastry between sheets of baking paper until 5mm (¼-inch) thick. Using 9cm (3½-inch) cutter, cut 12 rounds from pastry; press rounds into base and sides of foil cases. Spoon beef mixture into pastry cases; brush edges with egg.
5 Using 7cm (3-inch) cutter, cut 12 rounds from remaining pastry; place rounds on pies, press to seal edges. Brush pies with egg; cut two small slits in top of each pie.
6 Bake pies about 25 minutes. Serve with gluten-free tomato sauce (ketchup).

pastry Process flours and butter until mixture is fine. Add enough of the water and process until ingredients come together. Enclose with plastic wrap; refrigerate 30 minutes.

prep + cook time 1 hour (+ refrigeration) **makes** 12
nutritional count per pie 19.3g total fat (11g saturated fat); 1032kJ (247 cal); 7.8g carbohydrate; 10.7g protein; 0.7g fibre

This recipe is gluten-free, wheat-free, yeast-free and nut-free.

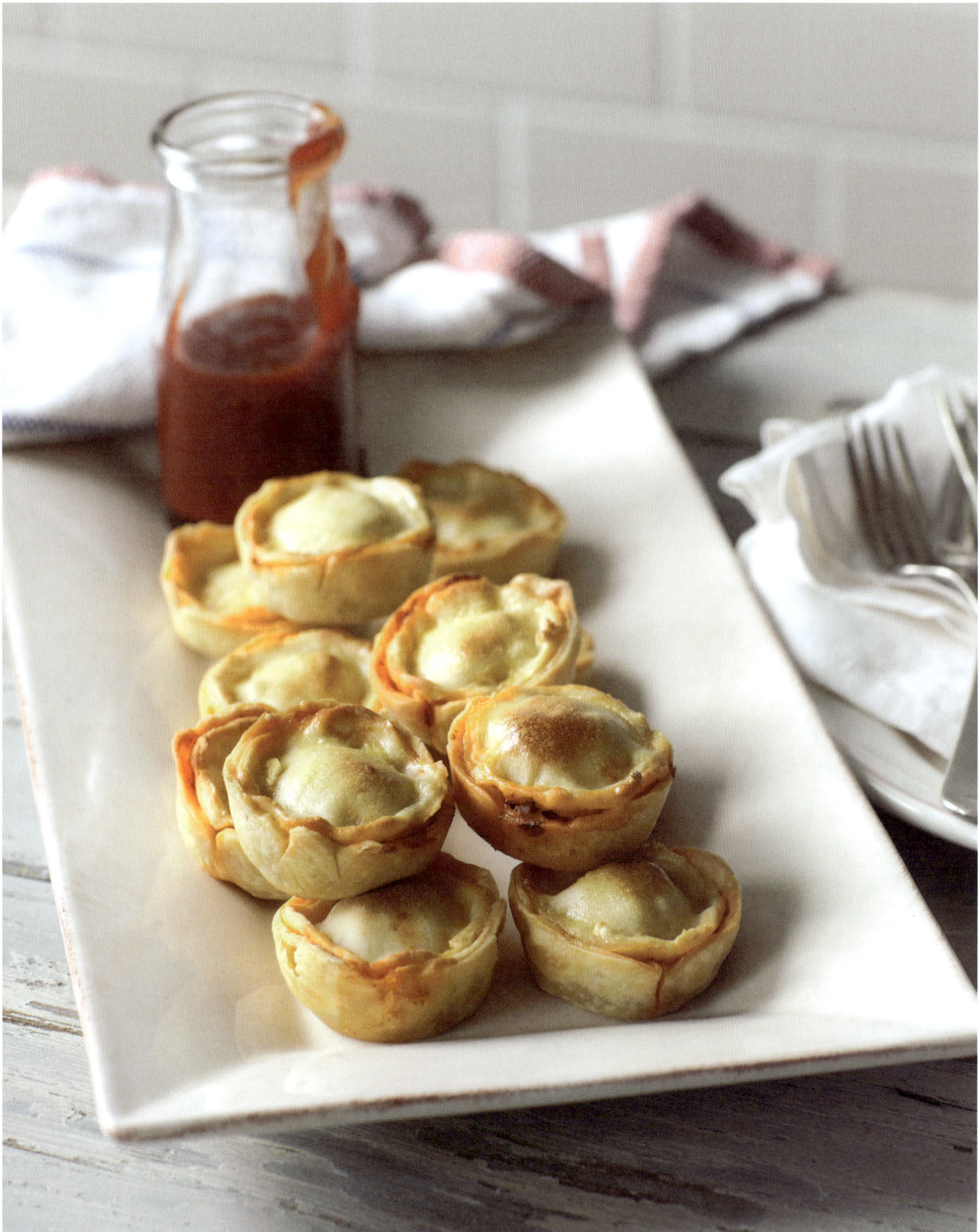

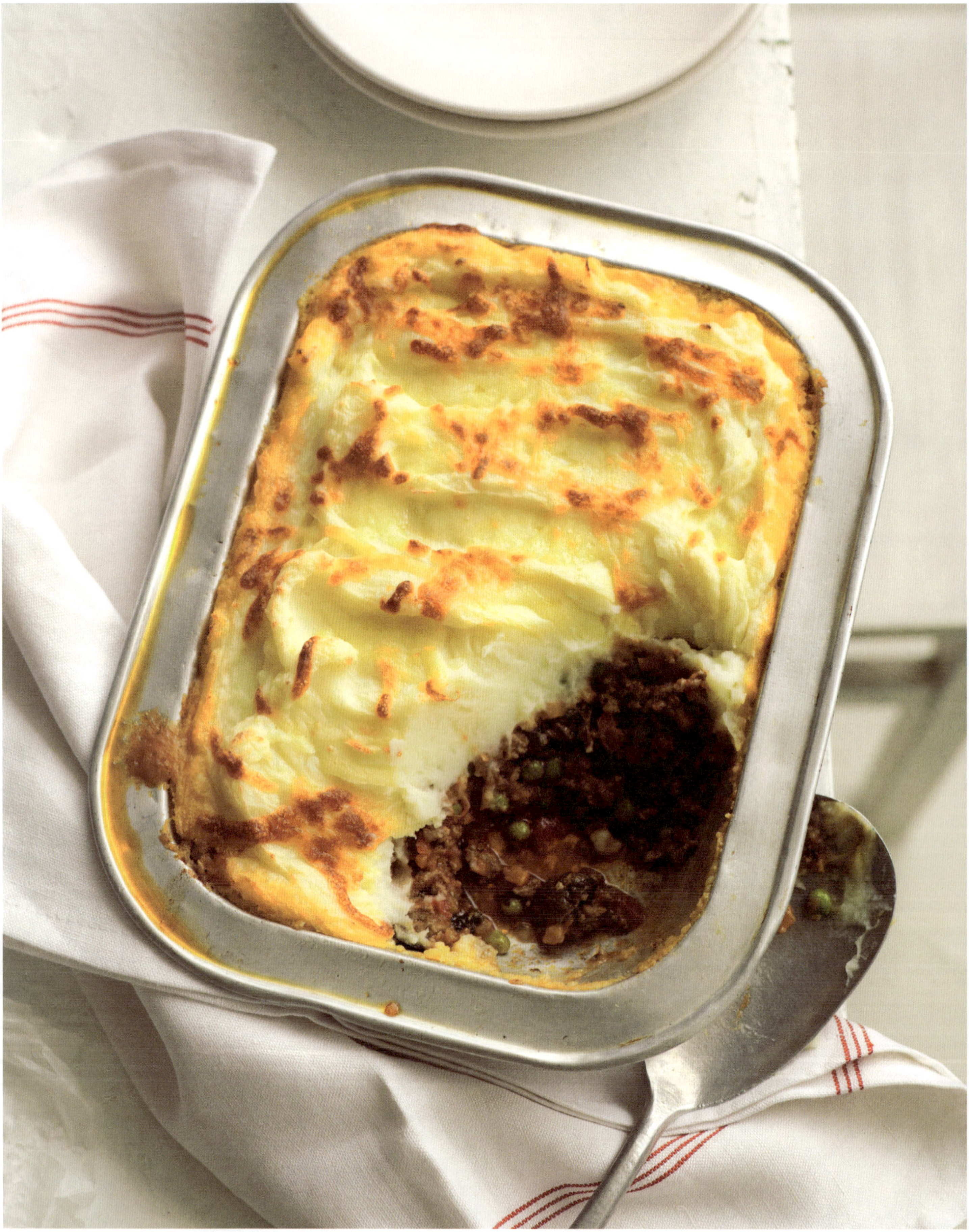

cottage pie

1 tablespoon olive oil
1 large brown onion (200g), chopped finely
2 cloves garlic, crushed
2 medium carrots (240g), chopped finely
1kg (2 pounds) minced (ground) beef
1 tablespoon worcestershire sauce
2 tablespoons tomato paste
2 x 425g (12½ ounces) canned crushed tomatoes
1 teaspoon dried mixed herbs
200g (6½ ounces) button mushrooms, quartered
1 cup (120g) frozen peas
1kg (2 pounds) sebago potatoes, chopped coarsely
¾ cup (180ml) hot milk
40g (1½ ounces) butter, softened
½ cup (50g) coarsely grated pizza cheese

1 Heat oil in large saucepan; cook onion, garlic and carrot, stirring, until onion softens. Add beef; cook, stirring, about 10 minutes or until changed in colour.
2 Add sauce, paste, undrained tomatoes and herbs to pan; bring to the boil. Reduce heat; simmer, uncovered, about 30 minutes or until mixture thickens slightly. Stir in mushrooms and peas.
3 Preheat oven to 180°C/350°F.
4 Meanwhile, boil, steam or microwave potato until tender; drain. Mash potato in large bowl with milk and butter.
5 Pour beef mixture into deep 3-litre (12-cup) ovenproof dish; top with mashed potato mixture, sprinkle with cheese.
6 Bake pie about 35 minutes or until heated through and top is browned lightly.

prep + cook time 2 hours **serves** 8
nutritional count per serving 20.7g total fat (9.5g saturated fat); 1806kJ (432 cal); 26.3g carbohydrate; 32.2g protein; 6.2g fibre

You can make the cottage pie up to two days in advance; keep, covered, in the refrigerator. Reheat, covered, in 180°C/350°F oven for about 40 minutes. The pie can also be frozen for up to three months; thaw overnight in the refrigerator before reheating as above.

meat

steak and kidney pie

300g (9½ ounces) beef ox kidneys
1.5kg (3 pounds) beef chuck steak, chopped coarsely
2 medium brown onions (300g), sliced thinly
1 cup (250ml) beef stock
1 tablespoon soy sauce
¼ cup (35g) plain (all-purpose) flour
½ cup (125ml) water
2 sheets puff pastry
1 egg, beaten lightly

1 Remove fat from kidneys; chop kidneys finely. Place kidneys, steak, onion, stock and sauce in large saucepan; simmer, covered, about 1 hour or until steak is tender.
2 Preheat oven to 200°C/400°F.
3 Stir blended flour and water into beef mixture; stir until mixture boils and thickens. Transfer to 1.5-litre (6-cup) ovenproof dish.
4 Cut pastry into 6cm (2¼-inch) rounds. Overlap rounds on beef mixture; brush with egg.
5 Bake pie about 30 minutes or until browned.

prep + cook time 2 hours 30 minutes **serves** 6
nutritional count per serving 25.8g total fat (12.2g saturated fat); 2546kJ (609 cal); 27.2g carbohydrate; 65.9g protein; 1.6g fibre

roast potato and bacon quiche

300g (9½ ounces) ruby lou potatoes, peeled, chopped coarsely
1 tablespoon olive oil
1 sheet puff pastry
2 teaspoons olive oil, extra
1 small brown onion (80g), sliced thinly
2 cloves garlic, crushed
3 rindless bacon slices (195g), chopped coarsely
⅓ cup (80ml) milk
⅓ cup (80ml) pouring cream
2 eggs
¼ cup (25g) coarsely grated mozzarella cheese

1 Preheat oven to 180°C/350°F.
2 Combine potato and oil in medium baking dish. Roast 30 minutes or until browned and cooked through.
3 Meanwhile, cut pastry into four squares; press pastry into four 1-cup (250ml) ovenproof dishes, prick pastry with fork. Place dishes on oven tray; bake 5 minutes.
4 Reduce oven to 160°C/325°F.
5 Heat extra oil in medium frying pan; cook onion, garlic and bacon, stirring, until onion softens and bacon is crisp. Drain on absorbent paper.
6 Divide potato among pastry cases; top with bacon mixture. Whisk milk, cream and eggs in medium jug, stir in cheese; pour into pastry cases.
7 Bake quiches about 25 minutes or until filling sets. Stand 5 minutes; carefully remove quiches from dishes.

prep + cook time 1 hour 25 minutes **makes** 4
nutritional count per quiche 34.5g total fat (15.7g saturated fat); 2128kJ (509 cal); 27.8g carbohydrate; 21.2g protein; 2.3g fibre

beef carbonade pies

2kg (4 pounds) beef round steak, cut into 3cm (1¼-inch) pieces
½ cup (75g) plain (all-purpose) flour
40g (1½ ounces) butter, melted
¼ cup (60ml) vegetable oil
4 medium brown onions (600g), sliced thickly
2 cloves garlic, crushed
2 large carrots (360g), chopped coarsely
2¾ cups (680ml) stout
1 tablespoon light brown sugar
¼ cup (60ml) cider vinegar
3 sprigs fresh thyme
1 bay leaf
2 sheets puff pastry
1 tablespoon milk
1 egg, beaten lightly

1 Coat beef in flour; shake off excess. Heat butter and 2 tablespoons of the oil in medium saucepan; cook beef, in batches, until browned all over. Remove from pan.
2 Heat remaining oil in same pan; cook onion, garlic and carrot, stirring, until onion softens. Return beef to pan with stout, sugar, vinegar, thyme and bay leaf; bring to the boil. Reduce heat; simmer, covered, 1½ hours.
3 Uncover; simmer, stirring occasionally, about 1 hour or until beef is tender and sauce thickens. Discard herbs.
4 Preheat oven to 220°C/425°F.
5 Divide beef mixture among eight 1¼-cup (310ml) ovenproof dishes. Cut each pastry sheet into four squares; top each dish with one pastry square, trim edges. Brush pastry with combined milk and egg; place dishes on oven tray.
6 Bake pies about 15 minutes or until pastry is puffed and browned lightly.

prep + cook time 3 hours 45 minutes **makes** 8
nutritional count per pie 33.9g total fat (14.4g saturated fat); 2930 kJ (701 cal); 32.4g carbohydrate; 58.2g protein; 3.1g fibre

Stout is a strong, dark beer that originated in Great Britain in the late 1700s. More redolent of hops than other beers, it is made with roasted barley, giving it its characteristic dark colour and bitter-sweet, almost coffee-like flavour.

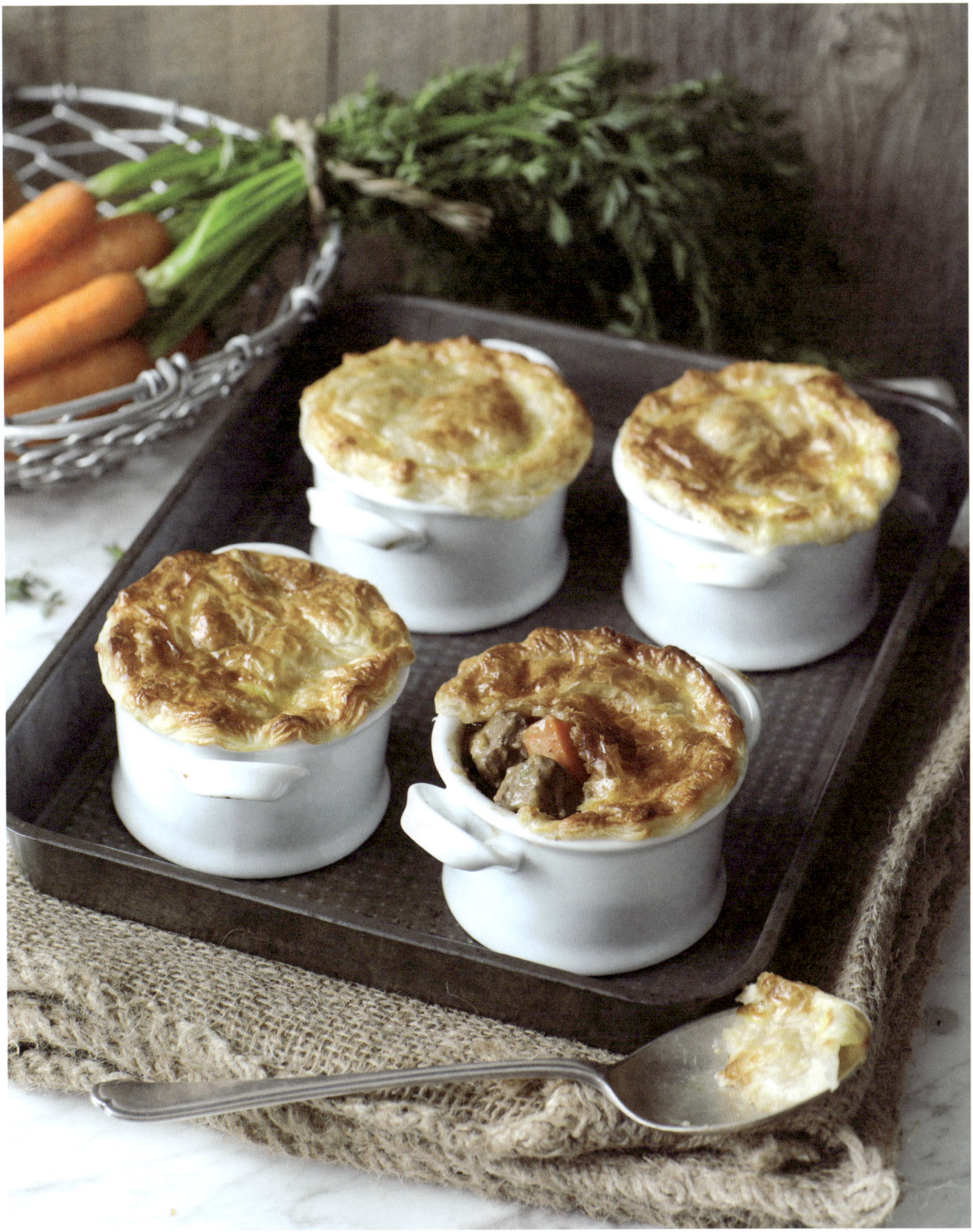

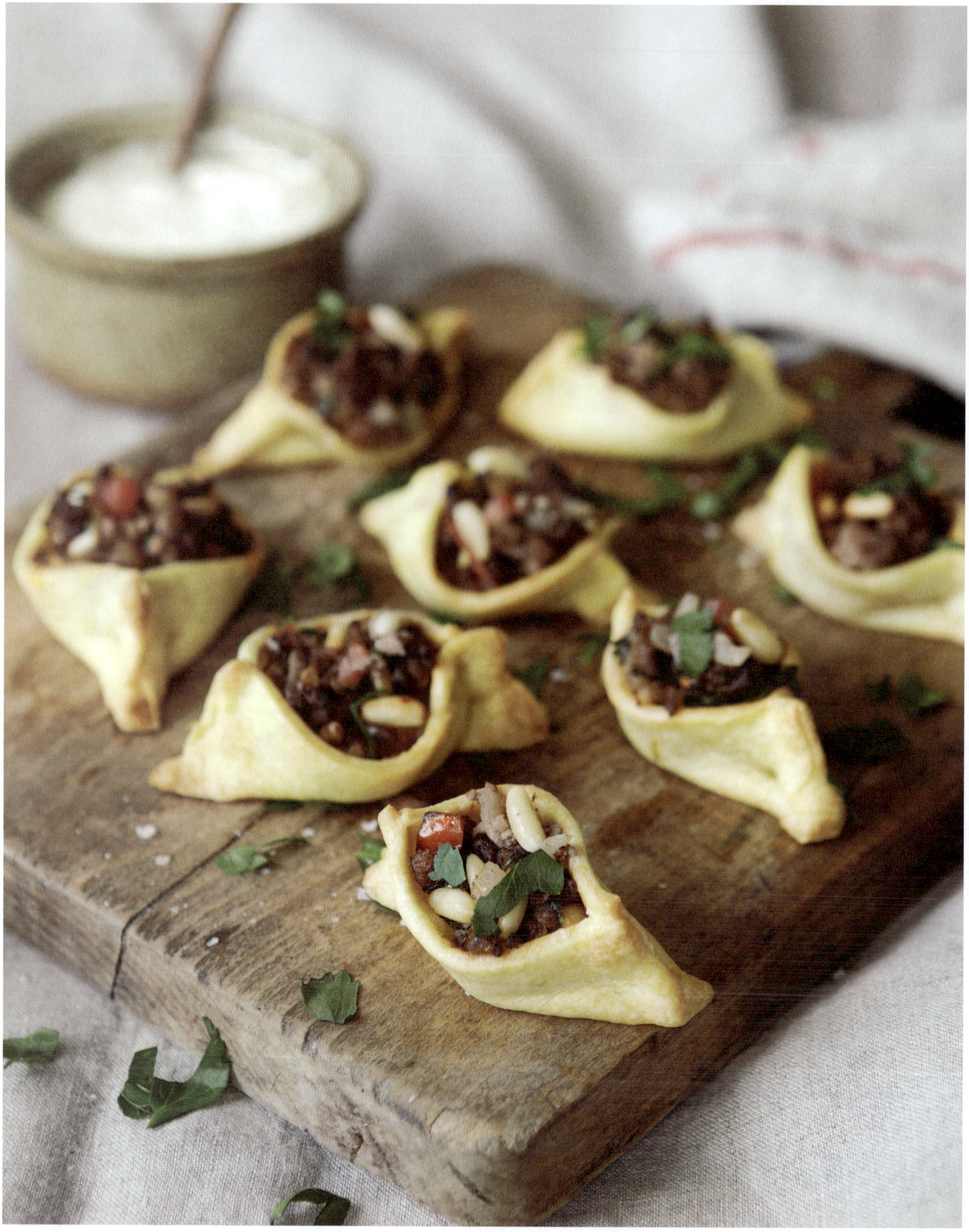

lamb and pine nut little boats

2 teaspoons olive oil
1 small brown onion (80g), chopped finely
2 cloves garlic, crushed
2 teaspoons ground cumin
400g (12½ ounces) minced (ground) lamb
2 medium tomatoes (300g), chopped finely
1 tablespoon finely chopped fresh flat-leaf parsley
1 tablespoon lemon juice
1 tablespoon sumac
3 sheets shortcrust pastry
1 egg, beaten lightly
2 tablespoons pine nuts
1 tablespoon finely chopped fresh flat-leaf parsley, extra
½ cup (140g) yogurt

1 Heat oil in small frying pan; cook onion, garlic and cumin, stirring, until onion softens.
2 Place onion mixture in medium bowl with lamb, tomato, parsley, juice and sumac; mix until combined.
3 Preheat oven to 200°C/400°F. Oil two oven trays.
4 Cut each pastry sheet into nine squares. Brush egg on two opposing sides of a pastry square; place a level tablespoon filling along centre of square. Bring egg-brushed sides together then push the two unbrushed sides inward to widen centre opening, making boat shape and showing filling. Sprinkle some of the pine nuts on exposed filling; place boat on oven tray. Repeat process with remaining pastry squares, egg, filling and pine nuts, spacing boats about 4cm (1½ inches) apart on oven trays.
5 Bake boats about 20 minutes or until browned lightly and cooked through. Serve boats sprinkled with extra parsley, and yogurt.

prep + cook time 50 minutes **makes** 27
nutritional count per boat 7.2g total fat (2.8g saturated fat); 510kJ (122 cal); 9g carbohydrate; 5g protein; 0.4g fibre

moroccan-spiced chunky lamb pies

2 tablespoons olive oil
2 medium red onions (340g), cut into thin wedges
4 cloves garlic, crushed
2 tablespoons plain (all-purpose) flour
1 tablespoon ground cumin
2 teaspoons sweet paprika
2 teaspoons ground cinnamon
1.5kg (3 pounds) trimmed diced lamb shoulder
1 litre (4 cups) chicken stock
400g (12½ ounces) canned diced tomatoes
2 medium kumara (orange sweet potato) (800g), cut into 2cm (¾-inch) pieces
12 sheets fillo pastry
50g (1½ ounces) butter, melted
1 tablespoon icing (confectioners') sugar
¼ teaspoon ground cinnamon
2 teaspoons finely grated lemon rind
2 tablespoons lemon juice
1¼ cups (150g) seeded green olives, halved
½ cup finely chopped fresh coriander (cilantro)
¾ cup (200g) greek-style yogurt

1 Preheat oven to 160°C/325°F.
2 Heat half the oil in large flameproof dish; cook onion, stirring, until softened. Add garlic; cook, stirring, until fragrant. Transfer to small bowl.
3 Combine flour, cumin, paprika and cinnamon in large bowl with lamb; shake off excess. Heat remaining oil in same dish; cook lamb, in batches, until browned. Remove from dish.
4 Add stock and undrained tomatoes to same dish; bring to the boil, stirring. Return onion mixture and lamb to dish; bring to the boil. Cover dish, transfer to oven; cook lamb 1 hour. Add kumara; cook, uncovered, further 30 minutes or until tender.
5 Increase oven to 200°C/400°F.
6 Meanwhile, layer six pastry sheets, brushing melted butter between each sheet; repeat with remaining fillo and most of the remaining butter. Using top of 2-cup (500ml) ovenproof dish as a guide, cut out six pastry lids for pies, allowing about 4cm (1½ inches) overhang. Brush lids with any remaining butter; dust with combined icing sugar and cinnamon.
7 Skim surface of lamb mixture to remove any fat; stir in rind, juice, olives and coriander. Divide among six 2-cup (500ml) ovenproof dishes; top each dish with pastry round, folding in overhanging edge. Place dishes on oven tray; bake about 20 minutes. Serve pies with yogurt.

prep + cook time 2 hours (+ refrigeration) **makes** 6
nutritional count per pie 39.5g total fat (17.7g saturated fat); 3336kJ (798 cal); 49.4g carbohydrate; 59.1g protein; 5.2g fibre

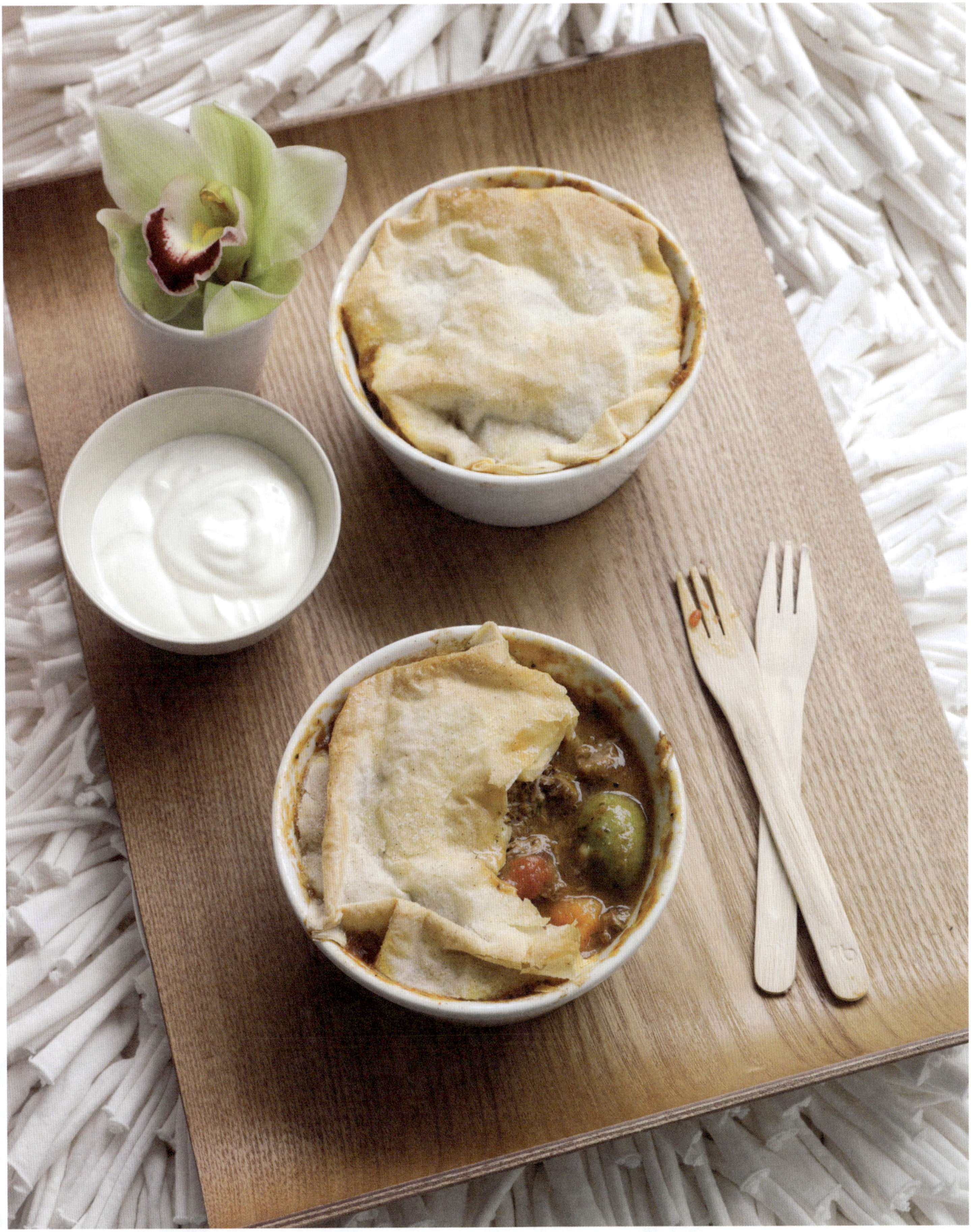

vegetable and egg

spinach pies

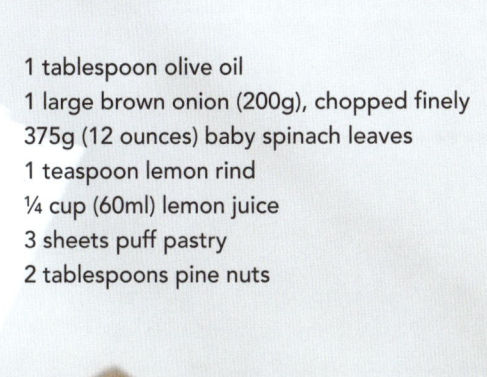

1 tablespoon olive oil
1 large brown onion (200g), chopped finely
375g (12 ounces) baby spinach leaves
1 teaspoon lemon rind
¼ cup (60ml) lemon juice
3 sheets puff pastry
2 tablespoons pine nuts

1 Preheat oven to 220°C/425°F. Line oven tray with baking paper.
2 Heat oil in large frying pan; cook onion, stirring, until softened. Add half the spinach leaves; cook, stirring, until wilted. Add remaining spinach leaves, rind and juice; cook, stirring, until liquid has evaporated. Cool 5 minutes.
3 Using 11cm (4½-inch) cutter, cut 12 rounds from pastry. Divide spinach mixture among rounds. Gather three points of each round together to form a triangle, leaving top of filling exposed. Pinch and twist each corner to secure pasty. Place pies on oven tray; sprinkle filling with pine nuts.
4 Bake pies about 15 minutes or until pastry is browned lightly.

prep + cook time 35 minutes **makes** 12
nutritional count per pie 11.1g total fat (5.3g saturated fat); 757kJ (181 cal); 16.3g carbohydrate; 3.4g protein; 1.6g fibre

spinach and pumpkin fillo pie

75g (2½ ounces) butter, melted
1 tablespoon olive oil
1 medium brown onion (150g), chopped finely
2 cloves garlic, crushed
1kg (2 pounds) butternut pumpkin, chopped finely
1 tablespoon light brown sugar
1 teaspoon ground cumin
½ teaspoon ground nutmeg
2 x 250g (8 ounces) frozen spinach, thawed, drained
1 cup (200g) fetta cheese
2 eggs, beaten lightly
6 sheets fillo pastry

1 Brush 24cm (9½-inch) ovenproof pie dish with some of the butter.
2 Heat oil in large frying pan; cook onion and garlic, stirring, until onion softens. Add pumpkin, sugar and spices; cook, covered, about 20 minutes or until pumpkin is tender. Stir in spinach and ¾ cup of the cheese. Cool 5 minutes. Stir in egg.
3 Preheat oven to 180°C/350°F.
4 Layer two sheets of pastry, brushing each with butter; fold pastry in half widthways, place in pie dish, edges overhanging. Brush pastry with butter again. Repeat with remaining pastry, overlapping the pieces clockwise around the dish. Fold over edges to make a rim around the edge of the pie; brush with remaining butter. Spoon pumpkin mixture into dish.
5 Bake pie about 40 minutes or until browned lightly. Sprinkle with remaining cheese.

prep + cook time 1 hour 20 minutes **serves** 6
nutritional count per serving 24.4g total fat (13.4g saturated fat); 1588kJ (380 cal); 23.2g carbohydrate; 15g protein; 5.1g fibre

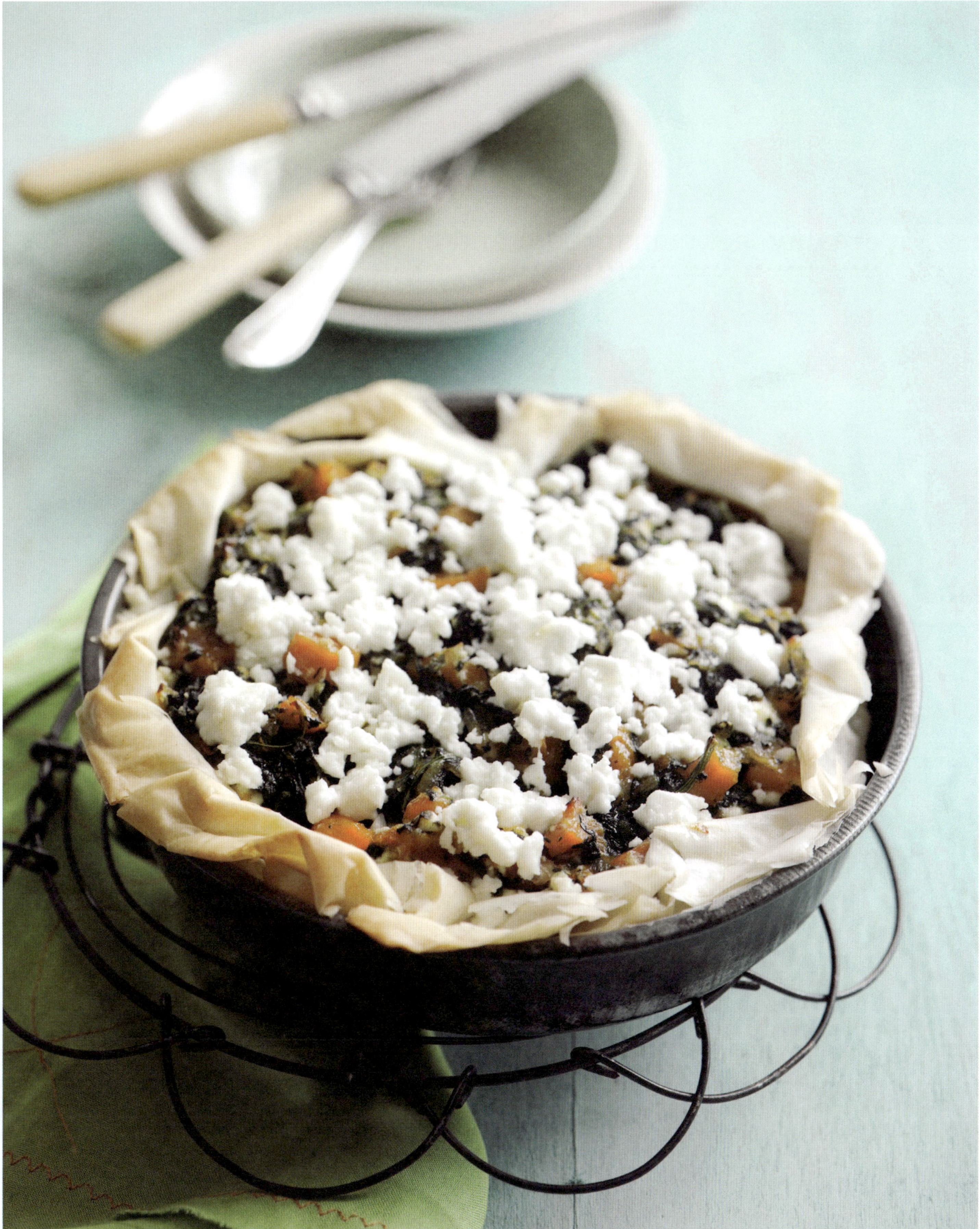

vegetable and egg

creamy leek, mushroom and baby pea pies

1 tablespoon olive oil
2 small leeks (400g), sliced thinly
1 clove garlic, crushed
300g (9½ ounces) mushrooms, chopped coarsely
2 tablespoons plain (all-purpose) flour
½ cup (125ml) low-fat milk
½ cup (125ml) vegetable stock
1 cup (120g) frozen baby peas
1 tablespoon finely chopped fresh chives
1 tablespoon wholegrain mustard
4 slices white mountain bread, quartered
cooking-oil spray

1 Preheat oven to 200°C/400°F.
2 Heat oil in large saucepan; cook leek and garlic, stirring, until leek softens. Add mushrooms; cook, stirring, about 5 minutes or until mushrooms are tender.
3 Add flour; cook, stirring, 1 minute. Gradually stir in milk and stock; cook, stirring, until mixture boils and thickens slightly. Stir in peas, chives and mustard; cook about 2 minutes or until peas are tender.
4 Divide mixture among four 1¼-cup (310ml) ovenproof dishes; place dishes on oven tray. Top each with four scrunched up pieces of bread; spray bread lightly with oil.
5 Bake pies about 10 minutes or until bread is browned.

prep + cook time 40 minutes **serves** 4
nutritional count per serving 6.2g total fat (0.8g saturated fat); 832kJ (199 cal); 24.7g carbohydrate; 11g protein; 7.1g fibre

tomato, pesto and olive tart

500g (1 pound) grape tomatoes
1 tablespoon balsamic vinegar
1 tablespoon olive oil
1 sheet puff pastry
2 tablespoons basil pesto
⅓ cup (55g) seeded black olives
1½ cups (360g) ricotta cheese
2 teaspoons fresh thyme leaves (optional)

1 Preheat oven to 220°C/425°F. Oil oven tray.
2 Combine tomatoes in medium bowl with vinegar and half the oil; place on oven tray. Roast about 10 minutes or until tomatoes collapse.
3 Place pastry on oven tray. Fold edges of pastry over to make a 5mm (¼-inch) border all the way around; prick base with fork. Place another oven tray on top of pastry; bake 10 minutes. Remove top tray from pastry; reduce oven to 200°C/400°F.
4 Spread pastry with pesto; top with tomatoes and olives. Sprinkle with cheese.
5 Bake tart about 10 minutes. Before serving, drizzle with remaining oil and sprinkle with thyme.

prep + cook time 30 minutes **serves** 4
nutritional count per serving 28.4g total fat (13.1g saturated fat); 1672kJ (400 cal); 22g carbohydrate; 13.5g protein; 2.9g fibre

quiche lorraine

1 medium brown onion (150g), chopped finely
3 rindless bacon slices (195g), chopped finely
3 eggs
1¼ cups (310ml) pouring cream
½ cup (125ml) milk
¾ cup (120g) coarsely grated gruyère cheese

pastry
1¾ cups (260g) plain (all-purpose) flour
150g (4½ ounces) cold butter, chopped coarsely
1 egg yolk
2 teaspoons lemon juice
⅓ cup (80ml) iced water, approximately

1 Make pastry.

2 Preheat oven to 200°C/400°F. Oil deep 24cm (9½-inch) loose-based fluted flan tin.

3 Roll pastry between sheets of baking paper until large enough to line tin. Lift pastry into tin; press pastry into base and side, trim edge. Place tin on oven tray; line pastry with baking paper, fill with dried beans or rice. Bake 10 minutes. Remove paper and beans; bake a further 10 minutes or until golden brown. Cool.

4 Reduce oven to 180°C/350°F.

5 Cook onion and bacon in heated oiled small frying pan until onion is soft; drain on absorbent paper. Cool. Sprinkle bacon mixture over pastry case.

6 Whisk eggs in medium bowl, then whisk in cream, milk and cheese; pour into pastry case.

7 Bake quiche about 35 minutes or until filling is set. Stand 5 minutes before removing from tin.

pastry Sift flour into bowl; rub in butter. Add egg yolk, juice and enough water to make ingredients come together. Knead on floured surface until smooth, enclose with plastic wrap; refrigerate 30 minutes.

prep + cook time 1 hour 30 minutes (+ refrigeration)
serves 6
nutritional count per serving 51.8g total fat (35.4g saturated fat); 3139kJ (751 cal); 35.4g carbohydrate; 22.1g protein; 2g fibre

It is fine to use just one 300ml carton of cream for this recipe.

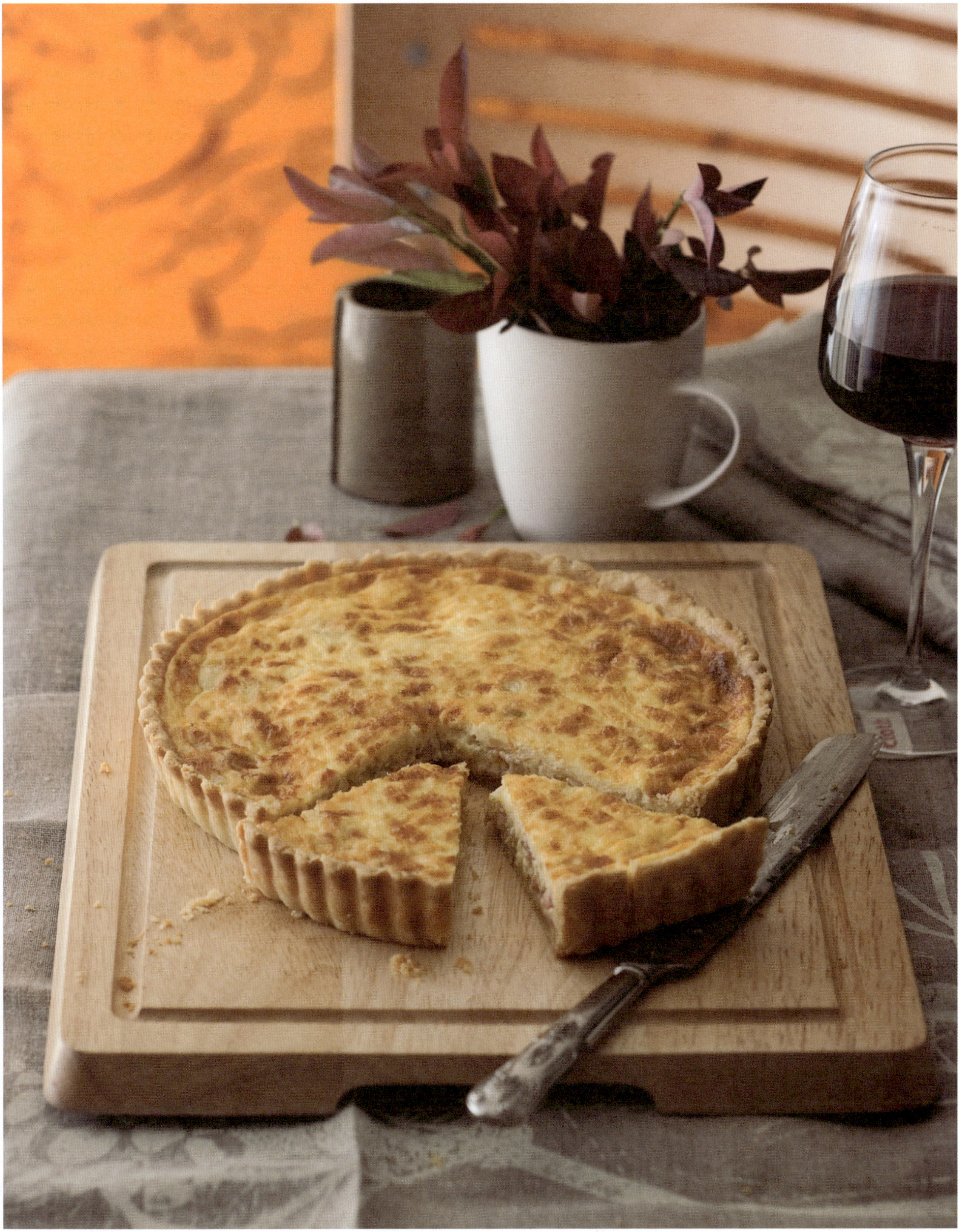

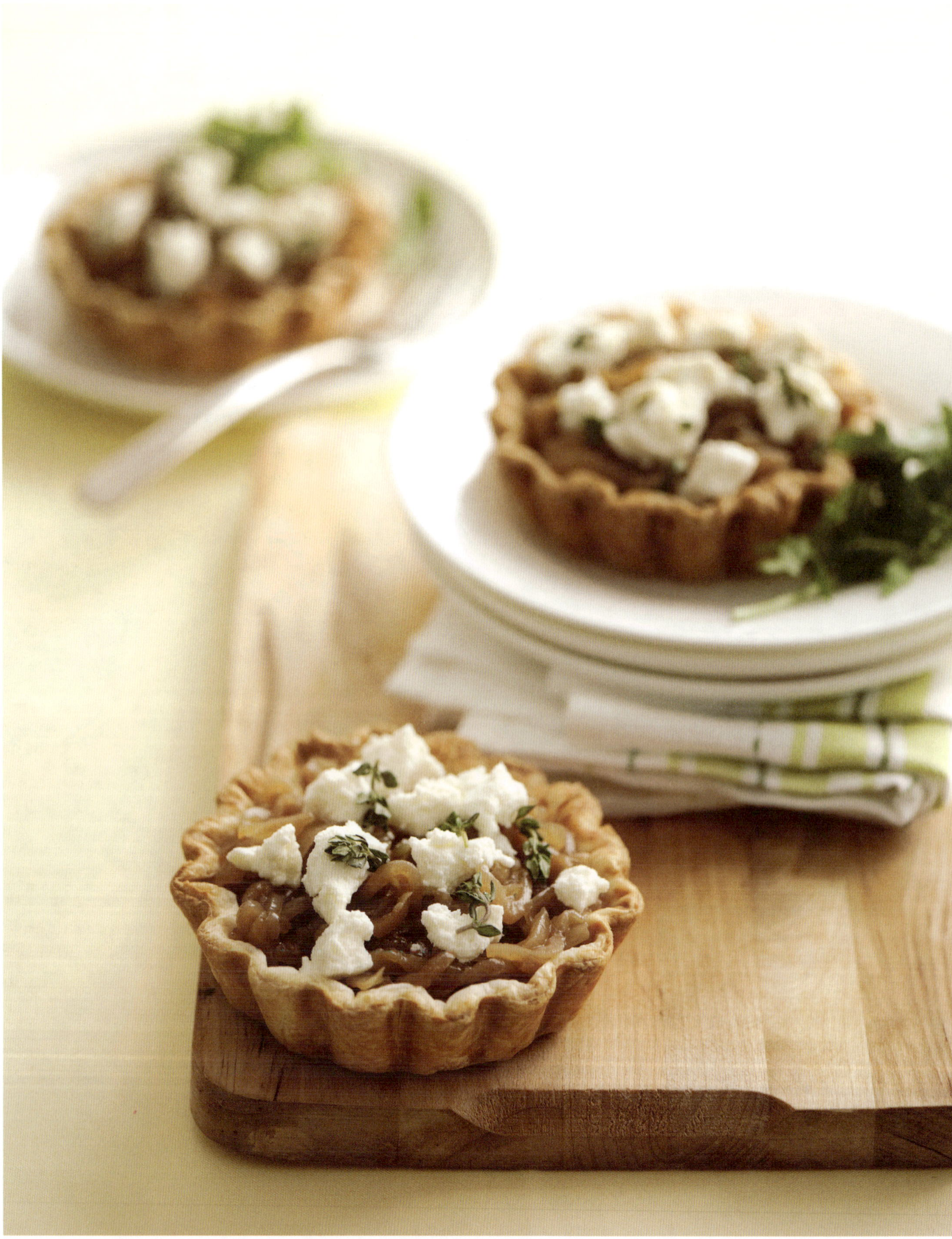

vegetable and egg

caramelised onion tarts

40g (1½ ounces) butter
1 tablespoon olive oil
3 large brown onions (600g), sliced thinly
2 tablespoons light brown sugar
2 tablespoons balsamic vinegar
½ cup (125ml) water
2 sheets puff pastry
¼ cup (60g) ricotta cheese
1 tablespoon fresh thyme leaves (optional)

1 Oil four 12cm (5-inch) loose-based fluted flan tins.
2 Melt butter with oil in large frying pan; cook onion, sugar and vinegar, stirring, until very soft and browned lightly. Add the water; cook, stirring, until water has evaporated.
3 Meanwhile, cut pastry sheets in half diagonally. Press pastry into base and side of tins; trim edge, prick bases with fork. Freeze 15 minutes.
4 Preheat oven to 220°C/425°F.
5 Place tins on oven tray; bake 15 minutes.
6 Top tarts with caramelised onion, gently push onion down to flatten pastry; sprinkle with cheese. Bake about 5 minutes. Just before serving, sprinkle with thyme.

prep + cook time 50 minutes (+ freezing) **makes** 4
nutritional count per tart 33.5g total fat (17.3g saturated fat); 2161kJ (517 cal); 44.6g carbohydrate; 8.4g protein; 3.1g fibre

serving suggestion Simple green salad.

These tarts are not baked with baking weights so the pastry will puff up. Gently push the pastry down when topping it with the onion, to create a rustic-looking tart.

vegetable and egg

spinach and beetroot tart

1 sheet puff pasty
250g (8 ounces) frozen spinach, thawed, drained
200g (6½ ounces) fetta cheese, crumbled
425g (13½ ounces) canned drained baby beetroot (beets), sliced thinly

1 Preheat oven to 220°C/425°F.
2 Place pastry on an oiled oven tray. Fold edges of pastry over to make 5mm (¼-inch) border all the way around pastry. Prick pastry base with fork. Place another oven tray on top of pastry; bake 10 minutes. Remove top tray from pastry.
3 Reduce oven to 200°C/400°F.
4 Meanwhile, combine spinach with half the cheese in medium bowl.
5 Top tart with spinach mixture, beetroot and remaining cheese. Bake about 10 minutes.

prep + cook time 30 minutes **serves** 4
nutritional count per serving 21.4g total fat (12.8g saturated fat); 1421kJ (340 cal); 22.1g carbohydrate; 13.4g protein; 4g fibre

Drain the spinach very thoroughly so that the moisture does not seep into the tart base and make the pastry soggy.

goat's cheese and zucchini flower quiches

3 sheets shortcrust pastry
12 baby zucchini with flowers (240g)
100g (3 ounces) firm goat's cheese, chopped finely
⅓ cup (25g) finely grated parmesan cheese
2 tablespoons finely chopped garlic chives
1¼ cups (310ml) pouring cream
¼ cup (60ml) milk
3 eggs

1 Preheat oven to 200°C/400°F. Oil 12-hole (⅓-cup/80ml) muffin pan.
2 Using 9cm (3½-inch) cutter, cut 12 rounds from pastry; press rounds into pan holes.
3 Remove flowers from zucchini; remove and discard stamens from flowers. Slice zucchini thinly. Divide combined sliced zucchini, cheeses and chives into pastry cases.
4 Whisk cream, milk and eggs in large jug; pour into pastry cases. Top each quiche with a zucchini flower.
5 Bake quiches about 25 minutes. Stand in pan 5 minutes before serving.

prep + cook time 50 minutes **makes** 12
nutritional count per quiche 25.8g total fat (15g saturated fat); 1421kJ (340 cal); 19.9g carbohydrate; 7.1g protein; 1.1g fibre

It is fine to use just one 300ml carton of cream for this recipe.

fetta and spinach fillo bundles

350g (11 ounces) spinach, trimmed
1 tablespoon olive oil
1 medium brown onion (150g), chopped finely
2 cloves garlic, crushed
½ teaspoon ground nutmeg
150g (4½ ounces) fetta cheese, crumbled
3 eggs
2 teaspoons finely grated lemon rind
¼ cup coarsely chopped fresh mint
2 tablespoons finely chopped fresh dill
80g (2½ ounces) butter, melted
6 sheets fillo pastry

1 Boil, steam or microwave spinach until wilted; drain. Refresh in cold water; drain. Squeeze out excess moisture. Chop spinach coarsely; spread out on absorbent paper.
2 Heat oil in small frying pan; cook onion and garlic, stirring, until onion softens. Add nutmeg; cook, stirring, until fragrant. Cool.
3 Combine onion mixture and spinach in medium bowl with cheese, eggs, rind and herbs.
4 Preheat oven to 200°C/400°F. Brush 6-hole (¾-cup/180ml) texas muffin pan with a little of the butter.
5 Brush each sheet of fillo with melted butter; fold in half to enclose buttered side. Gently press one sheet into each pan hole. Divide spinach mixture among pastry cases; fold fillo over filling to enclose. Brush with butter.
6 Bake fillo bundles about 15 minutes. Turn bundles out, top-side up, onto baking-paper-lined oven tray; bake about 5 minutes or until browned lightly. Stand 5 minutes before serving.

prep + cook time 45 minutes **makes** 6
nutritional count per bundle 22.9g total fat (12.3g saturated fat); 1200kJ (287 cal); 9.6g carbohydrate; 10.4g protein; 1.8g fibre

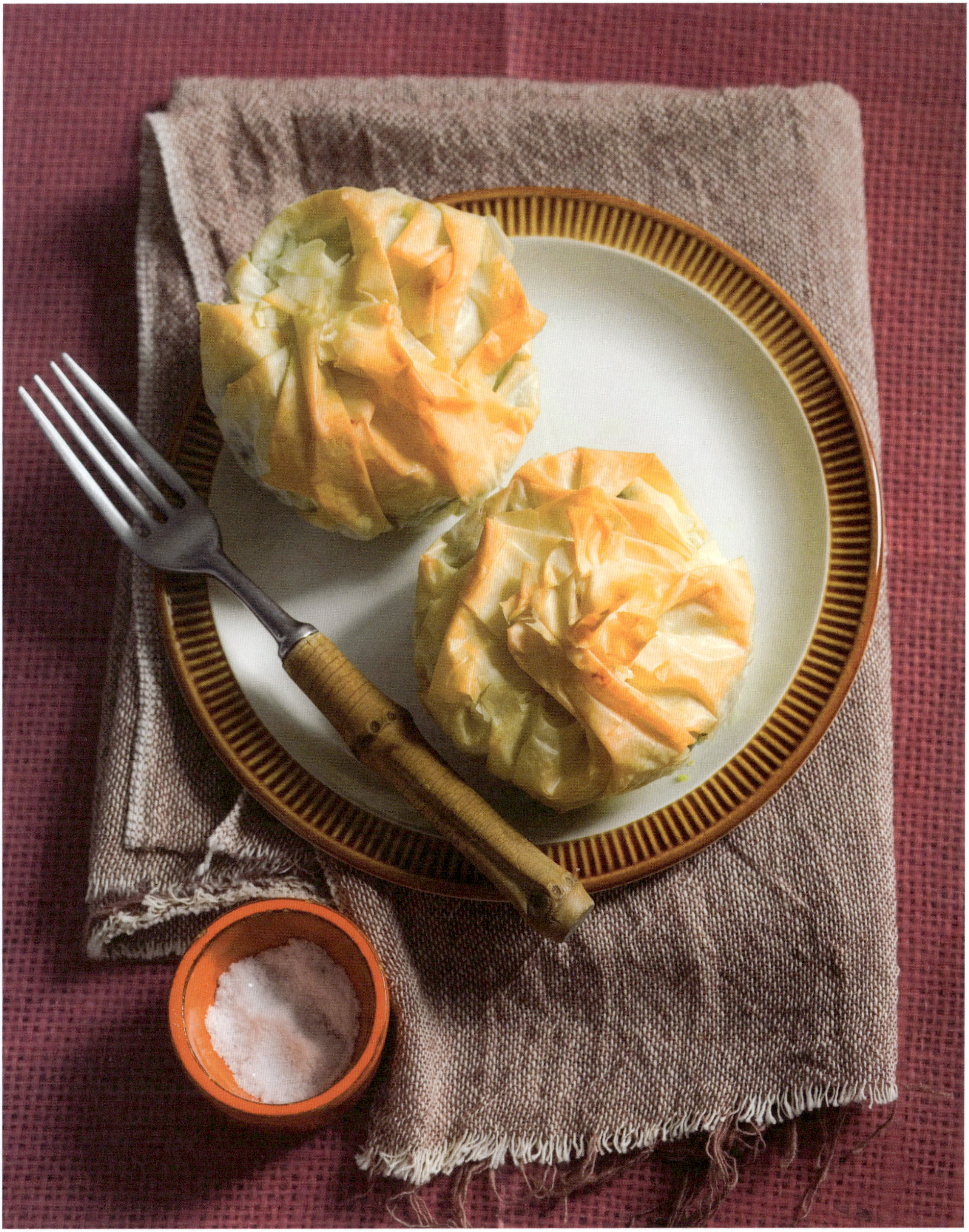

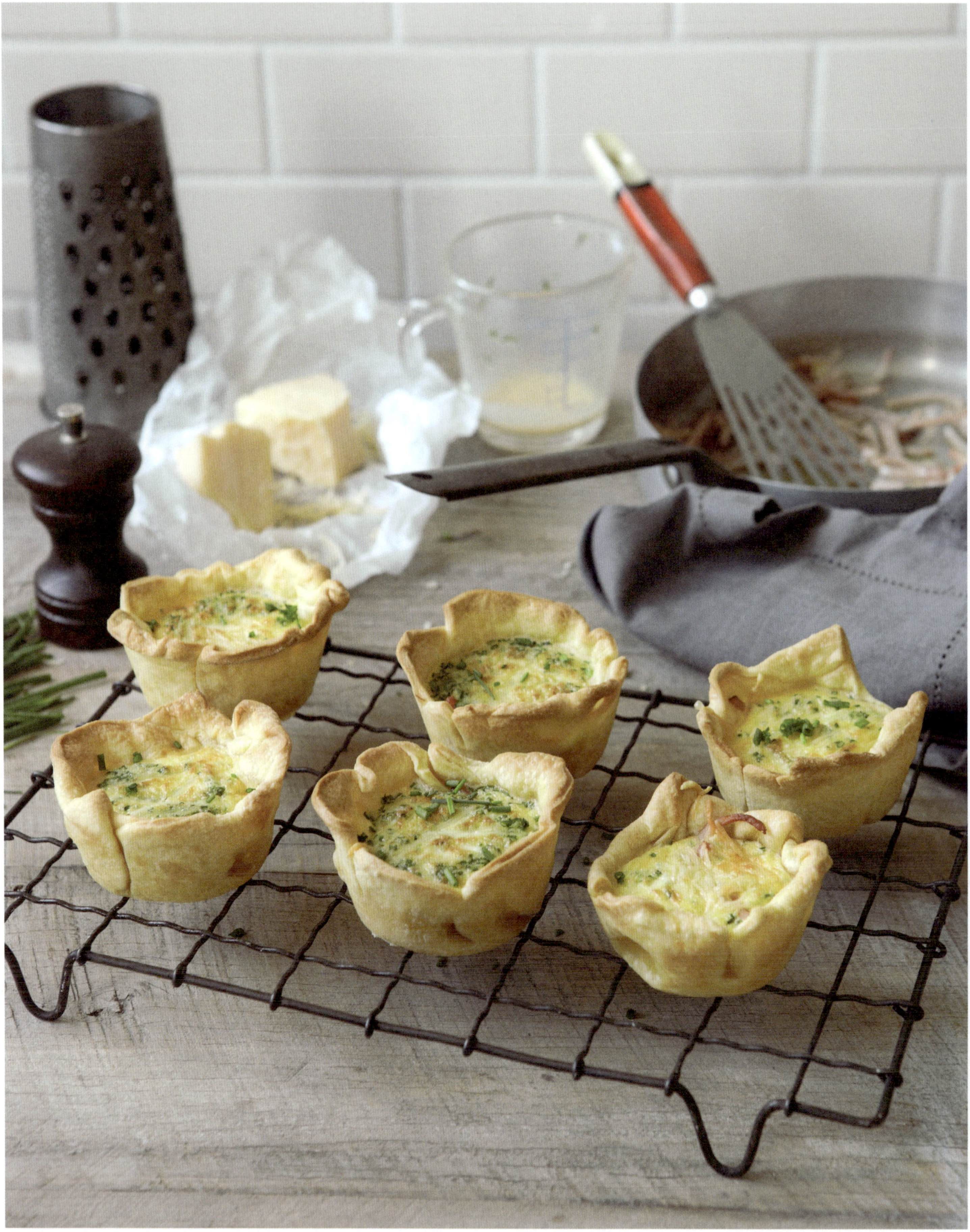

gluten-free egg, bacon and parmesan pies

2 teaspoons vegetable oil
6 rindless bacon slices (195g), sliced thinly
1 small brown onion (80g), chopped finely
2 cloves garlic, crushed
4 eggs
¼ cup (60ml) pouring cream
¼ cup (20g) finely grated parmesan cheese
1 tablespoon finely chopped fresh chives
pastry
1 cup (180g) rice flour
¼ cup (35g) (corn) cornflour (cornstarch)
¼ cup (30g) soya flour
¼ cup (20g) finely grated parmesan cheese
150g (4½ ounces) cold butter, chopped
2 tablespoons cold water, approximately

1 Make pastry.
2 Preheat oven to 220°C/425°F. Oil 6-hole (¾-cup/180ml) texas muffin pan.
3 Roll pastry between sheets of baking paper until 5mm (¼-inch) thick. Using 11cm (4½-inch) cutter, cut six rounds from pastry. Place rounds into pan holes, press into base and sides; prick bases with fork.
4 Bake pastry cases about 10 minutes or until browned lightly. Cool in pan.
5 Reduce oven to 200°C/400°F.
6 Meanwhile, heat oil in small frying pan; cook bacon, onion and garlic, stirring, until bacon is soft. Divide bacon mixture among pastry cases.
7 Whisk eggs and cream in medium jug; stir in cheese and chives. Pour egg mixture into pastry cases.
8 Bake pies about 25 minutes or until set.

pastry Process flours, cheese and butter until fine. Add enough of the water to make ingredients come together. Wrap pastry with plastic wrap; refrigerate 30 minutes.

prep + cook time 50 minutes (+ refrigeration) **makes** 6
nutritional count per pie 35.7g total fat (20.2g saturated fat); 2094kJ (501 cal); 32.3g carbohydrate; 18.2g protein; 1.4g fibre

This recipe is gluten-free, wheat-free and yeast-free.

vegetable and egg

freeform caramelised leek tarts

2 tablespoons olive oil
2 medium brown onions (300g), sliced thinly
2 medium leeks (700g), trimmed, sliced thinly
1 tablespoon fresh thyme leaves
2 cups (400g) ricotta cheese
⅓ cup (25g) coarsely grated parmesan cheese
1 egg, separated
4 sheets shortcrust pastry

1 Heat oil in large frying pan; cook onion and leek, stirring, about 15 minutes or until mixture starts to caramelise. Stir in thyme; cool.
2 Meanwhile, combine cheeses and egg yolk in small bowl.
3 Preheat oven to 200°C/400°F. Oil two oven trays; line with baking paper.
4 Using 20cm (8-inch) plate as a guide, cut one round from each pastry sheet; place two rounds on each tray. Divide ricotta mixture among rounds, leaving 4cm (1½-inch) border around edges.
5 Divide leek mixture over rounds. Turn border of each tart up around filling; brush upturned edges with egg white.
6 Bake tarts about 35 minutes or until pastry is browned lightly.

prep + cook time 1 hour 20 minutes **makes** 4
nutritional count per tart 70g total fat (34.3g saturated fat); 4531kJ (1084 cal); 83.2g carbohydrate; 28.3g protein; 7.1g fibre

vegetable and egg

cheese pastries

1½ cups (225g) plain (all-purpose) flour
1½ cups (225g) self-raising flour
½ teaspoon salt
¾ cup (180ml) warm water
¼ cup (60ml) olive oil
1 egg, beaten lightly
2 teaspoons sesame seeds
filling
1 egg, beaten lightly
100g (3 ounces) fetta cheese, crumbled
½ cup (120g) ricotta cheese
½ cup (40g) finely grated romano cheese

1 Preheat oven to 200°C/400°F. Oil oven trays; line with baking paper.
2 Process flours and salt until combined. While motor is operating, add enough of the combined water and oil so the mixture forms a ball (do not overmix). Wrap dough in plastic; refrigerate 30 minutes.
3 Meanwhile, combine ingredients for filling in bowl.
4 Divide dough in half. Roll each half on floured surface to 30cm x 40cm (12-inch x 16-inch) rectangle; using 8.5cm (3½-inch) cutter, cut 13 rounds from dough. Drop rounded teaspoons of filling onto rounds; brush edges with a little water. Fold rounds in half, press edges together with a fork to seal. Place pastries on trays; brush with egg, sprinkle with sesame seeds.
5 Bake pastries about 15 minutes or until browned lightly.

prep + cook time 1 hour 15 minutes (+ refrigeration)
makes 26
nutritional count per pastry 4.7g total fat (1.6g saturated fat); 456kJ (109 cal); 12.4g carbohydrate; 4g protein; 0.7g fibre

potato samosa

1½ cups (225g) plain (all-purpose) flour
1 tablespoon ghee
1 tablespoon cumin seeds
½ cup (125ml) warm water, approximately
vegetable oil, for deep-frying
potato masala filling
125g (4 ounces) coliban potatoes, chopped finely
1 teaspoon ghee
½ small brown onion (40g), chopped finely
1 clove garlic, crushed
½ fresh large green chilli, chopped finely
1 teaspoon grated fresh ginger
¼ teaspoon each coriander seeds and cumin seeds
½ teaspoon garam masala
1 tablespoon finely chopped fresh coriander (cilantro)
1 teaspoon lemon juice

1 Place flour in medium bowl; rub in ghee. Add seeds; gradually stir in enough of the water to make a firm dough. Knead on floured surface until smooth and elastic, enclose with plastic wrap; refrigerate 30 minutes.
2 Make potato masala filling.
3 Roll dough on floured surface until 3mm (⅛-inch) thick. Using 8cm (3¼-inch) cutter, cut 28 rounds from dough. Place level teaspoons of cold filling in centre of each round; brush around edge of rounds with water, press together to enclose filling.
4 Heat oil in large saucepan; deep-fry samosas, in batches, until browned and crisp. Drain on absorbent paper.

potato masala filling Boil, steam or microwave potato until just tender; drain. Mash half the potato in small bowl. Melt ghee in medium saucepan; cook onion, garlic, chilli, ginger, seeds and garam masala, stirring, until onion softens. Stir in coriander, juice and both mashed and chopped potato.

prep + cook time 1 hour (+ refrigeration) **makes** 28
nutritional count per samosa 2g total fat (0.7g saturated fat); 205kJ (49 cal); 6.5g carbohydrate; 1g protein; 0.4g fibre

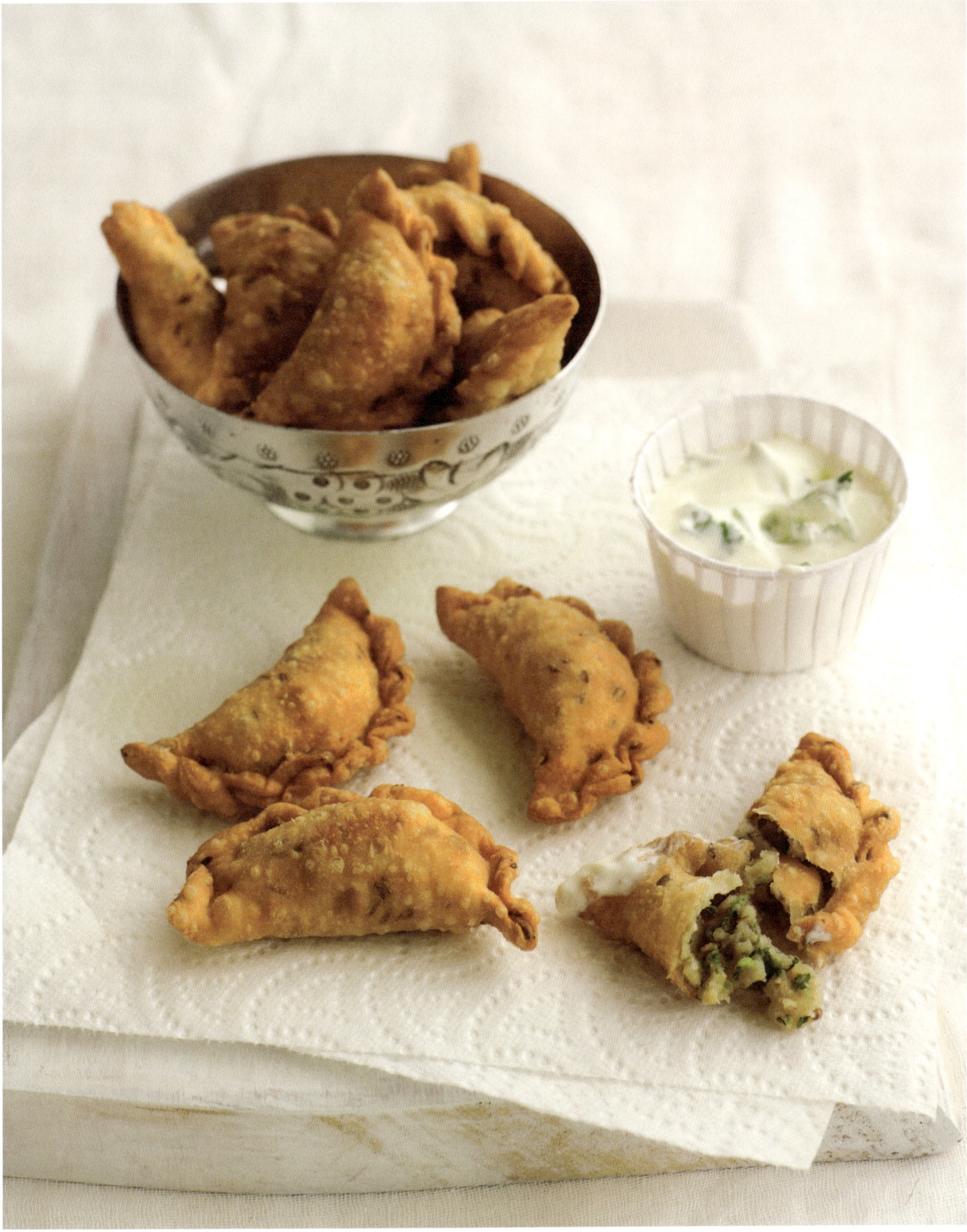

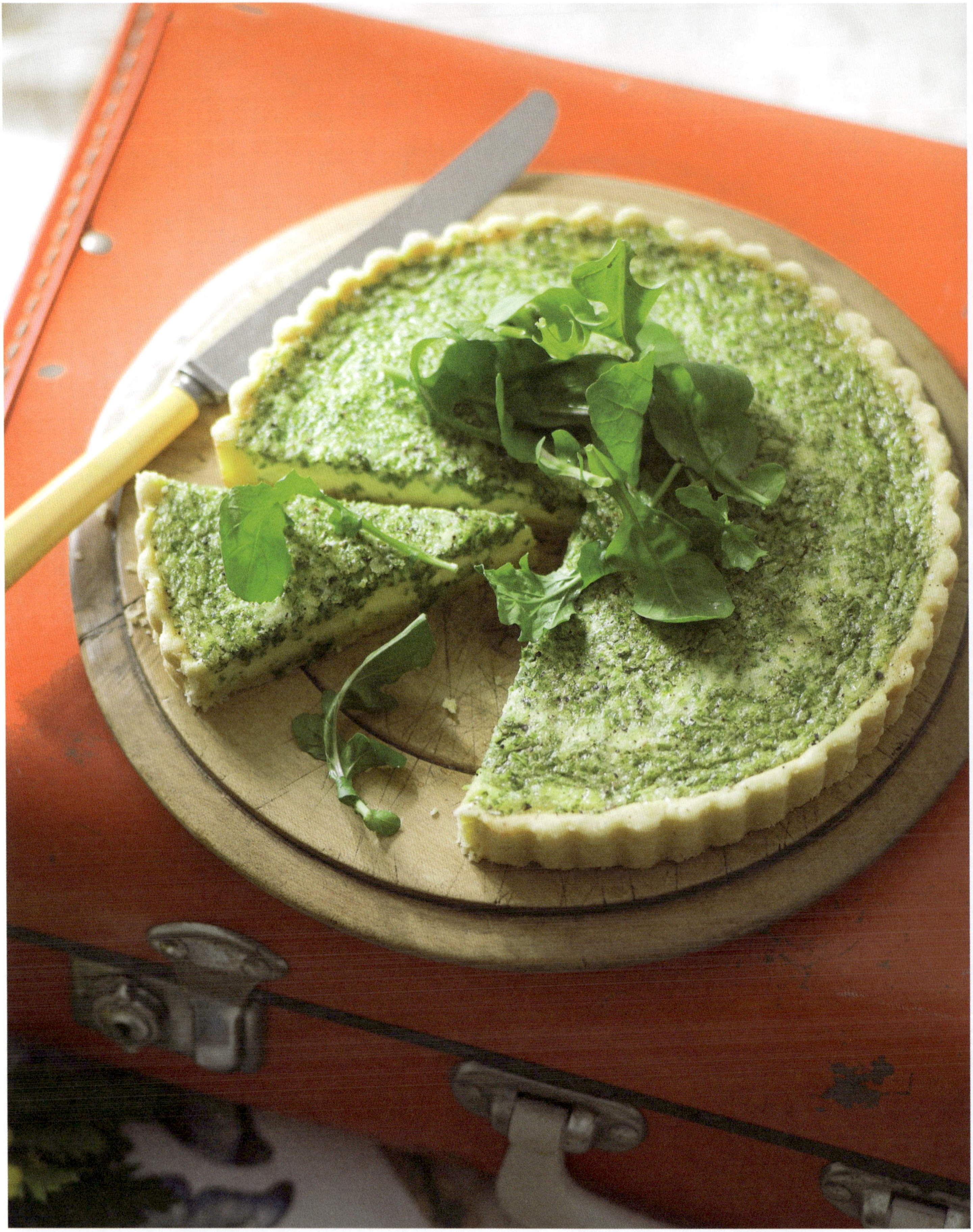

baby rocket quiche

50g (1½ ounces) baby rocket (arugula) leaves, chopped finely
3 eggs
1 egg yolk
¾ cup (180ml) pouring cream

pastry
1¼ cups (185g) plain (all-purpose) flour
125g (4 ounces) cold butter, chopped coarsely
1 egg yolk
2 teaspoons iced water

1 Make pastry.
2 Preheat oven to 200°C/400°F.
3 Oil shallow 20cm (8-inch) round loose-based fluted flan tin. Roll pastry out on floured surface until 5mm (¼-inch) thick. Lift pastry into tin; press into base and side, trim edge, prick base all over with fork. Cover; refrigerate 20 minutes.
4 Line pastry with baking paper, fill with dried beans or rice. Bake 12 minutes. Remove paper and beans; bake about 8 minutes or until pastry is browned lightly. Reduce oven to 160°C/325°F.
5 Sprinkle rocket into pastry case. Whisk eggs, egg yolk and cream in medium jug; pour over rocket.
6 Bake quiche about 40 minutes or until set. Cool.

pastry Process flour and butter until crumbly. Add egg yolk and the water, process until ingredients come together. Knead on floured surface until smooth, enclose with plastic wrap; refrigerate 20 minutes.

prep + cook time 1 hour 20 minutes (+ refrigeration)
serves 8
nutritional count per serving 25.9g total fat (15.6g saturated fat); 1375kJ (329 cal); 17.6g carbohydrate; 6.7g protein; 1g fibre

This quiche can be made a day ahead, keep covered in the refrigerator. You can also make and bake the pastry case a day or two ahead, then add and bake the filling on the day.

vegetable and egg

tomato tarts

4 medium vine-ripened tomatoes (600g), peeled, quartered, seeded
1 tablespoon light brown sugar
1 tablespoon balsamic vinegar
½ sheet puff pastry
16 sprigs fresh chervil

1 Preheat oven 220°C/425°F.
2 Combine tomato, sugar and vinegar in small baking dish; roast, about 20 minutes or until tomato is soft.
3 Meanwhile, cut pastry sheet in half lengthways, cut each half into four squares; cut each square into triangles (you will have 16). Place pastry triangles on oiled oven tray; top with another oiled oven tray (the second tray stops the pastry from puffing up). Bake pastry, alongside tomato, about 10 minutes or until crisp.
4 Place a tomato piece on each pastry triangle. Serve topped with chervil.

prep + cook time 40 minutes **makes** 16
nutritional count per tart 1.2g total fat (0.6g saturated fat); 117kJ (28 cal); 3.4g carbohydrate; 0.7g protein; 0.5g fibre

caramelised leek and brie tartlets

1 tablespoon olive oil
25g (¾ ounce) butter
2 medium leeks (700g), sliced finely
1 clove garlic, crushed
1 tablespoon light brown sugar
1 tablespoon white wine vinegar
3 sheets puff pastry
200g (6½-ounce) piece brie cheese
24 sprigs lemon thyme

1 Preheat oven to 200°C/400°F. Oil two 12-hole (2-tablespoons/40ml) deep flat-based patty pans.
2 Heat oil and butter in large frying pan; cook leek, stirring, about 5 minutes or until leek softens. Add garlic, sugar and vinegar; cook, stirring, about 8 minutes or until leek caramelises.
3 Cut eight squares from each pastry sheet; press one pastry square into each pan hole. Divide leek mixture into pastry cases.
4 Cut cheese into 24 pieces. Place a piece of cheese on top of each tartlet.
5 Bake tartlets about 20 minutes. Serve tartlets topped with thyme.

prep + cook time 40 minutes **makes** 24
nutritional count per tartlet 8.8g total fat (4.8g saturated fat); 535kJ (128 cal); 8.7g carbohydrate; 3.1g protein; 0.8g fibre

We used a 8.5cm (3½-inch) square cutter to make the pastry squares. The cutter is measured from corner to corner.

roasted vegetable tarts

90g (3 ounces) cold butter, chopped
1¼ cups (185g) plain (all-purpose) flour
½ cup (40g) grated parmesan cheese
1 egg yolk
3 teaspoons iced water
½ large butternut pumpkin (600g), chopped coarsely
10 baby beetroot (beets) (300g), trimmed
10 shallots (250g), peeled
8 cloves garlic
2 tablespoons olive oil
1 tablespoon chopped fresh chives
roast garlic cream
¾ cup (180g) sour cream
2 tablespoons milk
1 tablespoon chopped fresh chives

1 Process butter, flour and cheese until butter is combined. Add egg yolk and the water, process until ingredients just come together. Enclose with plastic wrap; refrigerate 30 minutes.
2 Preheat oven to 200°C/400°F. Combine pumpkin, beetroot, shallots and garlic with oil in large baking dish; bake about 45 minutes or until tender.
3 Meanwhile, oil six 6cm (2½-inch) round fluted ovenproof dishes. Divide dough into six portions. Roll each portion between two sheets of baking paper until large enough to line dishes. Lift pastry into dishes; press into base and side, trim edge. Place dishes on oven tray; refrigerate 30 minutes.
4 Peel beetroot, wearing disposable gloves. Squeeze flesh from garlic skins; reserve garlic for roast garlic cream. Cover vegetables to keep warm.
5 Reduce oven to 180°C/350°F. Line pastry in each dish with baking paper; fill with dried beans or rice. Bake 10 minutes. Remove paper and beans; bake further 5 minutes or until browned and crisp.
6 Place ingredients for roast garlic cream in small bowl with reserved garlic; stir to combine.
7 Fill pastry cases with roasted vegetables; sprinkle with chives. Serve tarts warm with roast garlic cream.

prep + cook time 1 hour 20 minutes (+ refrigeration)
makes 6
nutritional count per tart 34.6g total fat (19g saturated fat); 2061kJ (493 cal); 33.6g carbohydrate; 10.6g protein; 4.7g fibre

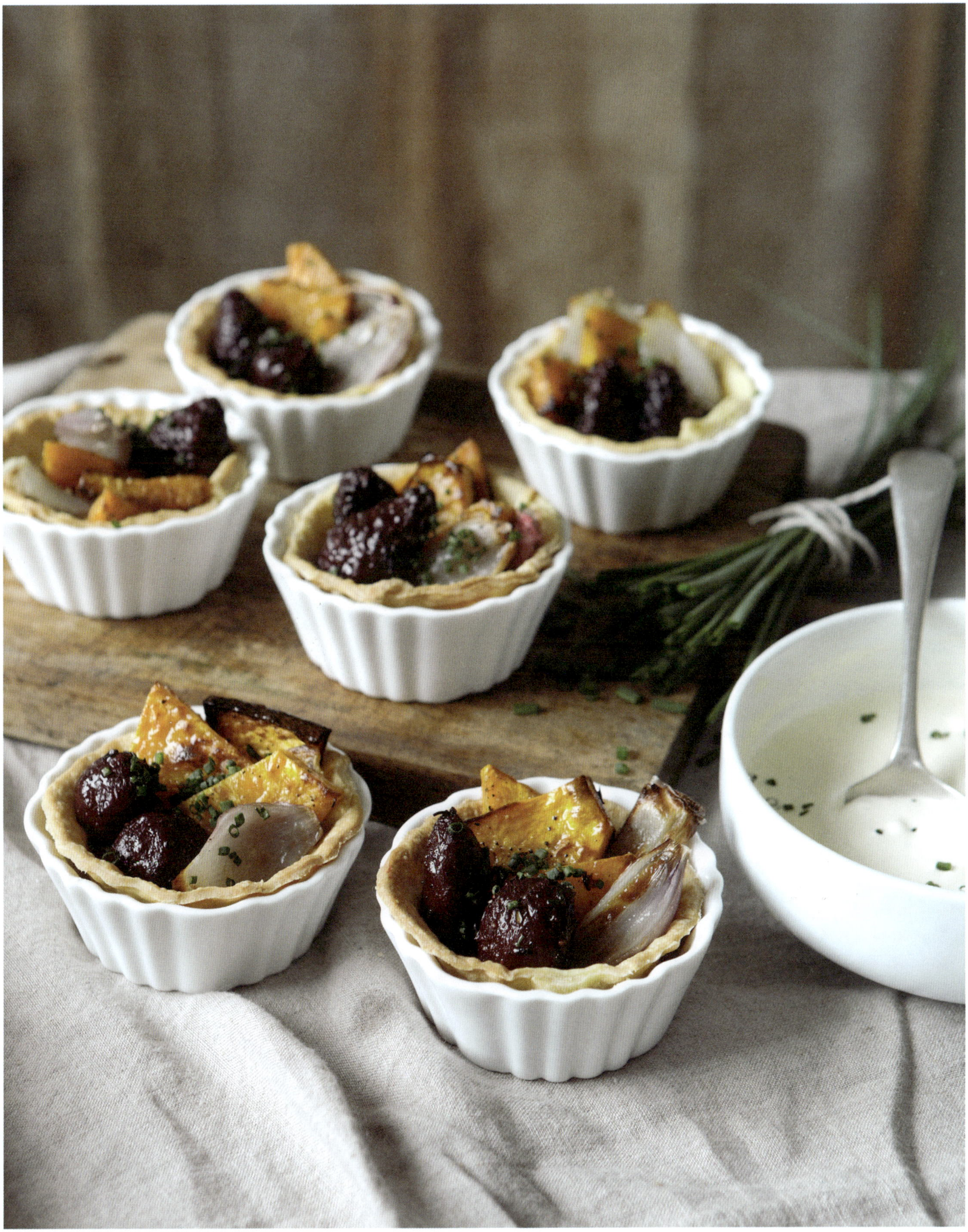

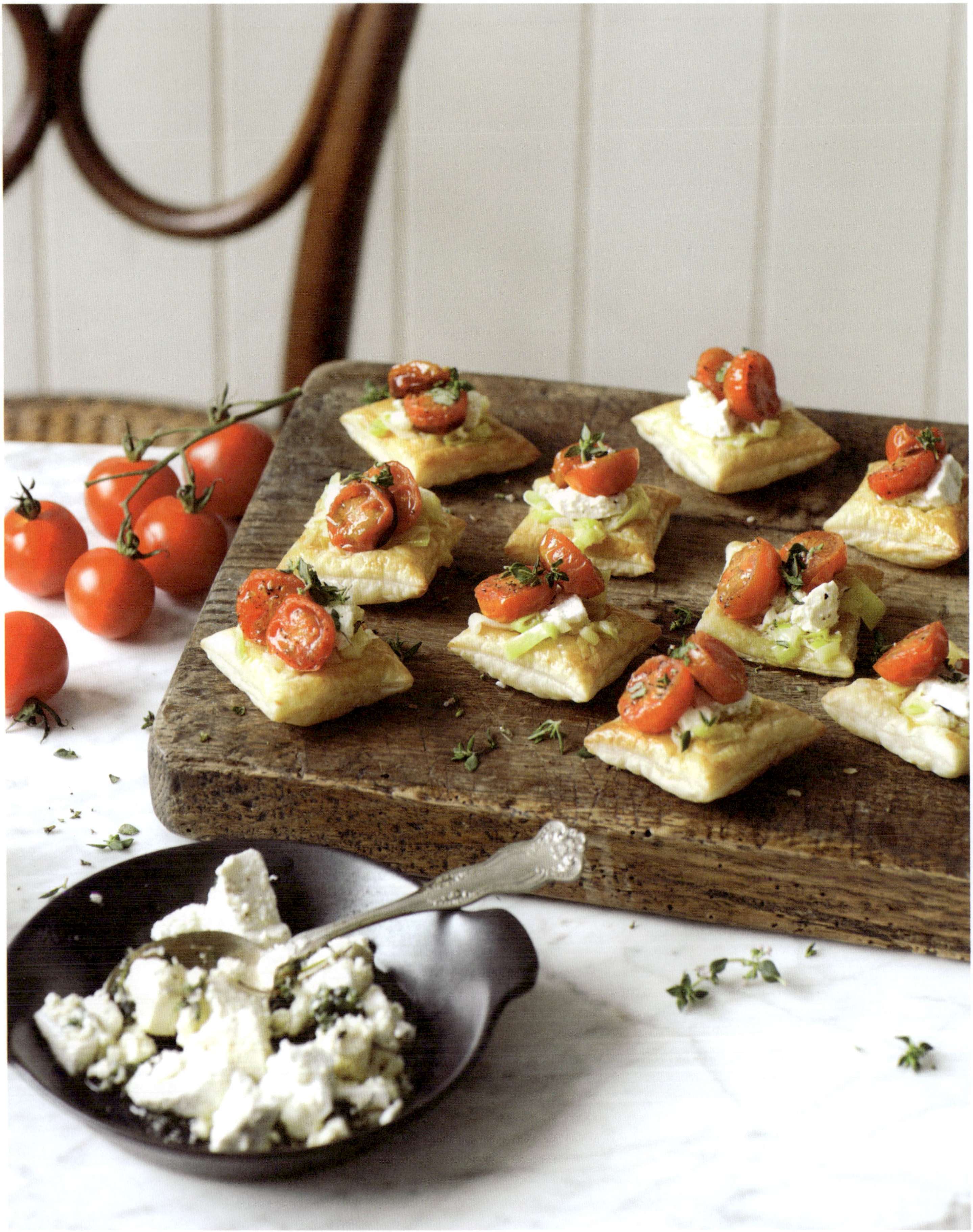

tomato, leek and marinated fetta tartlets

1 medium leek (350g)
20g (¾ ounce) butter
1 tablespoon olive oil
2 sheets puff pastry
500g (1 pound) cherry tomatoes, halved
1 tablespoon red wine vinegar
½ teaspoon fresh thyme leaves

marinated fetta
1 teaspoon finely grated lemon rind
¼ teaspoon cracked black pepper
2 cloves garlic, crushed
2 teaspoons fresh thyme leaves
200g (6½-ounce) piece fetta cheese, cut into 25 pieces
1¼ cups (310ml) olive oil

1 Make marinated fetta.
2 Preheat oven to 220°C/425°F.
3 Cut leek into 6cm (2¼-inch) pieces; cut pieces in half lengthways, slice halves lengthways into thin strips. Heat butter and oil in large frying pan; cook leek, stirring occasionally, about 20 minutes or until soft.
4 Meanwhile, cut pastry sheets into 25 x 5cm (2-inch) squares; place on oiled oven trays, prick pastry with fork. Bake about 10 minutes or until browned lightly. Reduce oven to 200°C/400°F.
5 Meanwhile, combine tomatoes and vinegar in medium bowl; season to taste.
6 Spread 1 tablespoon of the leek mixture on each pastry piece; crumble one piece of cheese over each, then top with tomato mixture.
7 Bake tartlets about 5 minutes or until tomato just softens. Serve immediately, sprinkled with thyme.

marinated fetta Place rind, pepper, garlic and thyme in medium sterilised glass jar with a tight-fitting lid; add cheese. Seal jar then shake gently to coat cheese in mixture. Open jar and pour in enough of the oil to completely cover cheese mixture. Reseal; refrigerate overnight.

prep + cook time 1 hour 25 minutes (+ refrigeration)
makes 25
nutritional count per tartlet 7g total fat (2.1g saturated fat); 401kJ (96 cal); 5.6g carbohydrate; 2.5g protein; 0.8g fibre

The fetta can be marinated up to two weeks before making the tartlets; keep, covered, in the refrigerator.
Work with one puff pastry sheet at a time, keeping the other in the freezer so that it doesn't become too soft.

vegetable and egg

lentil cottage pie

4 medium potatoes (800g), chopped coarsely
½ cup (125ml) milk, warmed
4 green onions (scallions), chopped finely
½ cup (100g) french-style green lentils
1 tablespoon olive oil
1 large brown onion (200g), chopped finely
2 cloves garlic, crushed
1 medium red capsicum (bell pepper) (200g), chopped coarsely
2 medium zucchini (240g), chopped coarsely
1 medium eggplant (300g), chopped coarsely
410g (13 ounces) canned crushed tomatoes

1 Boil, steam or microwave potato until tender; drain. Mash potato in large bowl with milk and green onion until smooth.
2 Meanwhile, cook lentils in small saucepan of boiling water until just tender; drain. Rinse; drain.
3 Preheat oven to 200°C/400°F.
4 Heat oil in medium saucepan; cook brown onion, garlic, capsicum, zucchini and eggplant, stirring, until vegetables soften. Add lentils and undrained tomato; bring to the boil. Reduce heat; simmer, about 10 minutes or until mixture has thickened.
5 Spoon mixture into oiled shallow 2.5-litre (10-cup) baking dish; spread with potato mixture.
6 Bake pie about 30 minutes or until top browns lightly.

prep + cook time 1 hour 35 minutes **serves** 4
nutritional count per serving 7.3g total fat (1.5g saturated fat); 1384kJ (331 cal); 44.8g carbohydrate; 15.4g protein; 11.8g fibre

corn, mushroom, capsicum and potato puddings

4 medium potatoes (800g), chopped coarsely
¼ cup (60ml) milk
40g (1½ ounces) low-fat dairy-free spread
3 trimmed corn cobs (750g)
2 teaspoons olive oil
2 cloves garlic, crushed
1 fresh long red chilli, chopped finely
1 medium brown onion (150g), chopped coarsely
1 medium red capsicum (bell pepper) (200g), chopped coarsely
150g (4½ ounces) mushrooms, chopped coarsely
¾ cup (90g) low-fat cheddar cheese, grated coarsely

1 Preheat oven to 200°C/400°F.
2 Boil, steam or microwave potato until tender; drain. Mash potato in large bowl with milk and dairy-free spread until smooth.
3 Meanwhile, using sharp knife, cut corn kernels from cobs. Heat oil in medium frying pan; cook garlic, chilli and onion, stirring, until onion softens. Add corn, capsicum and mushrooms; cook, stirring, until corn is tender. Stir in ½ cup of the cheese.
4 Spoon corn mixture into four 1¼-cup (310ml) ovenproof dishes; top with mashed potato and remaining cheese. Place dishes on oven tray.
5 Bake puddings about 25 minutes or until heated through and cheese is browned lightly.

prep + cook time 50 minutes **makes** 4
nutritional count per pudding 10.5g total fat (2.6g saturated fat); 1597kJ (382 cal); 50g carbohydrate; 20.7g protein; 11.1g fibre

caramelised fennel tarts

50g (1½ ounces) butter
4 baby fennel bulbs (520g), trimmed, halved lengthways
1 teaspoon finely grated orange rind
½ cup (125ml) orange juice
1 sheet puff pastry
2 teaspoons finely chopped fresh thyme

1 Preheat oven to 220°C/425°F. Oil two oven trays; line with baking paper.
2 Melt butter in large frying pan; cook fennel until browned lightly. Add rind and juice; bring to the boil. Reduce heat; simmer, uncovered, about 5 minutes or until fennel is caramelised and tender.
3 Cut pastry sheet into four squares; place on oven trays. Remove fennel from pan, leaving behind the pan juices; divide among pastry squares.
4 Bake tarts about 20 minutes or until pastry is browned lightly.
5 Meanwhile, return pan juices to the boil. Reduce heat; simmer, uncovered, until sauce thickens slightly.
6 Serve tarts drizzled with sauce and sprinkled with thyme.

prep + cook time 45 minutes **serves** 4
nutritional count per serving 19.8g total fat (11.9g saturated fat); 1145kJ (274 cal); 19.9g carbohydrate; 3.3g protein; 2.7g fibre

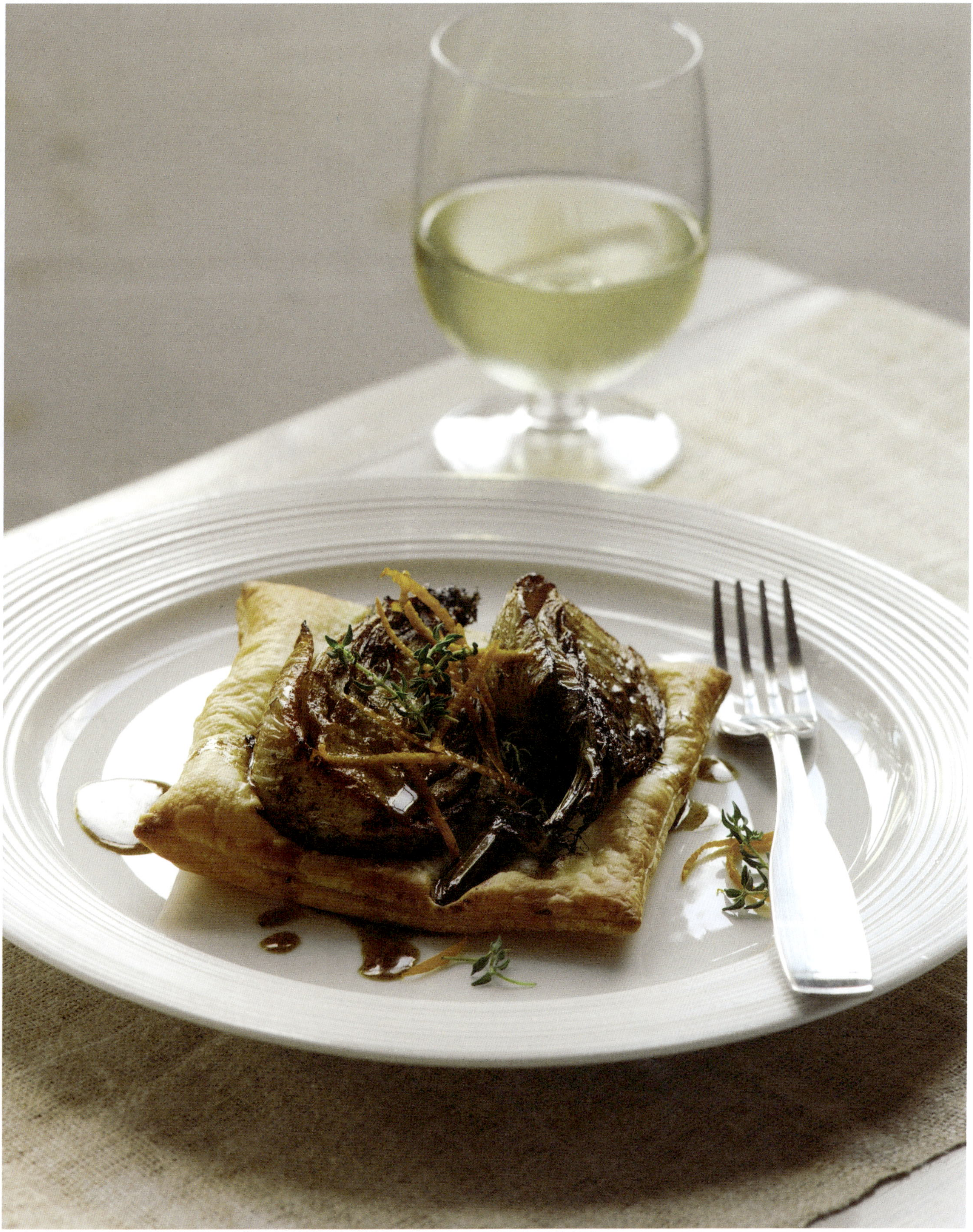

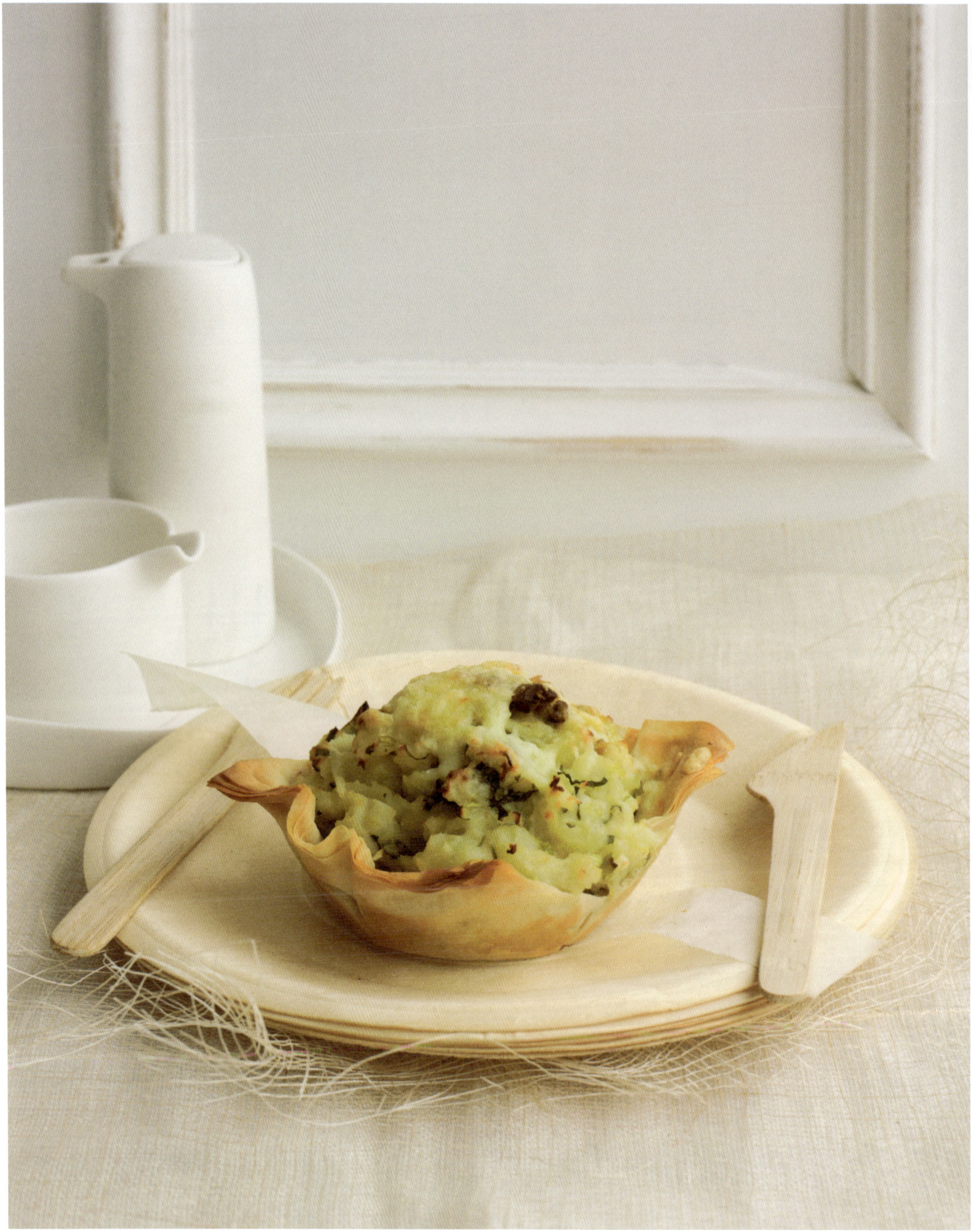

vegetarian tarts

1kg (2 pounds) lasoda potatoes, chopped coarsely
½ cup (125ml) hot vegetable stock
30g (1 ounce) butter
2 cloves garlic, crushed
200g (6½ ounces) mushrooms, sliced thickly
2 tablespoons finely shredded fresh basil
2 green onions (scallions), chopped finely
⅔ cup (80g) coarsely grated cheddar cheese
3 sheets fillo pastry
30g (1 ounce) butter, melted

1 Boil, steam or microwave potato until tender; drain. Mash potato in large bowl with stock.
2 Meanwhile, melt butter in small frying pan; cook garlic and mushroom, stirring, until mushroom softens. Stir mushroom mixture, basil, onion and half the cheese into potato mixture.
3 Preheat oven to 200°C/400°F. Oil four 1-cup (250ml) metal pie dishes. Place a 2.5cm x 30cm (1-inch x 12-inch) strip of baking paper over base of each dish, extending 5cm (2 inches) over sides of dishes.
4 Stack fillo sheets; cut stack in half crossways. Brush between layers with melted butter, then cut stack into four squares. Line dishes with pastry squares. Spoon potato mixture into dishes; sprinkle with remaining cheese. Place dishes on oven tray.
5 Bake tarts about 15 minutes or until pastry is browned lightly. Use baking paper strips to lift tarts out of dishes.

prep + cook time 45 minutes **serves** 4
nutritional count per serving 19.9g total fat (12.5g saturated fat); 1697kJ (406 cal); 39.3g carbohydrate; 14.5g protein; 5.9g fibre

sweet pies and tarts

apple pie

10 medium apples (1.5kg)
½ cup (125ml) water
¼ cup (55g) caster (superfine) sugar
1 teaspoon finely grated lemon rind
¼ teaspoon ground cinnamon
1 egg white
1 tablespoon caster (superfine) sugar, extra
pastry
1 cup (150g) plain (all-purpose) flour
½ cup (75g) self-raising flour
¼ cup (35g) cornflour (cornstarch)
¼ cup (30g) custard powder
1 tablespoon caster (superfine) sugar
100g (3 ounces) cold butter, chopped coarsely
1 egg yolk
¼ cup (60ml) iced water

1 Make pastry.
2 Peel, core and slice apple thickly. Place apple and the water in large saucepan; bring to the boil. Reduce heat; simmer, covered, about 10 minutes or until apples soften. Drain; stir in sugar, rind and cinnamon. Cool.
3 Preheat oven to 220°C/425°F. Grease deep 25cm (10-inch) pie dish.
4 Divide pastry in half. Roll one half between sheets of baking paper until large enough to line dish. Lift pastry into dish; press into base and side. Spoon apple mixture into pastry case; brush edge with egg white.
5 Roll remaining pastry large enough to cover filling; lift onto filling. Press edges together; trim away excess pastry. Brush pastry with egg white; sprinkle with extra sugar.
6 Bake pie 20 minutes. Reduce oven to 180°C/350°F; bake about 25 minutes or until golden brown.

pastry Process dry ingredients and butter until crumbly. Add egg yolk and the water; process until combined. Knead dough on floured surface until smooth, enclose with plastic wrap; refrigerate 30 minutes.

prep + cook time 1 hour 45 minutes (+ refrigeration)
serves 8
nutritional count per serving 11.4g total fat (7g saturated fat); 1438kJ (344 cal); 53.9g carbohydrate; 4.3g protein; 3.7g fibre

pecan pie

1 cup (120g) pecans, chopped coarsely
2 tablespoons cornflour (cornstarch)
1 cup (220g) firmly packed light brown sugar
60g (2 ounces) butter, melted
2 tablespoons pouring cream
1 teaspoon vanilla extract
3 eggs
⅓ cup (40g) pecans, extra
2 tablespoons apricot jam, warmed, sieved
pastry
1¼ cups (185g) plain (all-purpose) flour
⅓ cup (55g) icing (confectioners') sugar
125g (4 ounces) cold butter, chopped
1 egg yolk
1 teaspoon water

1 Make pastry.
2 Grease 24cm (9½-inch) round loose-based fluted flan tin. Roll pastry between sheets of baking paper until large enough to line tin. Lift pastry into tin; press into side, trim edge. Cover; refrigerate 20 minutes.
3 Preheat oven to 180°C/350°F.
4 Place tin on oven tray; line pastry with baking paper, fill with dried beans or rice. Bake 10 minutes. Remove paper and beans; bake about 5 minutes or until browned lightly. Cool.
5 Reduce oven to 160°C/325°F.
6 Combine chopped nuts and cornflour in medium bowl. Add sugar, butter, cream, extract and eggs; stir until combined. Pour mixture into pastry case, sprinkle with extra nuts.
7 Bake pie about 30 minutes. Cool; brush top of pie with jam.

pastry Process flour, icing sugar and butter until crumbly. Add egg yolk and the water; process until ingredients just come together. Knead dough on floured surface until smooth, enclose with plastic wrap; refrigerate 30 minutes.

prep + cook time 1 hour 15 minutes (+ refrigeration)
serves 10
nutritional count per serving 30.8g total fat (12.6g saturated fat); 1986kJ (475 cal); 46.4g carbohydrate; 6.1g protein; 2.1g fibre

Store pecan pie in refrigerator, in an airtight container, for up to three days.

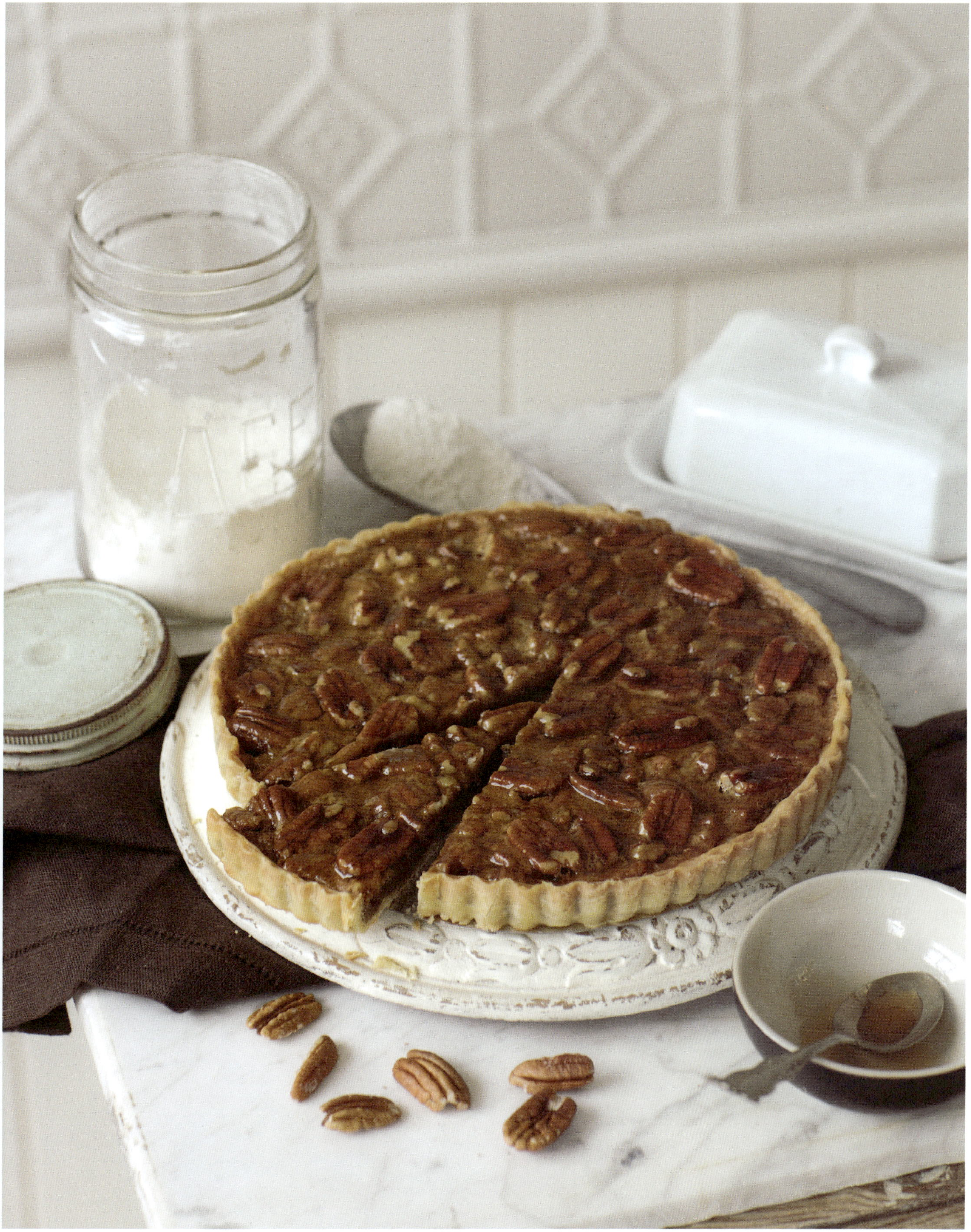

sweet pies and tarts

banoffee tart

1 sheet sweet shortcrust pastry
380g (12 ounces) canned caramel top 'n' fill
2 medium bananas (400g), sliced thinly
1¼ cups (310ml) thick double cream
½ teaspoon ground nutmeg

1 Preheat oven to 200°C/400°F. Grease 24cm (9½-inch) round loose-based fluted flan tin.
2 Lift pastry into tin; press into base and side, trim edge, prick base all over with fork. Cover; refrigerate 10 minutes.
3 Place tin on oven tray; line pastry case with baking paper, fill with dried beans or rice. Bake 15 minutes. Remove paper and beans; bake 10 minutes. Cool.
4 Fill pastry case with caramel; refrigerate overnight.
5 Top caramel with banana, then spread with cream. Serve sprinkled with nutmeg.

prep + cook time 30 minutes (+ refrigeration) **serves** 8
nutritional count per serving 28.7g total fat (18.2g saturated fat); 1839kJ (440 cal); 39.7g carbohydrate; 5.6g protein; 1.1g fibre

It is fine to use just one 300ml carton of cream for this recipe.

sweet pies and tarts

portuguese custard tarts

½ cup (110g) caster (superfine) sugar
2 tablespoons cornflour (cornstarch)
4 egg yolks
1¼ cups (310ml) pouring cream
⅓ cup (80ml) water
2cm (¾-inch) strip lemon rind
1 teaspoon vanilla extract
1 sheet sweet puff pastry

1 Preheat oven to 220°C/425°F. Grease 12-hole (⅓-cup/80ml) muffin pan.
2 Combine sugar and cornflour in medium saucepan; whisk in egg yolks, cream and the water. Add rind; stir over medium heat until mixture comes to the boil. Remove from heat; discard rind. Stir in extract.
3 Cut pastry sheet in half; place halves on top of each other. Roll pastry tightly (like a swiss roll) from one short side; cut roll into twelve 1cm (½-inch) rounds.
4 Place pastry rounds, cut-sides up, on floured surface; roll each into a 10cm (4-inch) round. Push rounds into pan holes; spoon in custard.
5 Bake tarts about 20 minutes. Stand 5 minutes, before lifting onto wire rack to cool.

prep + cook time 55 minutes **makes** 12
nutritional count per tart 14.3g total fat (8.3g saturated fat); 849kJ (203 cal); 16.5g carbohydrate; 2.4g protein; 0.2g fibre

It is fine to use just one 300ml carton of cream for this recipe.

131

spiced apricot and plum pie

2 x 825g (1¾-pound) canned dark plums in light syrup
2 cups (300g) dried apricots
1 cinnamon stick
3 cloves
½ teaspoon each mixed spice and ground ginger
2 sheets puff pastry
1 egg
spiced yogurt cream
½ cup (140g) yogurt
½ cup (120g) sour cream
1 tablespoon ground cinnamon
¼ teaspoon ground ginger

1 Preheat oven to 200°C/400°F. Grease 26cm (10½-inch) pie dish.
2 Drain plums; reserve 1 cup of the syrup. Halve plums, discard stones; place plums in dish.
3 Combine reserved syrup, apricots, cinnamon, cloves, mixed spice and ginger in medium saucepan, simmer, uncovered, until liquid is reduced to ½ cup. Remove and discard cinnamon stick and cloves; cool to room temperature. Pour mixture over plums.
4 Cut pastry into 2.5cm (1-inch) strips. Brush edge of dish with a little of the egg; press pastry strips around edge of dish. Twist remaining strips, place over filling in lattice pattern; trim ends, brush top with egg.
5 Bake pie about 40 minutes.
6 Make spiced yogurt cream; serve with pie.

spiced yogurt cream Combine ingredients in small bowl.

prep + cook time 1 hour 15 minutes (+ cooling)
serves 8
nutritional count per serving 16.5g total fat (5g saturated fat); 1655kJ (396 cal); 52.6g carbohydrate; 6.7g protein; 5.2g fibre

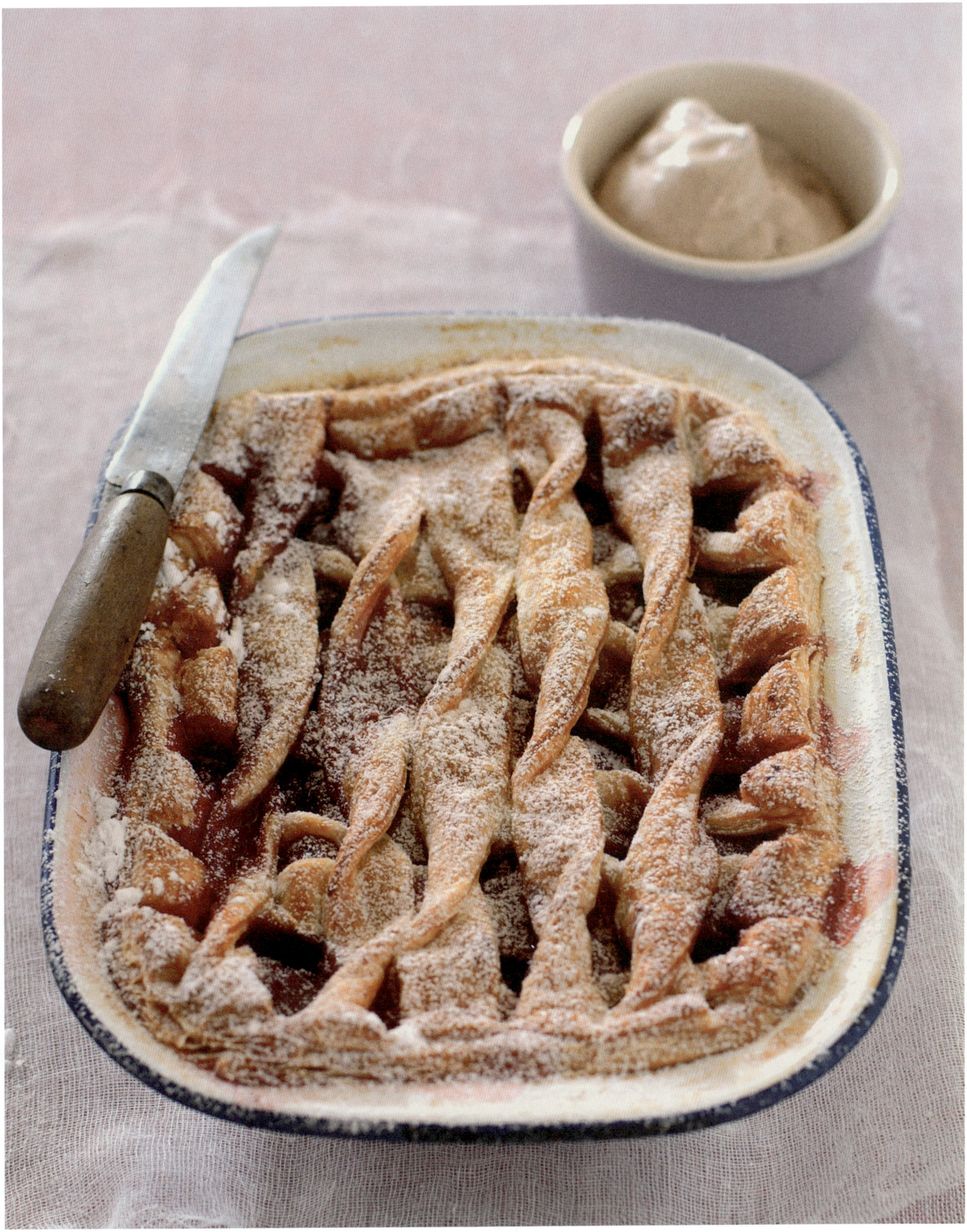

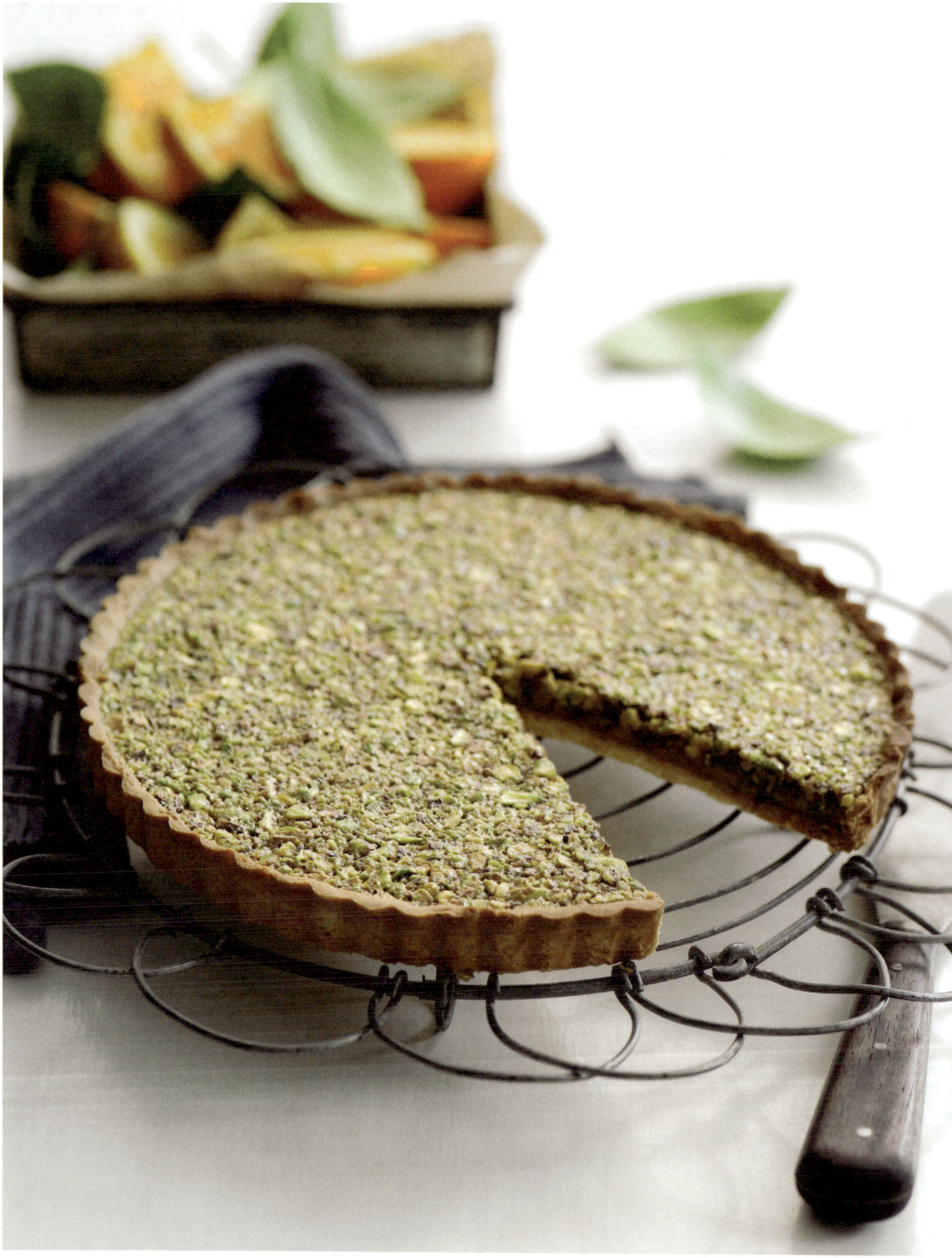

pistachio orange pie

1⅓ cups (185g) coarsely chopped unsalted pistachios
1 tablespoon plain (all-purpose) flour
2 tablespoons light brown sugar
40g (1½ ounces) butter, melted
2 eggs
¾ cup (180ml) maple syrup
2 teaspoons finely grated orange rind
1 tablespoon orange juice
2 tablespoons orange marmalade, warmed, sieved
pastry
1¼ cups (185g) plain (all-purpose) flour
⅓ cup (55g) icing (confectioners') sugar
125g (4 ounces) cold butter, chopped coarsely
1 egg yolk
1 teaspoon iced water, approximately

1 Make pastry.
2 Grease 24cm (9½-inch) round loose-based fluted flan tin. Roll pastry between sheets of baking paper until large enough to line tin. Lift pastry into tin, press into base and side; trim edge. Cover; refrigerate 30 minutes.
3 Preheat oven to 180°C/350°F.
4 Place tin on oven tray; line pastry with baking paper, fill with dried beans or rice. Bake 10 minutes. Remove paper and beans; bake 5 minutes. Cool.
5 Reduce oven to 160°C/325°F.
6 Combine nuts, flour, sugar, butter, eggs, syrup, rind and juice in medium bowl. Pour mixture into pastry case.
7 Bake pie about 45 minutes. Cool. Brush top of pie with marmalade.

pastry Process flour, icing sugar and butter until crumbly. Add egg yolk and enough of the water to process until ingredients come together. Knead dough on floured surface until smooth, enclose with plastic wrap; refrigerate 30 minutes.

prep + cook time 1 hour 20 minutes (+ refrigeration)
serves 10
nutritional count per serving 23.7g total fat (10.2g saturated fat); 1785kJ (427 cal); 44.9g carbohydrate; 7.4g protein; 2.5g fibre

pear cranberry pie

2 cups (300g) plain (all-purpose) flour
150g (4½ ounces) cold unsalted butter, chopped coarsely
½ cup (125ml) iced water
1 egg
1 tablespoon milk
1 tablespoon raw sugar
cranberry filling
½ cup (110g) caster (superfine) sugar
2 tablespoons water
400g (12½ ounces) frozen cranberries
pear filling
7 medium pears (1.6kg)
½ cup (125ml) water
⅓ cup (75g) caster (superfine) sugar

1 Process flour and butter until crumbly; add enough of the water to bring ingredients together. Press dough into a ball. Cover; refrigerate 1 hour.
2 Make cranberry filling. Make pear filling.
3 Preheat oven to 220°C/425°F.
4 Divide pastry in half. Roll one half between sheets of baking paper until large enough to line deep 25cm (10-inch) pie dish. Lift pastry into dish; ease into base and side. Spoon cranberry filling into pastry case; top with pear filling. Brush pastry edge with a little combined egg and milk.
5 Roll remaining pastry until large enough to cover top of pie; press edges together with fork to seal. Trim away excess pastry. Brush top of pie with egg mixture; sprinkle with sugar.
6 Bake pie 15 minutes. Reduce oven to 180°C/350°F; bake further 30 minutes.

cranberry filling Combine ingredients in medium saucepan; simmer, stirring, about 10 minutes or until syrupy. Remove from heat; cool.

pear filling Peel, quarter, core and slice pears thinly; place in large saucepan with the water. Simmer, stirring occasionally, about 10 minutes or until pear is tender. Drain pear; discard liquid. Stir sugar into pear; cool.

prep + cook time 1 hour 55 minutes (+ refrigeration)
serves 8
nutritional count per serving 16.8g total fat (10.5g saturated fat); 1580kJ (378 cal); 74.6g carbohydrate; 5.7g protein; 5.2g fibre

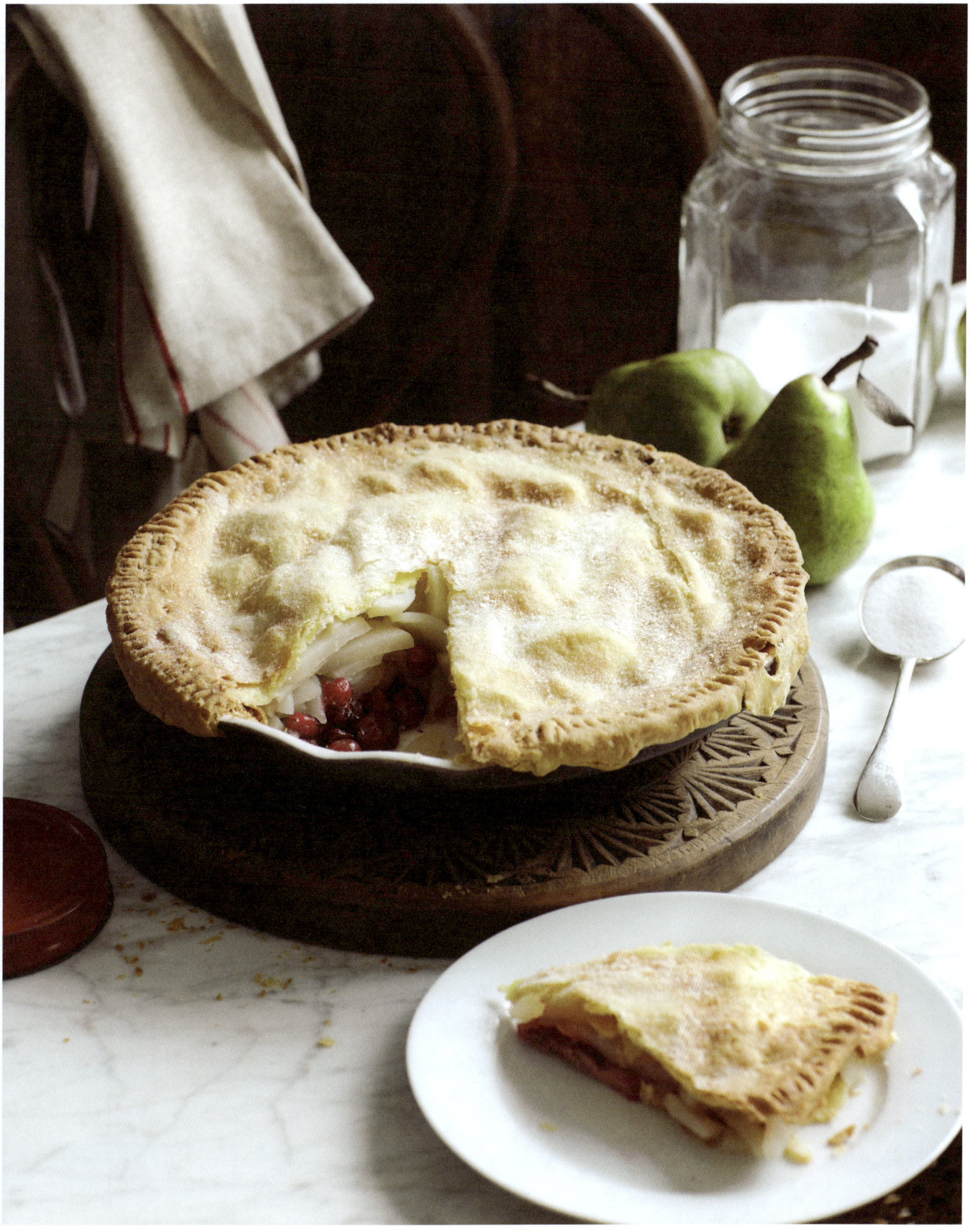

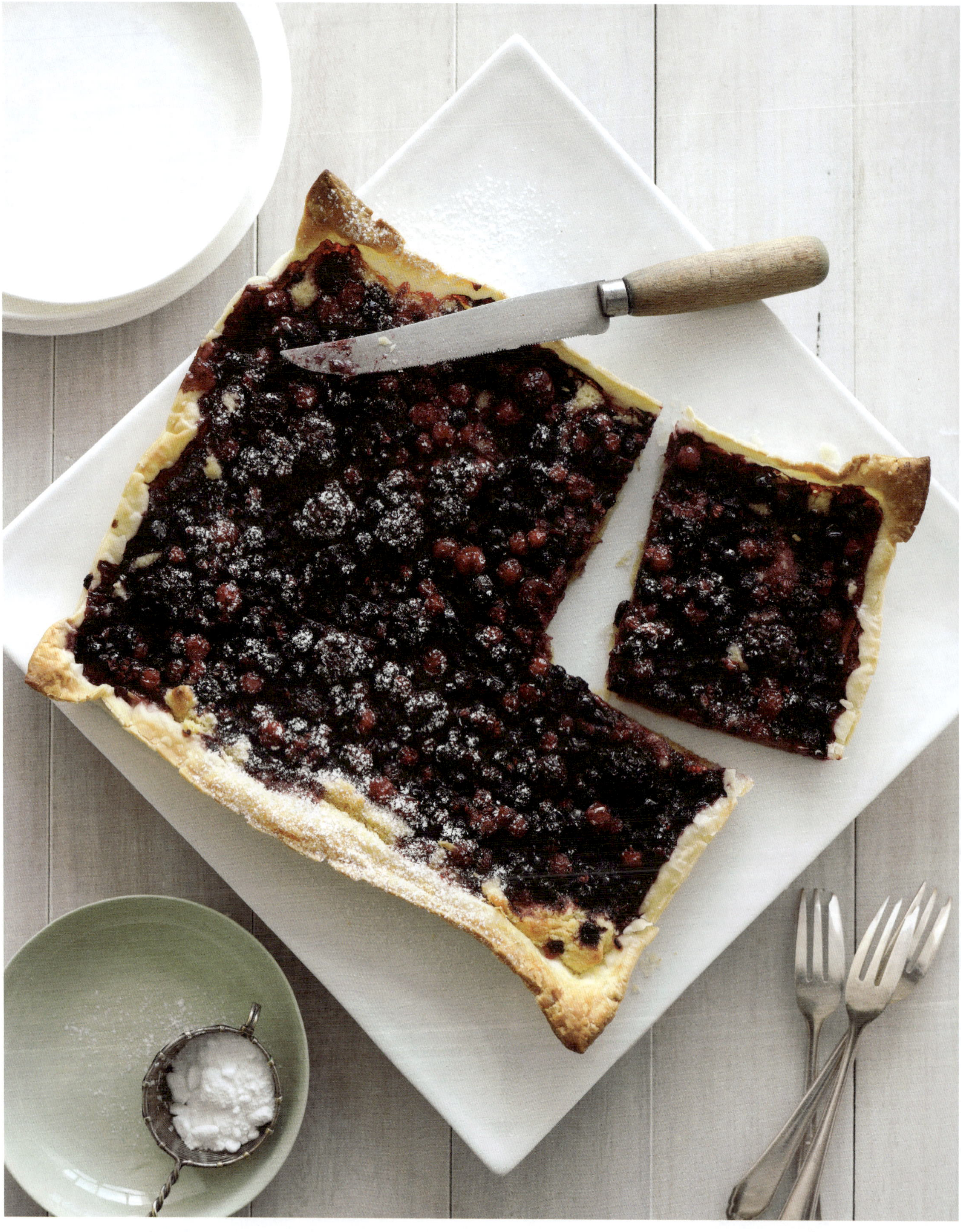

berry frangipane tart

1 sheet sweet puff pastry
300g (9½ ounces) frozen mixed berries
frangipane
80g (2½ ounces) butter, softened
½ teaspoon vanilla extract
⅓ cup (75g) caster (superfine) sugar
2 egg yolks
1 tablespoon plain (all-purpose) flour
1 cup (120g) ground almonds

1 Preheat oven to 220°C/425°F. Grease 20cm x 30cm (8-inch x 12-inch) lamington pan.
2 Roll pastry until large enough to line base and sides of pan. Lift pastry into pan; press into base and sides, prick base all over with fork. Freeze 5 minutes.
3 Place another lamington pan on top of pastry; bake 5 minutes. Remove top pan; bake 5 minutes or until pastry is browned lightly. Cool 5 minutes. Reduce oven to 180°C/350°F.
4 Meanwhile, make frangipane.
5 Spread frangipane over pastry base. Sprinkle with berries, press into frangipane.
6 Bake tart about 30 minutes or until browned lightly.

frangipane Beat butter, extract, sugar and egg yolks in small bowl with electric mixer until light and fluffy. Stir in flour and ground almonds.

prep + cook time 50 minutes **serves** 6
nutritional count per serving 30.2g total fat (11.9g saturated fat); 1722kJ (412 cal); 26.4g carbohydrate; 7.7g protein; 3.3g fibre

Frangipane is a delicious almond-flavoured filling for pies, tarts and cakes.
We've used mixed berries in this recipe, however, you can use any berries you like.
It is important to use frozen berries to prevent the colour bleeding dramatically through the frangipane as it cooks.

sweet pies and tarts

The reason this pie is "impossible" is because the ingredients separate into three layers while baking. The heavy flour sinks to the bottom of the dish and pretends it's pastry, the light coconut floats to the top of the mixture to make a kind of crust or topping. The egg and milk stay happily in the middle making a delicious custard.

impossible pie

½ cup (75g) plain (all-purpose) flour
1 cup (220g) caster (superfine) sugar
¾ cup (60g) desiccated coconut
4 eggs
1 teaspoon vanilla extract
125g (4 ounces) butter, melted
½ cup (40g) flaked almonds
2 cups (500ml) milk

1 Preheat oven to 180°C/350°F. Grease deep 24cm (9½-inch) pie dish.
2 Combine sifted flour, sugar, coconut, eggs, extract, butter and half the nuts in large bowl. Gradually add milk, stirring, until combined. Pour mixture into dish.
3 Bake pie 35 minutes. Remove pie from oven, sprinkle with remaining nuts; bake further 10 minutes.

prep + cook time 55 minutes **serves** 8
nutritional count per serving 25.7g total fat (15.4g saturated fat); 1747kJ (418 cal); 38.2g carbohydrate; 8.1g protein; 1.9g fibre

caramel meringue pies

18 (220g) butternut snap biscuits
380g (12 ounces) canned caramel top 'n' fill
2 egg whites
⅓ cup (75g) caster (superfine) sugar
2 tablespoons shredded coconut

1 Preheat oven to 160°C/325°F. Grease 18 holes of two 12-hole (1½-tablespoons/30ml) shallow round-based patty pans.
2 Place one biscuit over top of each greased pan hole; bake about 4 minutes or until biscuits soften. Using the back of a teaspoon, gently push softened biscuits into pan holes; cool.
3 Increase oven to 240°C/475°F.
4 Place caramel in small bowl; whisk until smooth. Spoon caramel into biscuit cases.
5 Beat egg whites in small bowl with electric mixer until soft peaks form; gradually add sugar, beating until sugar dissolves.
6 Spread meringue over caramel; sprinkle with coconut.
7 Bake pies about 3 minutes or until browned lightly.

prep + cook time 30 minutes **makes** 18
nutritional count per pie 3.4g total fat (2.3g saturated fat); 493kJ (118 cal); 25g carbohydrate; 1.5g protein; 0.8g fibre

crème brûlée praline tarts

1⅓ cups (330ml) pouring cream
⅓ cup (80ml) milk
1 vanilla bean
4 egg yolks
¼ cup (55g) caster (superfine) sugar
pastry
1¼ cups (185g) plain (all-purpose) flour
¼ cup (55g) caster (superfine) sugar
125g (4 ounces) cold butter, chopped coarsely
1 egg yolk
praline
¼ cup (55g) caster (superfine) sugar
2 tablespoons water
1 tablespoon roasted hazelnuts
2 tablespoons unsalted roasted pistachios

1 Make pastry.
2 Grease 6-hole (¾-cup/180ml) texas muffin pan. Using 11cm (4½-inch) cutter, cut six rounds from pastry. Press rounds into pan holes; prick bases all over with fork. Refrigerate 30 minutes.
3 Preheat oven to 160°C/325°F.
4 Combine cream and milk in small saucepan. Split vanilla bean in half lengthways; scrape seeds into pan. Bring to the boil. Beat egg yolks and sugar in small bowl with electric mixer until thick and creamy. Gradually whisk hot cream mixture into egg mixture. Pour warm custard into pastry cases.
5 Bake tarts about 30 minutes or until set. Cool 15 minutes. Refrigerate 1 hour.
6 Meanwhile, make praline.
7 Preheat grill (broiler).
8 Remove tarts from pan; place on oven tray. Sprinkle custard with praline; grill until praline caramelises. Serve immediately.

pastry Process flour, sugar and butter until coarse. Add egg yolk; process until combined. Knead on floured surface until smooth. Roll pastry between sheets of baking paper until 5mm (¼-inch) thick. Refrigerate 15 minutes.

praline Stir sugar and the water in small saucepan over heat until sugar dissolves. Boil, uncovered, without stirring, about 8 minutes or until golden in colour. Place nuts, in single layer, on greased oven tray. Pour toffee over nuts; stand about 15 minutes or until set. Break toffee into large pieces; process until chopped finely.

prep + cook time 1 hour 20 minutes (+ refrigeration, standing & cooling) **makes** 6
nutritional count per tart 49.8g total fat (29.1g saturated fat); 2901kJ (694 cal); 52.8g carbohydrate; 8.7g protein; 1.8g fibre

It is fine to use just one 300ml carton of cream for this recipe.

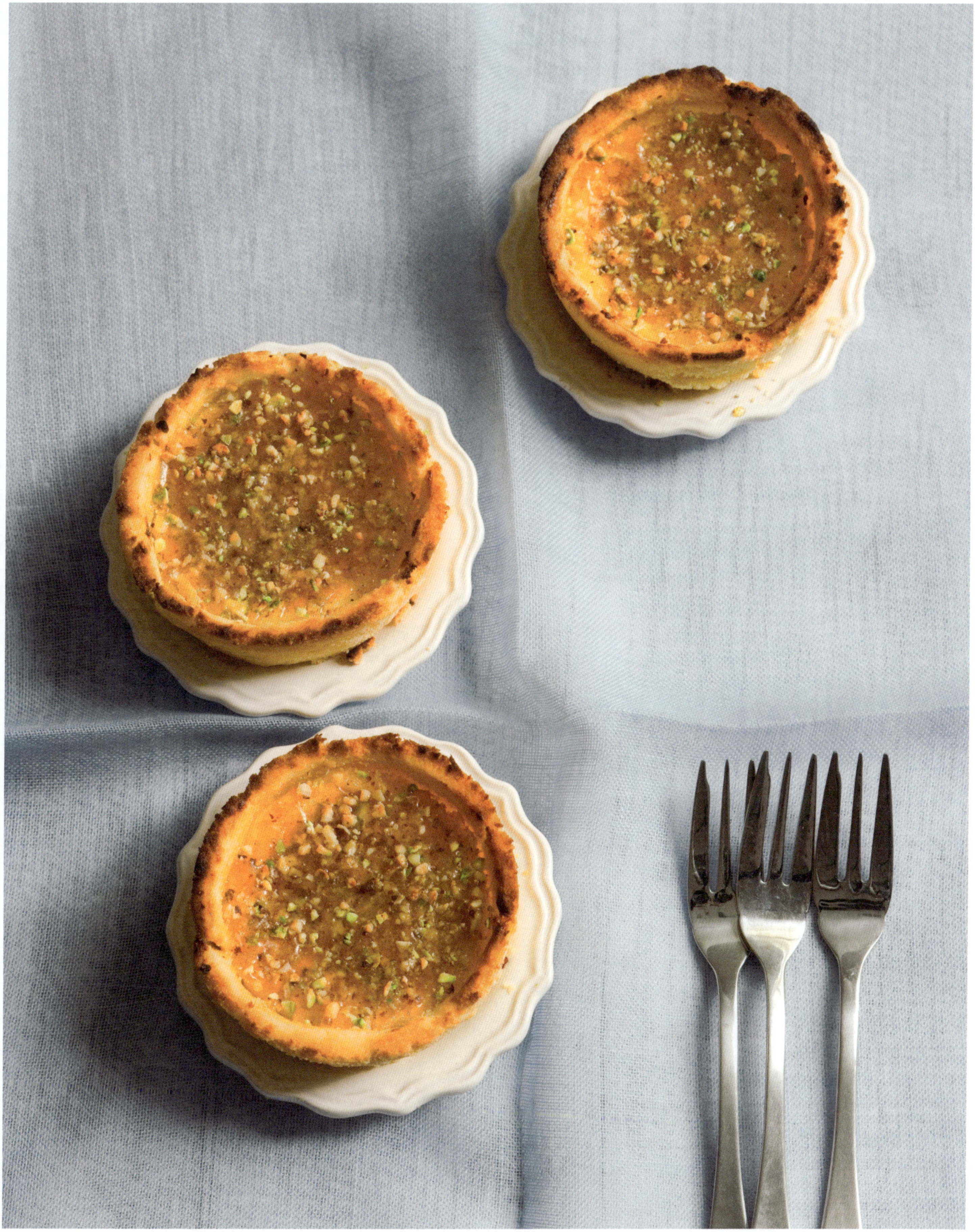

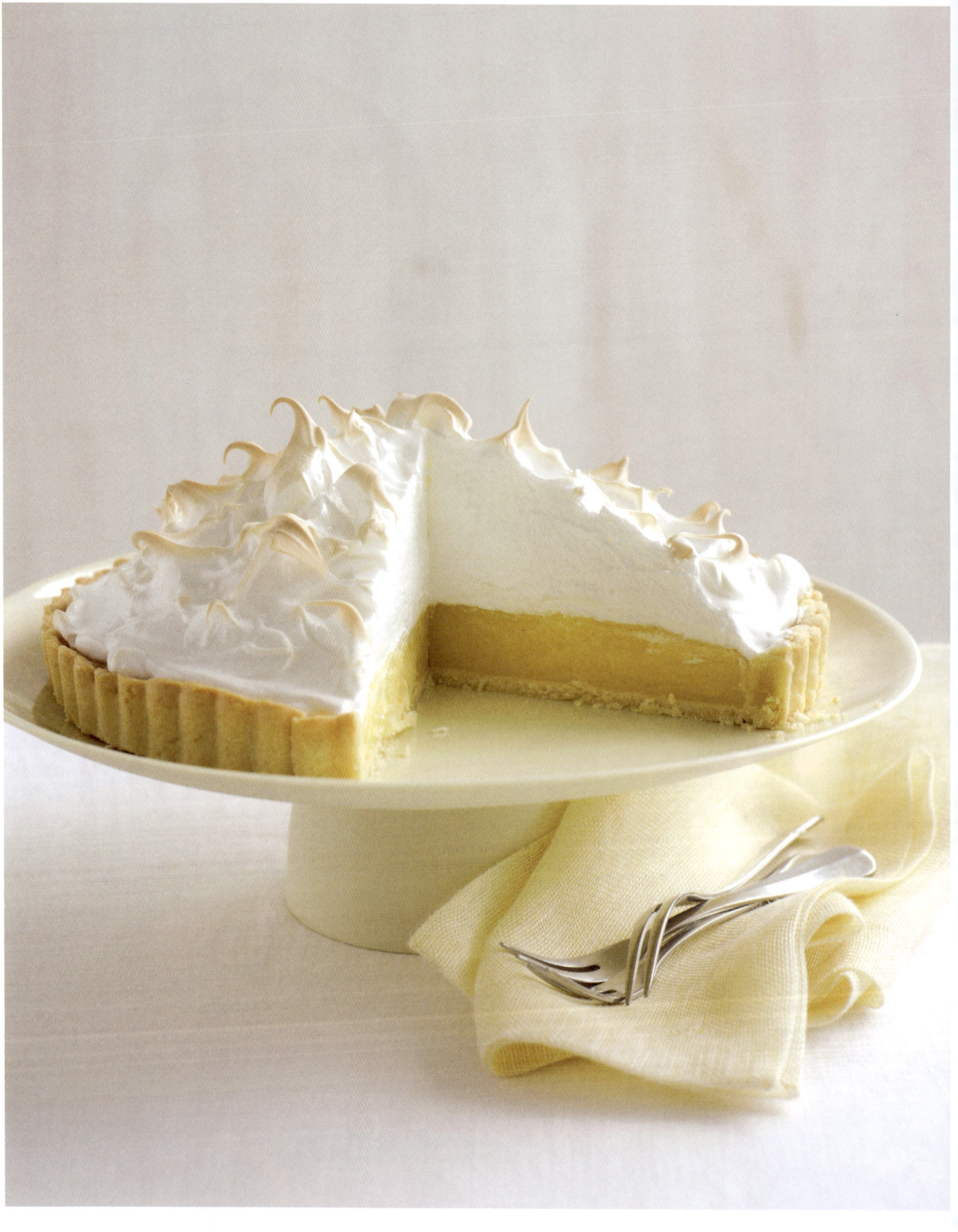

lemon meringue pie

½ cup (75g) cornflour (cornstarch)
1 cup (220g) caster (superfine) sugar
½ cup (125ml) lemon juice
1¼ cups (310ml) water
2 teaspoons finely grated lemon rind
60g (2 ounces) unsalted butter, chopped
3 eggs, separated
½ cup (110g) caster (superfine) sugar, extra
pastry
1½ cups (225g) plain (all-purpose) flour
1 tablespoon icing (confectioners') sugar
140g (4½ ounces) cold butter, chopped
1 egg yolk
2 tablespoons cold water

1 Make pastry.
2 Grease 24cm (9½-inch) round loose-based fluted flan tin. Roll pastry between sheets of baking paper until large enough to line tin. Lift pastry into tin; press into base and side, trim edge. Cover; refrigerate 30 minutes.
3 Preheat oven to 240°C/475°F.
4 Place tin on oven tray; line pastry with baking paper, fill with dried beans or rice. Bake 15 minutes. Remove paper and beans; bake about 10 minutes. Cool pastry case, turn oven off.
5 Meanwhile, combine cornflour and sugar in medium saucepan; gradually stir in juice and the water until smooth. Cook, stirring, over high heat, until mixture boils and thickens. Reduce heat; simmer, stirring, 1 minute. Remove from heat; stir in rind, butter and egg yolks. Cool 10 minutes.
6 Spread filling into pastry case. Cover; refrigerate 2 hours.
7 Preheat oven to 240°C/475°F.
8 Beat egg whites in small bowl with electric mixer until soft peaks form; gradually add extra sugar, beating until sugar dissolves.
9 Roughen surface of filling with fork before spreading with meringue mixture. Bake about 2 minutes or until browned lightly.

pastry Process flour, icing sugar and butter until crumbly. Add egg yolk and the water; process until ingredients come together. Knead dough on floured surface until smooth, enclose with plastic wrap; refrigerate 30 minutes.

prep + cook time 1 hour 10 minutes (+ refrigeration)
serves 10
nutritional count per serving 18.9g total fat (11.6g saturated fat); 1772kJ (424 cal); 57.7g carbohydrate; 5g protein; 0.9g fibre

lemon tart

1¼ cups (185g) plain (all-purpose) flour
⅓ cup (55g) icing (confectioners') sugar
¼ cup (30g) ground almonds
125g (4 ounces) cold butter, chopped
1 egg yolk
2 tablespoons iced water
lemon filling
3 teaspoons finely grated lemon rind
⅓ cup (80ml) lemon juice
3 eggs
½ cup (110g) caster (superfine) sugar
⅔ cup (160ml) thickened (heavy) cream

1 Process flour, icing sugar, ground almonds and butter until crumbly. Add egg yolk and the water; process until ingredients come together. Knead dough on floured surface until smooth, enclose with plastic wrap; refrigerate 30 minutes.
2 Roll pastry between sheets of baking paper until large enough to line shallow 24cm (9½-inch) round loose-based fluted flan tin. Lift pastry into tin; press into base and side, trim edge. Cover; refrigerate 30 minutes.
3 Meanwhile, preheat oven to 200°C/400°F.
4 Place tin on oven tray; line pastry with baking paper, fill with dried beans or rice. Bake 15 minutes. Remove paper and beans; bake about 10 minutes or until browned lightly.
5 Meanwhile, make lemon filling.
6 Reduce oven to 180°C/350°F.
7 Pour lemon filling into pastry case. Bake tart about 30 minutes or until filling has set slightly; cool. Refrigerate until cold.
8 Serve tart dusted with a little sifted icing sugar.

lemon filling Whisk ingredients in medium bowl; stand 5 minutes.

prep + cook time 1 hour 30 minutes (+ refrigeration) **serves** 8
nutritional count per serving 25.3g total fat (14.3g saturated fat); 1714kJ (410 cal); 38.5g carbohydrate; 6.7g protein; 1.3g fibre

Don't overcook the filling. The custard should feel firm around the outside of the tart, but still a bit wobbly in the middle – it will set as the tart cools.
This tart is best made a day ahead and stored in the refrigerator.

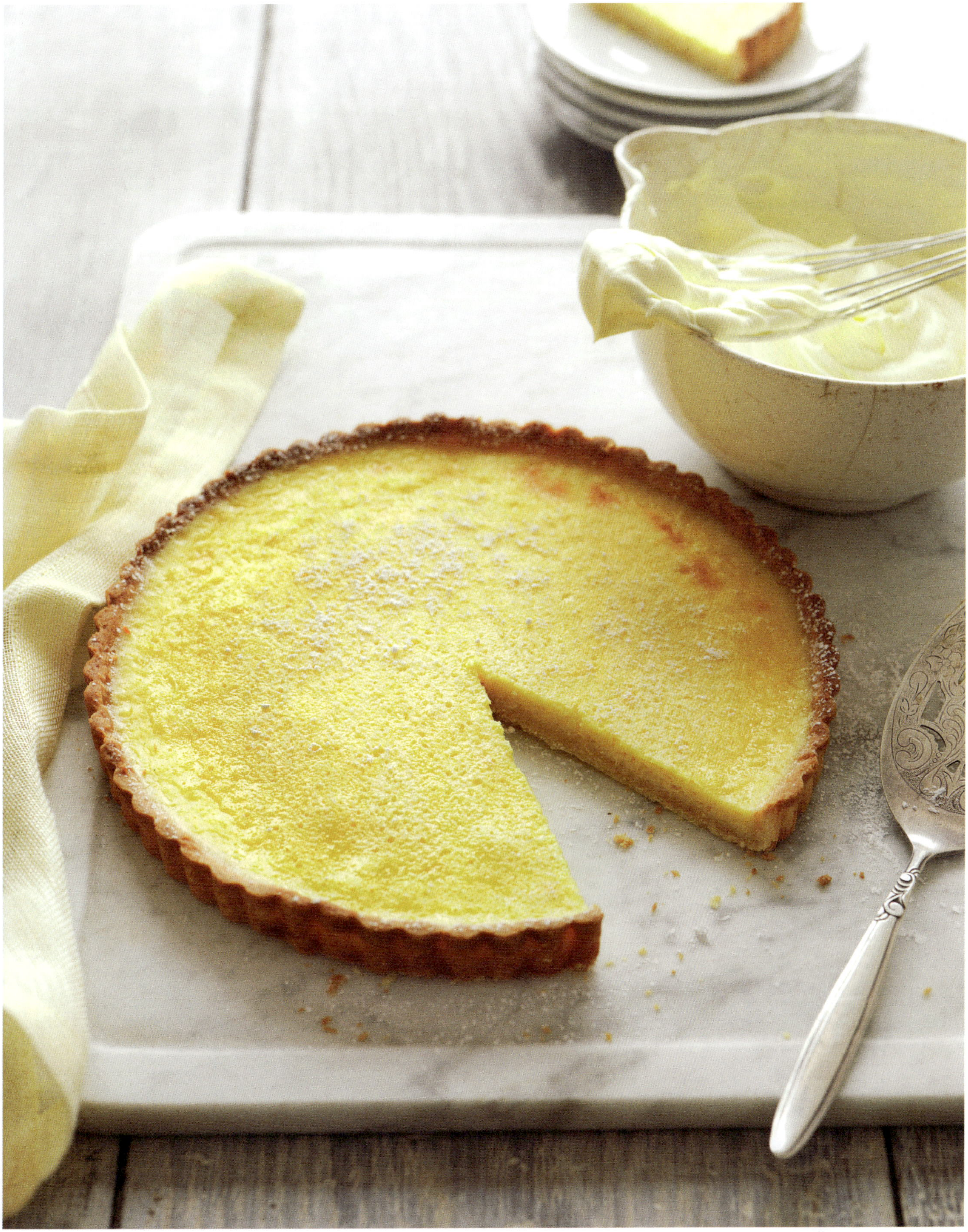

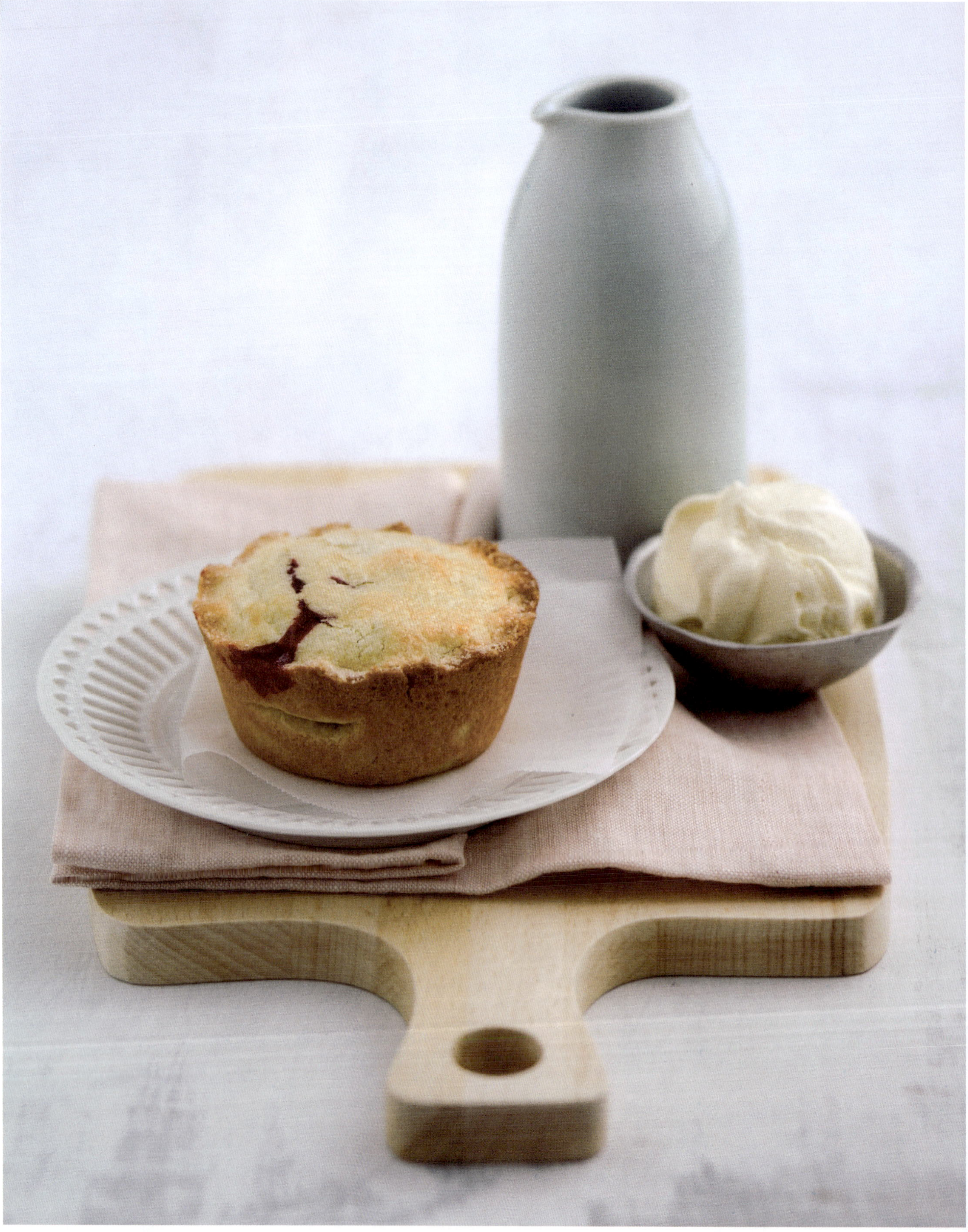

berry and rhubarb pies

2 cups (220g) coarsely chopped rhubarb
¼ cup (55g) caster (superfine) sugar
2 tablespoons water
1 tablespoon cornflour (cornstarch)
2 cups (300g) frozen mixed berries
1 egg white
2 teaspoons caster (superfine) sugar, extra

pastry
1⅔ cups (250g) plain (all-purpose) flour
⅓ cup (75g) caster (superfine) sugar
150g (4½ ounces) cold butter, chopped coarsely
1 egg yolk

1 Make pastry.
2 Place rhubarb, sugar and half the water in medium saucepan; bring to the boil. Reduce heat; simmer, covered, about 3 minutes or until rhubarb is tender. Blend cornflour with the remaining water; stir into rhubarb mixture. Stir over heat until mixture boils and thickens. Remove from heat; stir in berries. Cool.
3 Grease 6-hole (¾-cup/180ml) texas muffin pan. Roll two-thirds of the pastry between sheets of baking paper until 5mm (¼-inch) thick. Using 12cm (5-inch) cutter, cut six rounds from pastry. Press rounds into pan holes. Refrigerate 30 minutes.
4 Preheat oven to 200°C/400°F.
5 Roll remaining pastry between sheets of baking paper until 5mm (¼-inch) thick. Using 9cm (3½-inch) cutter, cut six rounds from pastry.
6 Divide fruit mixture among pastry cases.
7 Brush edge of 9cm (3½-inch) rounds with egg white; place over filling. Press edges firmly to seal. Brush tops with egg white; sprinkle with extra sugar.
8 Bake pies about 30 minutes. Stand in pan 10 minutes. Using palette knife, loosen pies from edge of pan before lifting out. Serve warm.

pastry Process flour, sugar and butter until coarse. Add egg yolk; process until combined. Knead dough on floured surface until smooth, enclose with plastic wrap; refrigerate 30 minutes.

prep + cook time 1 hour 10 minutes (+ refrigeration)
makes 6
nutritional count per pie 22.1g total fat (13.9g saturated fat); 1946kJ (464 cal); 57.1g carbohydrate; 7.2g protein; 3.9g fibre

You need four large stems of rhubarb to get the required amount of chopped rhubarb.

mixed berry coulis cheese tart

250g (8 ounces) granita biscuits
125g (4 ounces) butter, melted
2 teaspoons finely grated lemon rind
1 teaspoon gelatine
2 tablespoons water
250g (8 ounces) cream cheese
395g (12½ ounces) canned sweetened condensed milk
2 tablespoons lemon juice

berry coulis
1 cup (150g) frozen mixed berries, thawed
¼ cup (60ml) lemon juice
2 tablespoons icing (confectioners') sugar

1 Grease 24cm (9½-inch) shallow, loose-based fluted flan tin.
2 Blend or process biscuits until mixture resembles fine breadcrumbs. Add butter and rind; process until combined. Press biscuit mixture evenly over base and three-quarters of the way up side of tin. Cover; refrigerate about 1 hour or until firm.
3 Blend or process ingredients for berry coulis until smooth.
4 Sprinkle gelatine over the water in small heatproof jug; stand jug in small saucepan of simmering water. Stir until gelatine dissolves; cool 5 minutes.
5 Meanwhile, blend or process cream cheese, condensed milk and juice until smooth.
6 Stir gelatine into cream cheese mixture; pour mixture into biscuit case. Drizzle 2 tablespoons of the berry coulis over the top of cream cheese mixture; using skewer, gently swirl coulis into cream cheese mixture for marbled effect. Cover; refrigerate 4 hours or overnight. Refrigerate remaining coulis, covered, until required.
7 Serve tart with remaining coulis.

prep + cook time 35 minutes (+ refrigeration)
serves 10
nutritional count per serving 24.4g total fat (15.1g saturated fat); 1751kJ (419 cal); 43.2g carbohydrate; 8.4g protein; 1.8g fibre

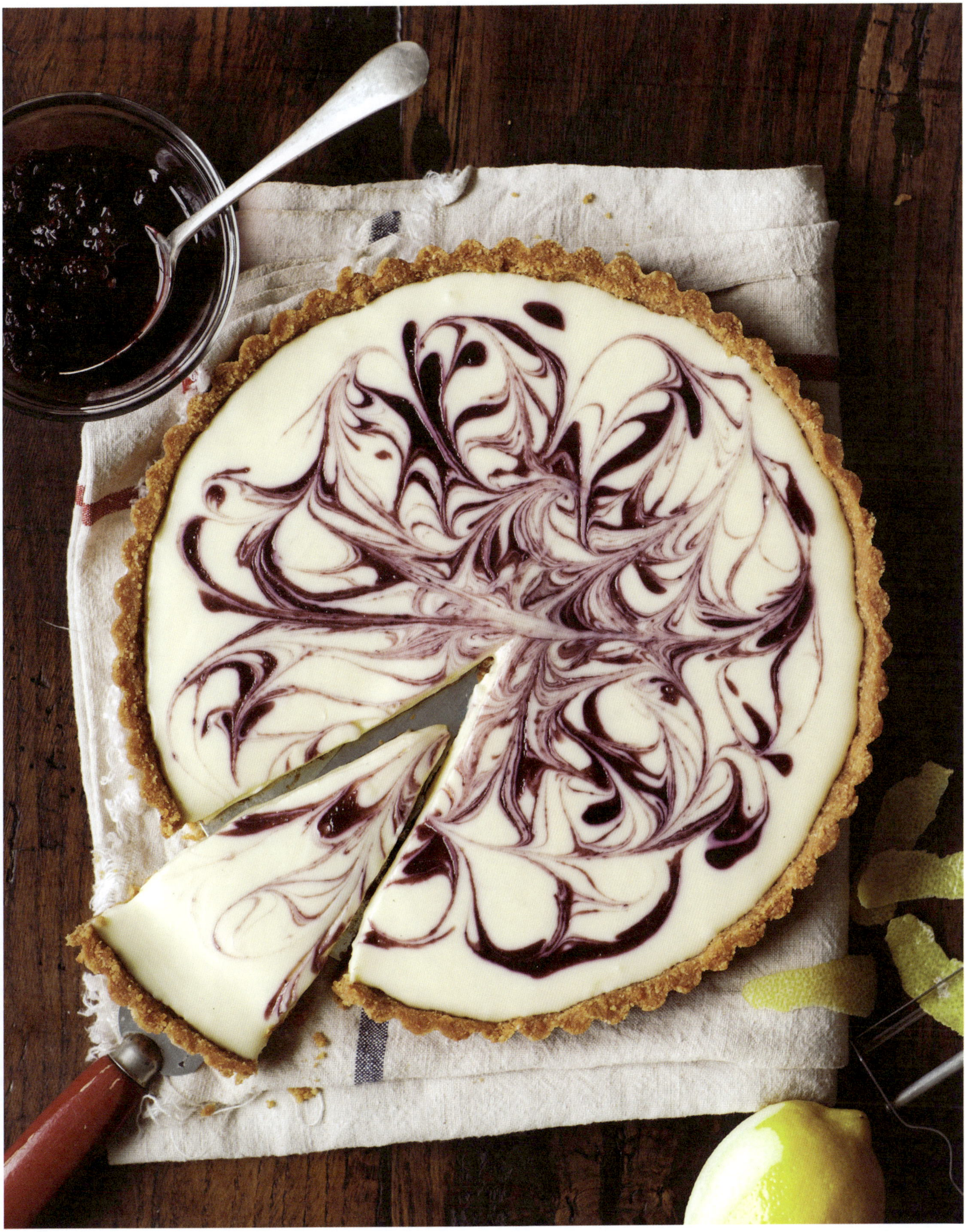

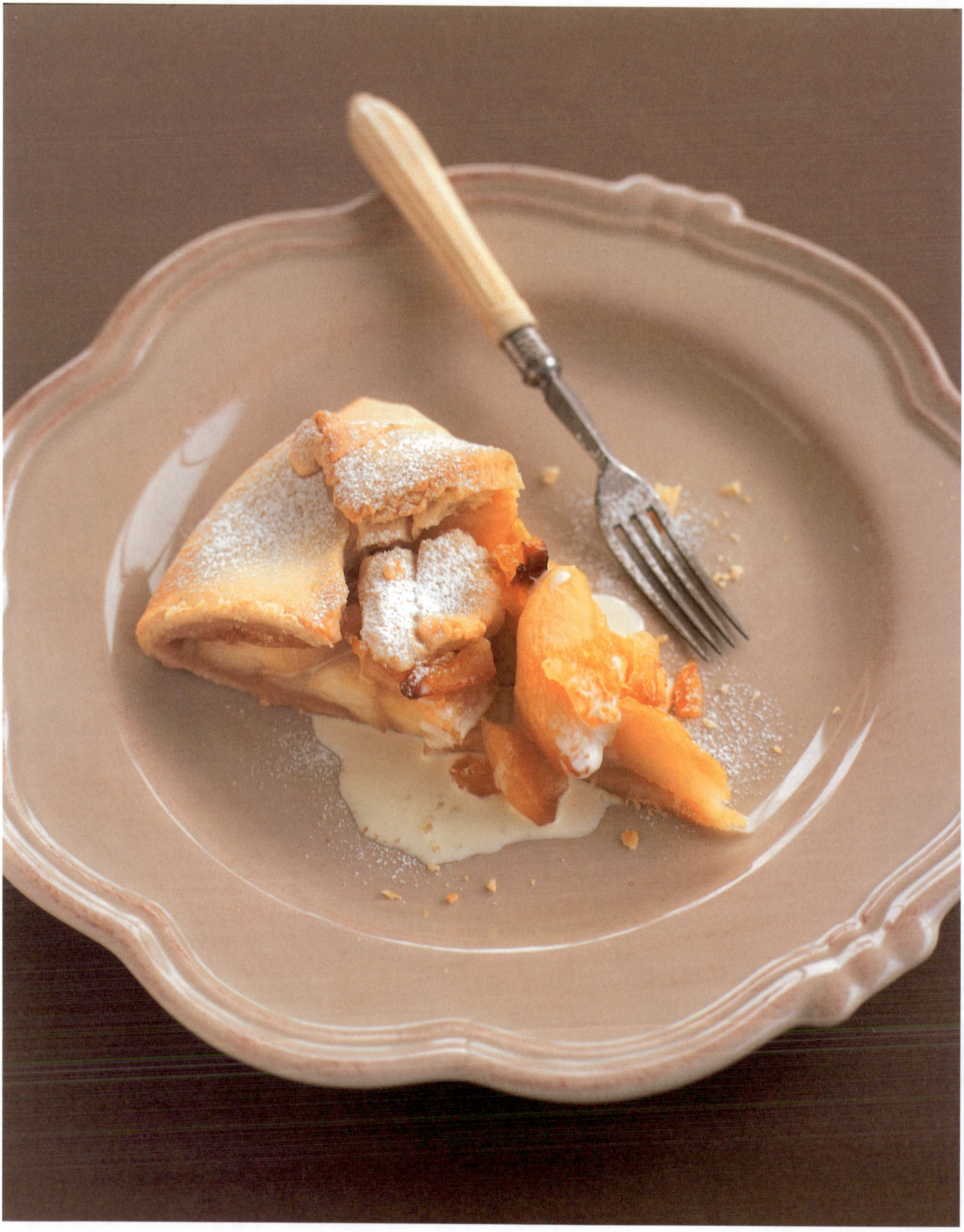

apple and marmalade freeform pie

2½ cups (375g) plain (all-purpose) flour
185g (6 ounces) cold butter, chopped
2 egg yolks
½ cup (60g) finely grated cheddar cheese
¼ cup (60ml) water, approximately
6 medium apples (900g)
2 tablespoons water, extra
2 tablespoons light brown sugar
2 teaspoons milk
citrus marmalade
1 small orange (180g)
1 medium lemon (140g)
1 tablespoon water
1½ cups (375ml) water, extra
2 cups (440g) caster (superfine) sugar, approximately

1 Make citrus marmalade.
2 Process flour and butter until crumbly; add egg yolks, cheese and enough water to form a soft dough. Knead dough on floured surface until smooth, enclose with plastic wrap; refrigerate 30 minutes.
3 Preheat oven to 200°C/400°F.
4 Peel, core and halve apples; cut each half into six wedges. Cook apple with the extra water and sugar in medium saucepan, covered, stirring occasionally, about 5 minutes or until apple has just softened. Cool to room temperature.
5 Roll pastry between sheets of baking paper to form 40cm (16-inch) circle. Remove top sheet of paper, turn pastry onto oven tray. Remove remaining sheet of baking paper.
6 Spread apple mixture over pastry, leaving a 5cm (2-inch) border. Dollop six rounded teaspoons of the marmalade onto apple mixture. Fold pastry up to partly enclose fruit; brush pastry evenly with milk.
7 Bake pie about 30 minutes or until pastry is cooked and browned lightly. Dust with icing (confectioners') sugar, before serving.

citrus marmalade Cut orange and lemon in half; slice thinly. Remove seeds; place seeds in small bowl with the water. Cover; stand overnight. Place fruit in medium microwave-safe bowl; cover with the extra water. Cover; stand overnight. Strain seed mixture into fruit mixture; discard seeds. Cook fruit mixture, covered, in microwave oven on MEDIUM (50%), stirring every 5 minutes, about 30 minutes or until rind softens. Measure fruit mixture, then mix with equal measure of caster sugar in same microwave-safe bowl. Cook, uncovered, in microwave on MEDIUM (50%), stirring every 5 minutes, about 30 minutes or until marmalade jells when tested. Skim surface of marmalade; stand 10 minutes. Pour into hot sterilised jars, seal while hot. (Makes 2 cups.)

prep + cook time 2 hours 20 minutes (+ refrigeration & standing) **serves** 6
nutritional count per serving 31.5g total fat (19.6g saturated fat); 2479kJ (593 cal); 137.6g carbohydrate; 11.3g protein; 5.3g fibre

Purchased marmalade can be used in this recipe.
To test if marmalade has jelled, dip a wooden spoon into marmalade, then hold spoon up with the bowl of the spoon facing you. When marmalade is ready, two or three drops will roll down the spoon and join in a heavy drop.
You can use the remaining marmalade on slices of toasted ciabatta whenever you feel like it. Make the marmalade the day before you make the pie, if possible.

sweet pies and tarts

coconut and passionfruit custard pie

½ cup (75g) plain (all-purpose) flour
1 cup (220g) caster (superfine) sugar
1 cup (80g) desiccated coconut
4 eggs, beaten lightly
2 teaspoons vanilla extract
125g (4 ounces) butter, melted
1⅓ cups (330ml) milk
½ cup (125ml) passionfruit pulp
1 tablespoon icing (confectioners') sugar

1 Preheat oven to 200°C/400°F. Grease straight-sided 24cm (9½-inch) pie dish.
2 Sift flour into large bowl; stir in remaining ingredients, except for icing sugar. Pour mixture into pie dish.
3 Bake pie about 1 hour or until browned lightly and set.
4 Serve pie dusted with sifted icing sugar.

prep + cook time 1 hour 10 minutes **serves** 8
nutritional count per serving 23.8g total fat (15.6g saturated fat); 1647kJ (394 cal); 38.1g carbohydrate; 7g protein; 4.1g fibre

serving suggestion Thick (double) cream.

You will need about six passionfruit for this recipe. The base of this dish should have a layer of custard after baking.

mini berry pies

300g (9½ ounces) frozen mixed berries
¼ cup (55g) caster (superfine) sugar
2 teaspoons cornflour (cornstarch)
1 tablespoon water
5 sheets shortcrust pastry
1 egg white
1 tablespoon caster (superfine) sugar, extra

1 Preheat oven to 200°C/400°F. Grease three 12-hole (1-tablespoon/20ml) mini muffin pans.
2 Stir berries and sugar in small saucepan over heat until sugar dissolves. Bring to the boil. Blend cornflour with the water; stir into berry mixture. Stir over heat until mixture boils and thickens. Cool.
3 Using 6cm (2¼-inch) cutter, cut 36 rounds from pastry; press rounds into pan holes. Divide berry mixture into pastry cases.
4 Using 4cm (1½-inch) cutter, cut 36 rounds from remaining pastry; top pies with rounds. Press edges firmly to seal. Brush tops with egg white; sprinkle with extra sugar. Make small cut in top of each pie.
5 Bake pies about 20 minutes. Stand in pan 10 minutes before turning, top-side up, onto wire rack. Serve pies warm or cold.

prep + cook time 45 minutes **makes** 36
nutritional count per pie 0.4g total fat (3.4g saturated fat); 460kJ (110 cal); 12.9g carbohydrate; 1.7g protein; 0.7g fibre

quince tart tatin

4 medium quinces (1.2kg)
1 cup (220g) caster (superfine) sugar
1 litre (4 cups) water
1 teaspoon finely grated orange rind
¼ cup (60ml) orange juice
40g (1½ ounces) butter

pastry
1 cup (150g) plain (all-purpose) flour
¼ cup (40g) icing (confectioners') sugar
100g (3 ounces) butter, chopped
1 egg yolk
1 tablespoon cold water, approximately

1 Peel and core quinces; quarter lengthways.
2 Place quince in large saucepan with sugar, the water, rind and juice; bring to the boil. Reduce heat; simmer, covered, about 2½ hours or until quince is rosy in colour. Using slotted spoon, remove quince from syrup; bring syrup to the boil. Boil, uncovered, until syrup reduces to ¾ cup. Stir in butter.
3 Meanwhile, make pastry.
4 Preheat oven to 200°C/400°F. Line base of deep 22cm (9-inch) round cake pan with baking paper.
5 Place quince, rounded-sides down, in pan; pour syrup over quince.
6 Roll pastry between sheets of baking paper until large enough to line base of pan. Lift pastry into pan, tucking pastry down side of pan.
7 Bake tart about 30 minutes or until pastry is browned lightly. Cool 5 minutes. Turn tart onto serving plate.

pastry Process flour, sugar and butter until crumbly. Add egg yolk and enough of the water to make ingredients just come together. Knead dough on floured surface until smooth, enclose with plastic wrap; refrigerate 30 minutes.

prep + cook time 3 hours 20 minutes (+ refrigeration)
serves 6
nutritional count per serving 20.7g total fat (12.9g saturated fat); 2098kJ (502 cal); 77.5g carbohydrate; 4.1g protein; 11.3g fibre

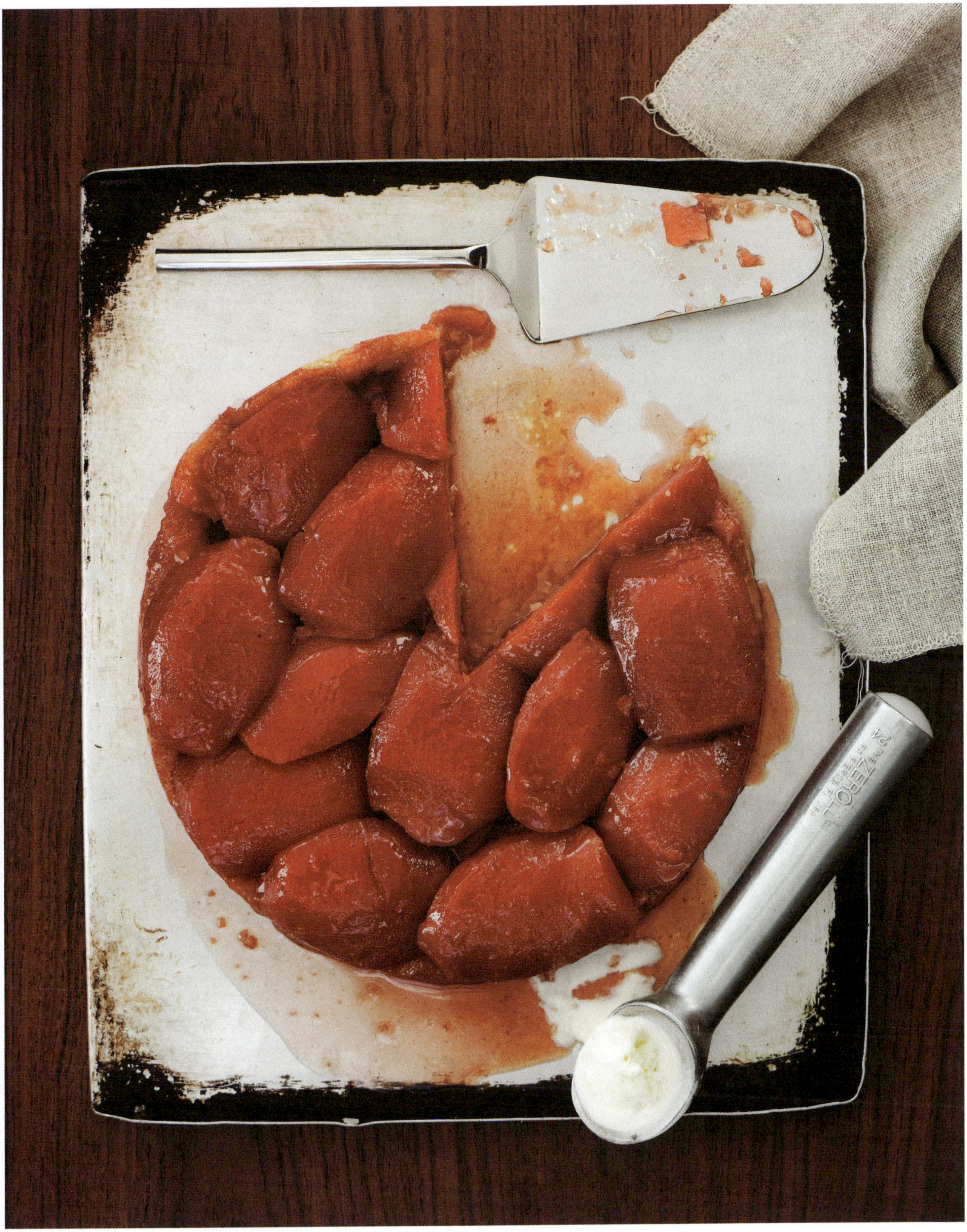
ZEROLL

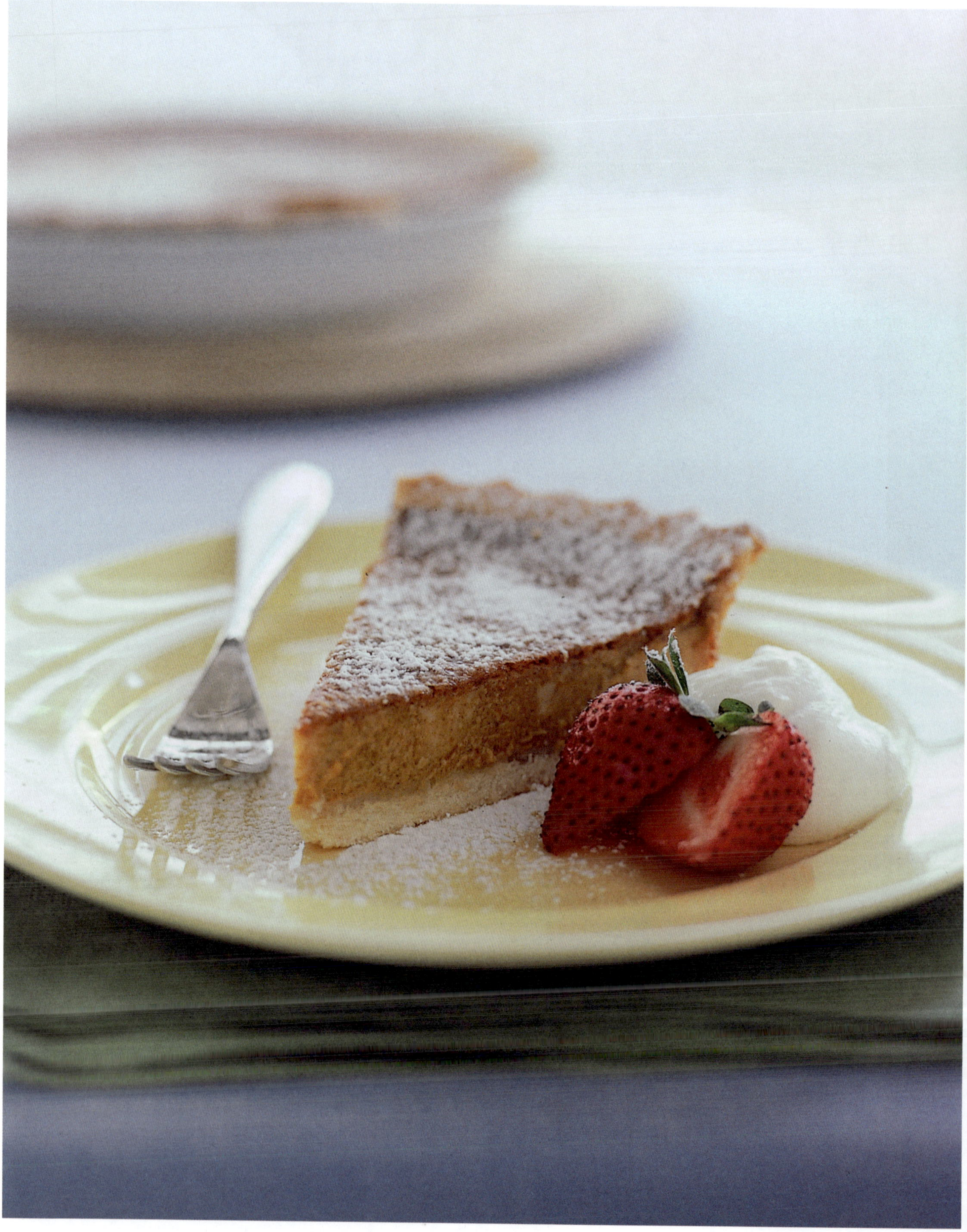

pumpkin pie

1 cup (150g) plain (all-purpose) flour
¼ cup (35g) self-raising flour
2 tablespoons cornflour (cornstarch)
2 tablespoons icing (confectioners') sugar
125g (4 ounces) cold butter, chopped coarsely
2 tablespoons cold water, approximately
filling
2 eggs
¼ cup (55g) firmly packed light brown sugar
2 tablespoons maple syrup
1 cup cooked mashed pumpkin
⅔ cup (160ml) evaporated milk
1 teaspoon ground cinnamon
½ teaspoon ground nutmeg
pinch ground allspice

1 Sift flours and sugar into medium bowl; rub in butter. Add enough water to make ingredients come together. Knead dough on floured surface until smooth. Wrap in plastic wrap; refrigerate 30 minutes.
2 Preheat oven to 200°C/400°F. Grease 22cm (9-inch) pie dish.
3 Roll pastry between sheets of baking paper until large enough to line dish. Lift pastry into dish; press into base and side, trim edge. Use scraps of pastry to make a double edge of pastry; trim and decorate edge.
4 Place dish on oven tray; line pastry with baking paper, fill with dried beans or rice. Bake 10 minutes. Remove paper and beans; bake further 10 minutes. Cool.
5 Reduce oven to 180°C/350°F.
6 Make filling; pour into pastry case.
7 Bake pie about 50 minutes; cool.

filling Beat eggs, sugar and syrup in small bowl with electric mixer until thick. Stir in pumpkin and remaining ingredients.

prep + cook time 1 hour 40 minutes (+ refrigeration) **serves** 8
nutritional count per serving 15.8g total fat (9.8g saturated fat); 1287kJ (308 cal); 37.4g carbohydrate; 6.6g protein; 1.3g fibre

serving suggestion Dust pie with a little sifted icing (confectioners') sugar and serve with cream or ice-cream.

roasted nectarine tart

8 nectarines (1.3kg), halved, stones removed
¼ cup (60ml) orange juice
½ cup (110g) firmly packed light brown sugar
pastry
1⅔ cups (250g) plain (all-purpose) flour
⅔ cup (110g) icing (confectioners') sugar
125g (4 ounces) cold butter, chopped
1 egg yolk
1½ tablespoons cold water, approximately
crème pâtissière
1¼ cups (310ml) thickened (heavy) cream
1 cup (250ml) milk
½ cup (110g) caster (superfine) sugar
1 vanilla bean
3 egg yolks
2 tablespoons cornflour (cornstarch)
80g (2½ ounces) unsalted butter, chopped

1 Make pastry.
2 Grease 10cm x 34cm (4-inch x 13½-inch) loose-based fluted flan tin; place tin on oven tray.
3 Roll pastry between sheets of baking paper until large enough to line tin. Lift pastry into tin; press into base and sides, trim edges. Cover; refrigerate 30 minutes.
4 Preheat oven to 180°C/350°F.
5 Line pastry with baking paper, fill with dried beans or rice. Bake 10 minutes. Remove paper and beans; bake about 10 minutes or until browned lightly. Cool.
6 Meanwhile, make crème pâtissière.
7 Increase oven to 220°C/425°F. Place nectarines, in single layer, in large shallow baking dish; sprinkle with juice and sugar. Roast, uncovered, about 20 minutes or until nectarines are soft. Cool.
8 Meanwhile, spoon crème pâtissière into pastry case. Cover; refrigerate 30 minutes or until firm.
9 Arrange nectarines on tart; drizzle with pan juices.

pastry Process flour, sugar and butter until crumbly. Add egg yolk and enough of the water until ingredients just come together. Knead dough on floured surface until smooth, enclose with plastic wrap; refrigerate 30 minutes.

crème pâtissière Combine cream, milk and sugar in medium saucepan. Split vanilla bean in half lengthways, scrape seeds into pan, then add pod; bring to the boil. Remove from heat; discard pod. Beat egg yolks in small bowl with electric mixer until thick and creamy; beat in cornflour. Gradually beat in hot cream mixture. Strain mixture into same cleaned saucepan; stir over heat until mixture boils and thickens. Remove from heat; whisk in butter. Cover surface of custard with plastic wrap; cool to room temperature.

prep + cook time 1 hour 30 minutes (+ refrigeration)
serves 8
nutritional count per serving 40.7g total fat (25.5g saturated); 3043kJ (728 cal); 80g carbohydrate; 8.6g protein; 4.6g fibre

It is fine to you just one 300ml carton of cream for this recipe.

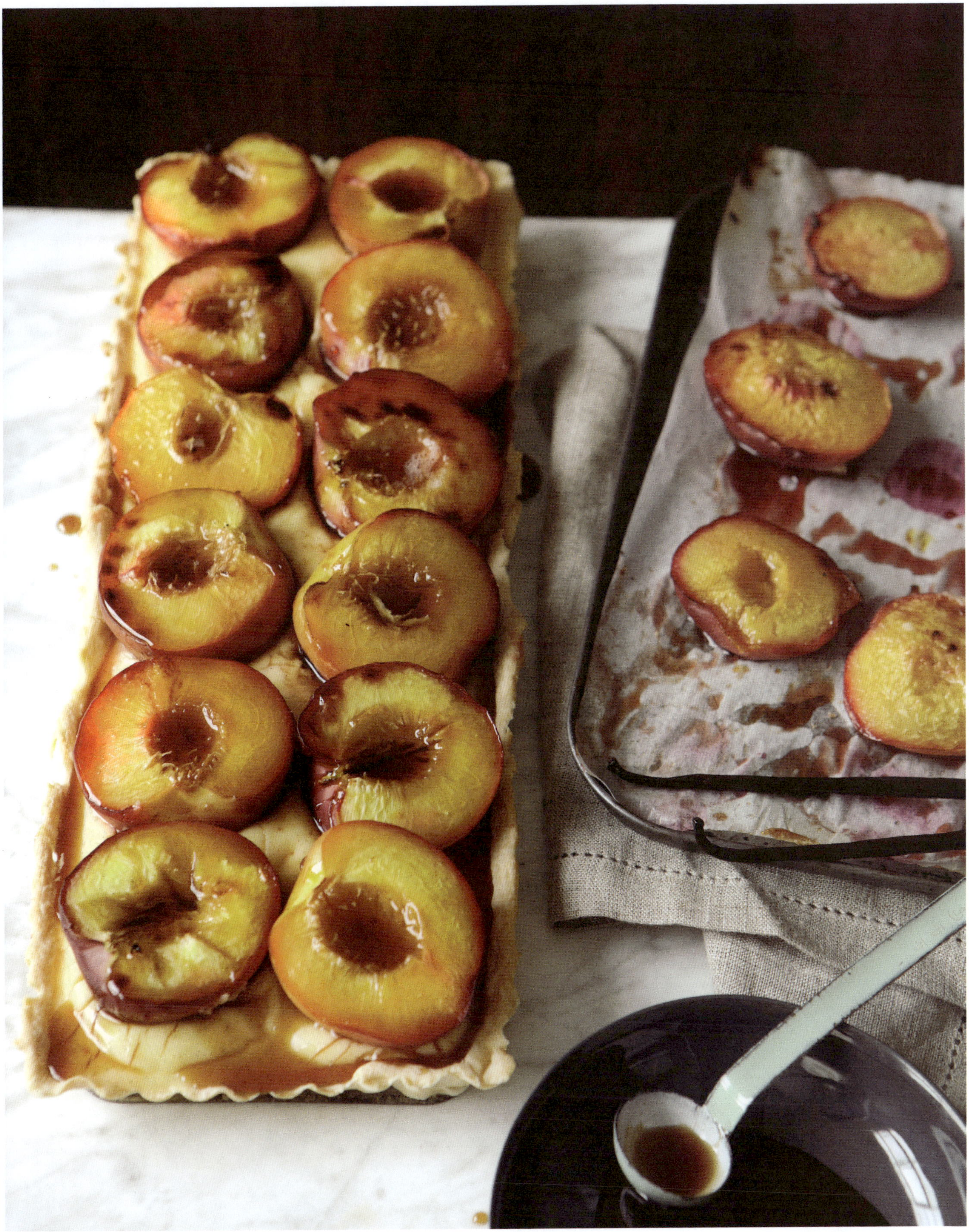

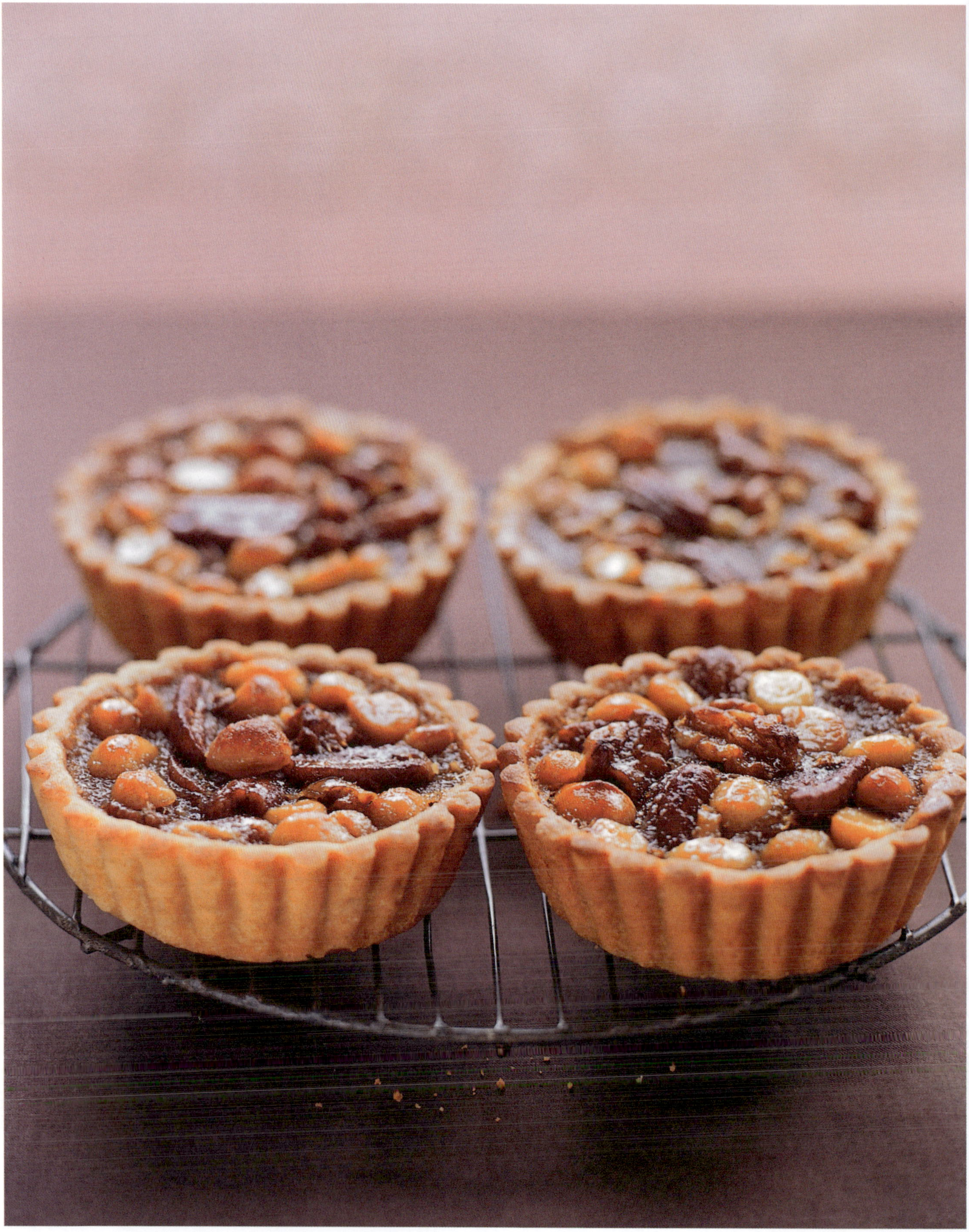

pecan, macadamia and walnut tartlets

1¼ cups (185g) plain (all-purpose) flour
⅓ cup (55g) icing (confectioners') sugar
¼ cup (30g) ground almonds
125g (4 ounces) cold butter, chopped coarsely
1 egg yolk
filling
⅓ cup (50g) roasted macadamias
⅓ cup (35g) roasted pecans
⅓ cup (35g) roasted walnuts
2 tablespoons light brown sugar
1 tablespoon plain (all-purpose) flour
40g (1½ ounces) butter, melted
2 eggs
¾ cup (180ml) pure maple syrup

1 Process flour, sugar and ground almonds with butter until combined. Add egg yolk and process until ingredients just come together. Knead dough on floured surface until smooth, enclose with plastic wrap; refrigerate 30 minutes.
2 Grease four 10cm (4-inch) round loose-based fluted flan tins. Divide pastry into four portions. Roll each portion between sheets of baking paper until large enough to line tins. Lift pastry into tins; press into base and side, trim edge. Cover; refrigerate 1 hour.
3 Preheat oven to 200°C/400°F.
4 Place tins on oven tray; line each pastry case with baking paper, fill with dried beans or rice. Bake 10 minutes. Remove paper and beans; bake about 7 minutes or until browned lightly. Cool.
5 Reduce oven to 180°C/350°F.
6 Make filling; spoon into pastry cases.
7 Bake tartlets about 25 minutes. Cool.

filling Combine ingredients in medium bowl.

prep + cook time 45 minutes (+ refrigeration)
makes 4
nutritional count per tartlet 64.7g total fat (26g saturated fat); 4268kJ (1021 cal); 97.5g carbohydrate; 14.6g protein; 4.6g fibre

chocolate tart

1½ cups (225g) plain (all-purpose) flour
½ cup (110g) caster (superfine) sugar
140g (4½ ounces) cold butter, chopped coarsely
1 egg, beaten lightly
1 teaspoon cocoa powder
chocolate filling
2 eggs
2 egg yolks
¼ cup (55g) caster (superfine) sugar
250g (8 ounces) dark eating (semi-sweet) chocolate, melted
200g (6½ ounces) butter, melted

1 Process flour, sugar and butter until crumbly. Add egg, process until ingredients come together. Knead dough on floured surface until smooth, enclose with plastic wrap; refrigerate 30 minutes.
2 Grease 24cm (9½-inch) round loose-based fluted flan tin. Roll pastry between sheets of baking paper until large enough to line tin. Lift pastry into tin; press into base and side, trim edge, prick base all over with fork. Cover; refrigerate 30 minutes.
3 Meanwhile, preheat oven to 200°C/400°F.
4 Make chocolate filling.
5 Place tin on oven tray; line pastry with baking paper, fill with dried beans or rice. Bake 10 minutes. Remove paper and beans; bake about 5 minutes or until pastry has browned lightly. Cool.
6 Reduce oven to 180°C/350°F.
7 Pour chocolate filling into pastry case.
8 Bake tart about 10 minutes or until filling has set; cool 10 minutes. Refrigerate 1 hour. Serve dusted with sifted cocoa powder; top with strawberries, if you like.

chocolate filling Whisk eggs, egg yolks and sugar in medium heatproof bowl over medium saucepan of simmering water (don't let water touch base of bowl) about 15 minutes or until light and fluffy. Gently whisk chocolate and butter into egg mixture.

prep + cook time 1 hour 30 minutes (+ refrigeration)
serves 8
nutritional count per serving 48.1g total fat (32.7g saturated fat); 2934kJ (702 cal); 59.1g carbohydrate; 7.9g protein; 2.5g fibre

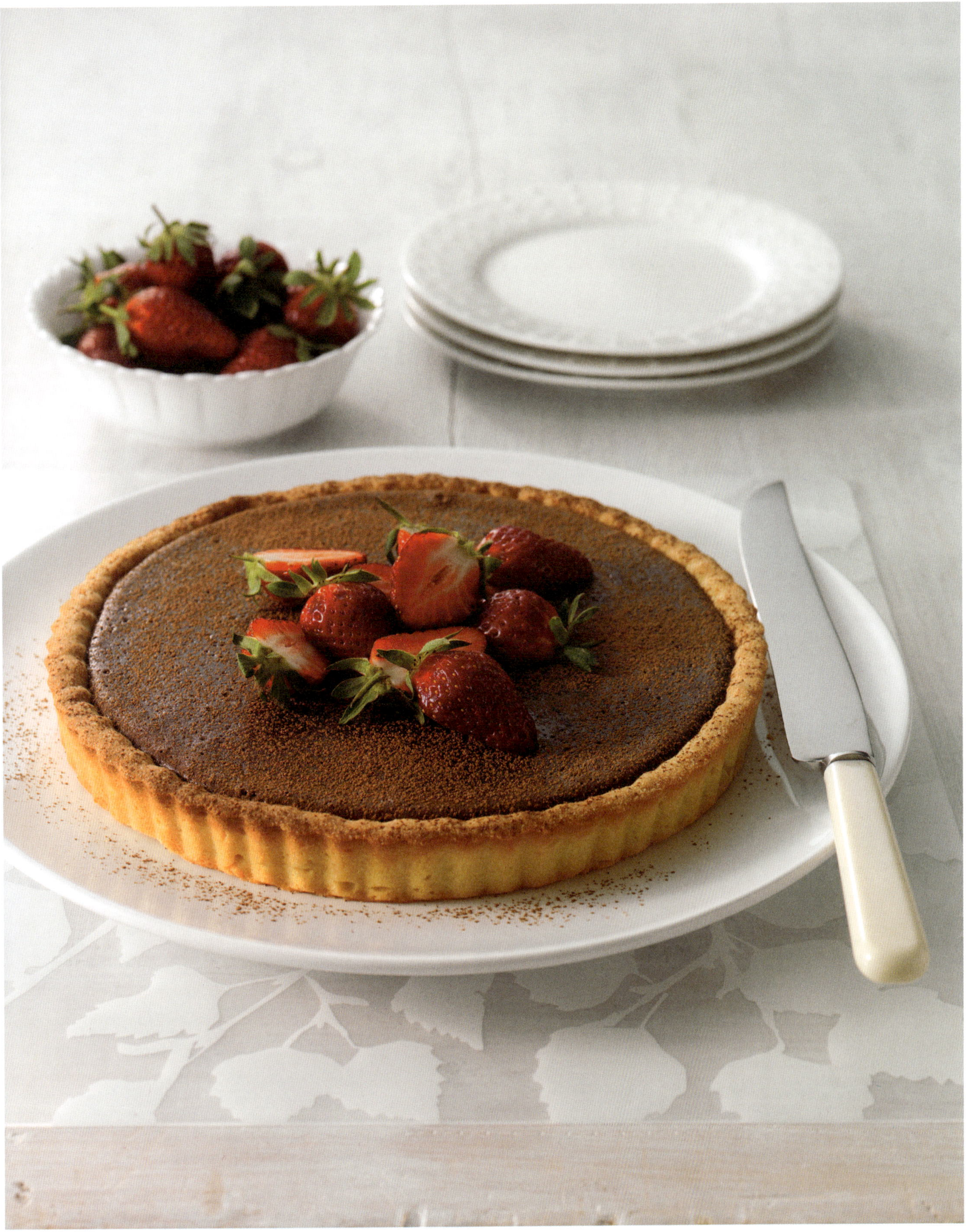

sweet pies and tarts

roasted pear tarts

3 medium pears (700g)
1 tablespoon pure maple syrup
¼ cup (55g) raw sugar
40g (1½ ounces) butter, chopped
1 sheet butter-puff pastry
1 egg, beaten lightly

1 Preheat oven to 180°C/350°F.
2 Peel pears, leaving stems intact; cut in half lengthways. Remove cores carefully. Place pears in baking dish, cut-side up; top with syrup, sugar and butter.
3 Bake pears about 20 minutes or until tender, brushing occasionally with pan juices and turning pears over after 10 minutes.
4 Increase oven to 200°C/400°F. Grease oven tray.
5 Cut pastry sheet in half; place pastry halves about 2cm (¾ inch) apart on oven tray.
6 Place three pear halves, cut-side down, on each pastry half. Brush pears and pastry with pan juices; brush pastry only with a little of the egg.
7 Bake tarts about 20 minutes or until pastry is puffed and browned lightly. To serve, cut pastry so each serving contains a pear half.

prep + cook time 1 hour **serves** 6
nutritional count per serving 12.8g total fat (7.3g saturated fat); 1091kJ (261 cal); 33.9g carbohydrate; 3g protein; 2g fibre

serving suggestion Ice-cream or hot custard.

Pears can be roasted several hours ahead. Tart is best cooked close to serving.

lime chiffon pie

250g (8 ounces) plain sweet biscuits
125g (4 ounces) butter, melted
4 eggs, separated
⅓ cup (75g) caster (superfine) sugar
3 teaspoons gelatine
2 teaspoons finely grated lime rind
⅓ cup (80ml) lime juice
⅓ cup (80ml) water
⅓ cup (75g) caster (superfine) sugar, extra

1 Grease deep 24cm (9½-inch) pie dish.
2 Process biscuits until fine; add butter, process until combined. Press mixture firmly over base and side of dish; refrigerate 30 minutes.
3 Place egg yolks, sugar, gelatine, rind, juice and the water in medium heatproof bowl; whisk over medium saucepan of simmering water until mixture thickens slightly. Remove from heat; pour into large bowl. Cover; cool.
4 Beat egg whites in small bowl with electric mixer until soft peaks form; gradually add extra sugar, beating until sugar dissolves. Fold meringue into filling mixture, in two batches.
5 Spread filling into crumb crust; refrigerate 3 hours.

prep + cook time 35 minutes (+ refrigeration) **serves** 6
nutritional count per serving 27.8g total fat (15.8g saturated fat); 2094kJ (501 cal); 54.8g carbohydrate; 9.3g protein; 0.9g fibre

Store chiffon pie in refrigerator, covered, for up to two days.

fruit mince tarts

2 cups (300g) plain (all-purpose) flour
2 tablespoons custard powder
⅓ cup (75g) caster (superfine) sugar
185g (6 ounces) cold butter, chopped
1 egg yolk
2 tablespoons cold water, approximately
1 egg white, beaten lightly
1 tablespoon icing (confectioners') sugar
fruit mince filling
475g (15 ounces) bottled fruit mince
2 tablespoons brandy
¼ cup (35g) glacé peaches, chopped
¼ cup (35g) glacé apricots, chopped
1 teaspoon grated lemon rind
½ teaspoon grated orange rind

1 Grease two 12-hole deep patty pan trays.
2 Process flour, custard powder, sugar and butter until combined. Add egg yolk and enough of the water to make ingredients just come together. Knead dough on floured surface until smooth, enclose with plastic wrap; refrigerate 30 minutes.
3 Roll two-thirds of the dough between sheets of baking paper until 3mm (⅛-inch) thick. Using 7.5cm (3-inch) cutter, cut 24 rounds from pastry. Lift rounds into pan holes; press into base and side. Reserve pastry scraps. Cover; refrigerate until required.
4 Meanwhile, make fruit mince filling.
5 Preheat oven to 200°C/400°F.
6 Spoon one heaped teaspoon of fruit mince into pastry cases. Roll remaining pastry until 3mm (⅛-inch) thick. Using 4.5cm (1¾-inch) star cutter, cut out 24 stars. Place pastry shapes in centre of tarts; brush with egg white.
7 Bake tarts about 20 minutes or until browned lightly. Serve dusted with sifted icing sugar.

fruit mince filling Combine ingredients in medium bowl.

prep + cook time 1 hour 20 minutes (+ refrigeration)
makes 24
nutritional count per tart 7.3g total fat (4.5g saturated fat); 698kJ (167 cal); 25.6g carbohydrate; 2g protein; 1.1g fibre

These tarts can be made three days ahead; keep, covered, in refrigerator. Reheat in oven about 5 minutes before serving.

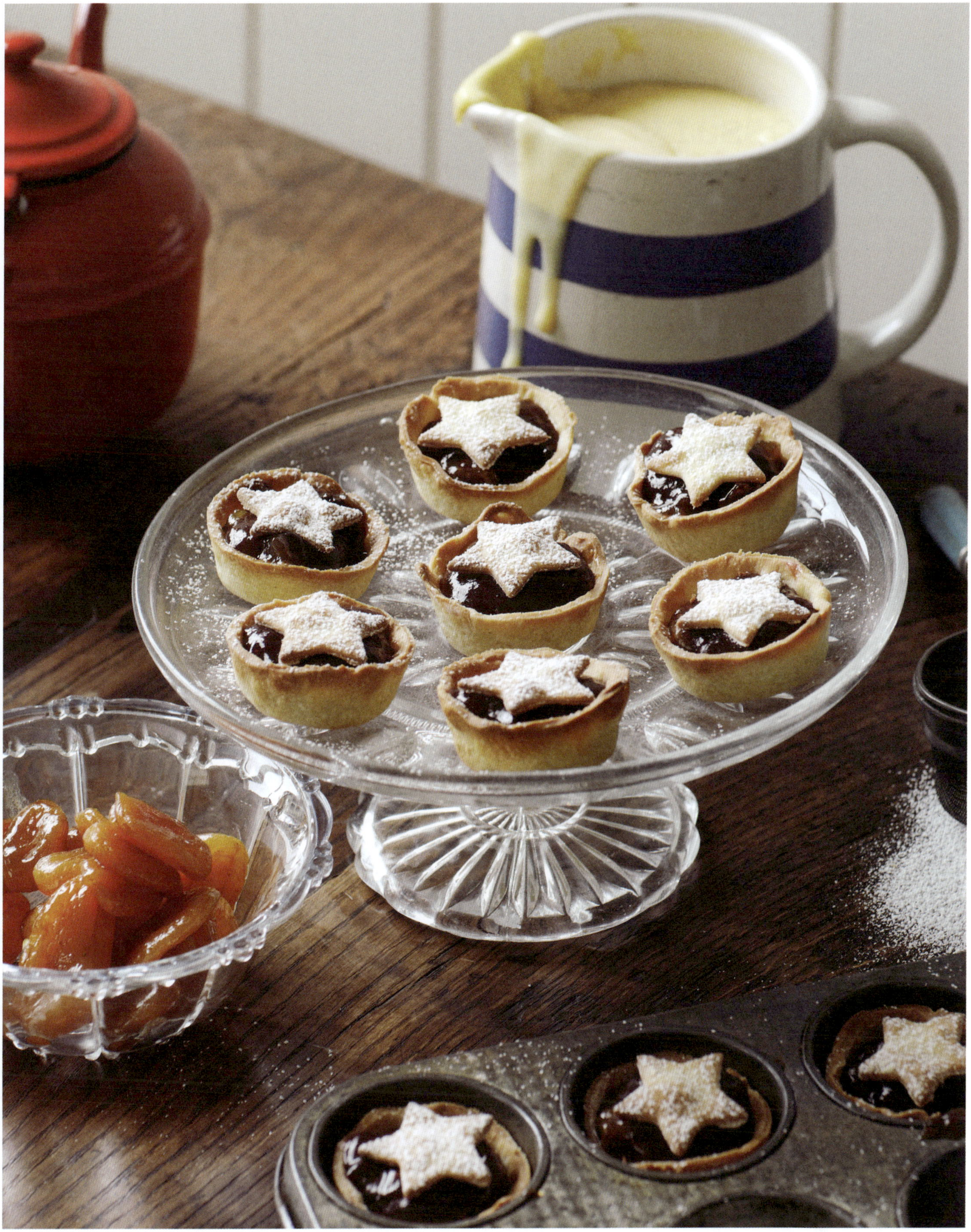

glossary

ALMONDS
blanched whole nuts with the brown skins removed.
flaked paper-thin slices.
ground also called almond meal.

ARROWROOT a starch made from a rhizome, used mostly as a thickening agent. Cornflour can be substituted but does not make as clear a glaze and imparts its own taste.

BAKING PAPER also called parchment paper; a silicone-coated paper used to line baking pans and oven trays so cakes and biscuits won't stick, making removal easy.

BEEF
gravy boneless stewing beef from the shin.
skirt steak lean, flavourful coarse-grained cut from the inner thigh; needs slow-cooking.

BEETROOT also called red beets; firm, round root vegetable.

BICARBONATE OF SODA also called baking or carb soda.

BISCUITS
butternut snap crunchy biscuit made from rolled oats, coconut and golden syrup.
granita also called digestives; made from wheat flakes.
plain chocolate a crisp sweet biscuit with added cocoa powder but having no icing or filling.
plain sweet also called cookies; a crisp sweet biscuit without icing or filling.

BREADCRUMBS, STALE crumbs made by grating, blending or processing 1- or 2-day-old bread.

BUTTER use salted or unsalted butter; 125g is equal to one stick (4 ounces) of butter.

CARAMEL TOP 'N' FILL a caramel filling made from milk and sugar cane. Use straight from the can for slices, tarts and cheesecakes. Has similar qualities to sweetened condensed milk, only having a thicker, more caramel consistency.

CARAWAY SEEDS the small, half-moon-shaped dried seed from a member of the parsley family; adds a sharp anise flavour.

CELERIAC tuberous root with knobbly brown skin, white flesh and a celery-like flavour.

CHEESE
cream cheese commonly known as philadelphia or philly; a soft cow-milk cheese with a fat content ranging from 14% to 33%. Sold in supermarkets.
fetta Greek in origin; a crumbly textured goat- or sheep-milk cheese having a sharp, salty taste. Ripened and stored in salted whey.
goat's made from goat's milk, has an earthy, strong taste. Available soft, crumbly and firm, in various shapes and sizes.
parmesan also called parmigiano; a hard, grainy cow-milk cheese originating in the Parma region of Italy. Curd is salted in brine for a month then aged for up to 2 years.
pizza cheese a commercial blend of grated mozzarella, cheddar and parmesan in varying proportions.
ricotta a soft, sweet, moist, white cow-milk cheese with 8.5% fat content and slightly grainy texture.

CHICKPEAS also called garbanzos, hummus or channa; an irregularly round, sandy-coloured legume. Firm texture even after cooking, a floury mouth-feel and robust nutty flavour; available canned or dried (soak in cold water before use).

CHILLIES use rubber gloves when seeding and chopping fresh chillies as they can burn your skin.

CHOCOLATE, DARK EATING also called semi-sweet; made of cocoa liquor, cocoa butter and sugar.

CINNAMON available both in the piece (sticks or quills) and ground.

CLOVES dried flower buds; used whole or ground. Has a strong scent and taste; use sparingly.

COCONUT
milk not the liquid inside but the diluted liquid from the second pressing. Available in cans and cartons at most supermarkets.
shredded strips of dried coconut.

CORIANDER also called cilantro, pak chee or chinese parsley; bright-green-leafed herb with both pungent aroma and taste. Coriander stems and roots are also used: wash well before use.

CORNFLOUR also known as cornstarch, used as a thickening agent. Available as 100% corn (maize) and wheaten cornflour.

COS LETTUCE also known as romaine lettuce; the traditional caesar salad lettuce.

CREAM
pouring also called pure cream. It has no additives, and contains a minimum fat content of 35%.

glossary

thick we used thick cream with 48% fat content.
thickened a whipping cream containing a thickener. Minimum fat content 35%.
CUMIN also called zeera or comino; resembling caraway in size, is the dried seed of a plant related to the parsley family. Has a spicy, curry-like flavour; also available ground.
CUSTARD POWDER instant mixture used to make pouring custard; similar to North American instant pudding mixes.
EGGPLANT also called aubergine; ranges in size and colour.
EGGS if a recipe calls for raw or barely cooked eggs, exercise caution if there is a salmonella problem in your area.
FENNEL also called finocchio or anise. A crunchy green vegetable slightly resembling celery; eaten raw in salad, cooked or used as an ingredient.
FISH SAUCE called naam pla (Thai) and nuoc naam (Vietnamese). Made from pulverised salted fermented fish; has a pungent smell and strong taste, use according to taste.
FLOUR
plain an all-purpose flour made from wheat.
rice a very fine flour made from ground white rice.
self-raising plain flour sifted with baking powder in the proportion of 1 cup flour to 2 teaspoons baking powder.
soya made from dried soyabeans.
wholemeal flours milled from the whole wheat grain (bran, germ and endosperm). Available in both plain and self-raising varieties.
GARAM MASALA literally meaning blended spices; based on varying proportions of cloves, cardamom, cinnamon, coriander, fennel and cumin, roasted and ground together.
GELATINE we used powdered gelatine. It is also available in sheet form, known as leaf gelatine.
GHEE clarified butter; with the milk solids removed, this fat can be heated to a high temperature without burning.
GINGER, GROUND also called powdered ginger; cannot be substituted for fresh.
GOLDEN SYRUP a by-product of refined sugar cane; pure maple syrup or honey can be substituted.
HAZELNUTS also called filberts; plump, grape-sized, rich, sweet nut.
ground known as hazelnut meal.
KAFFIR LIME LEAVES also called bai magrood and looks like two glossy dark green leaves joined end to end, forming a rounded hourglass shape. Sold fresh, dried or frozen, the dried leaves are less potent so double the number if using them as a substitute for fresh; a strip of fresh lime peel may be substituted for each kaffir lime leaf.
KUMARA the polynesian name of an orange-fleshed sweet potato often confused with yam.
LEMON GRASS also called takrai, serai or serah. A tall, clumping, lemon-smelling and tasting, sharp-edged aromatic tropical grass; the white lower part of the stem is used, finely chopped. Can be found, fresh, dried, powdered and frozen, in supermarkets and Asian food shops.
MAPLE SYRUP, PURE a thin syrup distilled from the sap of the maple tree. Maple-flavoured syrup or pancake syrup is not an adequate substitute for the real thing.
MARMALADE a preserve, usually based on citrus fruit.
MARSALA a sweet, fortified wine.
MILK
evaporated unsweetened canned milk from which water has been extracted by evaporation.
sweetened condensed from which 60% of the water has been removed; the remaining milk is then sweetened with sugar.
MIXED SPICE a blend of ground spices usually consisting of cinnamon, allspice and nutmeg.
MUSHROOMS
button small, cultivated white mushrooms with a mild flavour; use when a recipe calls for an unspecified mushroom.
swiss brown also called roman or cremini. Light to dark brown in colour with full-bodied flavour.
MUSTARD
dijon also called french. Pale brown, creamy, distinctively flavoured, mild french mustard.
wholegrain also called seeded; french-style coarse-grain mustard made from crushed mustard seeds and dijon-style french mustard.

171

glossary

NUTMEG a strong and pungent spice ground from the dried nut of an Indonesian evergreen tree. Usually bought ground, the flavour is more intense if freshly ground from the whole nut (buy in spice shops).

NUTS, HOW TO ROAST place shelled, peeled nuts, in a single layer, on an oven tray; roast in a moderate oven for 8-10 minutes. Be careful to avoid burning nuts.

OIL
peanut pressed from ground peanuts; the most commonly used oil in Asian cooking due to its capacity to handle high heat without burning.
vegetable any number of oils from plant rather than animal fats.

ONION
brown strongly-flavoured onions with a brown skin and creamy flesh; most commonly used onion.
green also called scallion or (incorrectly) shallot; an immature onion picked before the bulb has formed, having a long, bright-green edible stalk.

PINE NUTS also called pignoli; not a nut but a small, cream-coloured kernel from pine cones. They are best roasted before use.

POLENTA also cornmeal; a flour-like cereal made of dried corn (maize). Also the name of the dish made from it.

PRAWNS also called shrimp; varieties include, school, king, royal red, sydney harbour, tiger. Can be bought uncooked (green) or cooked, with or without shells.

PRESERVED LEMON whole or quartered salted lemons preserved in olive oil and lemon juice. Available from delicatessens and specialty food shops. Use the rind only and rinse well under cold water before using.

RHUBARB only eat its thick, celery-like stalks, as the leaves contain a toxic substance.

ROCKET also called arugula, rugula and rucola; peppery green leaf used raw in salads or in cooking.

SESAME SEEDS black and white are the most common of this small oval seed; toast in a heavy-based frying pan over low heat.

SHALLOTS also called french shallots, golden shallots or eschalots; small, elongated, brown-skinned members of the onion family.

SILVER BEET also called swiss chard or, incorrectly, spinach; has fleshy stalks and large leaves.

SPINACH also called english spinach and incorrectly, silver beet.

SUGAR
brown soft, finely granulated sugar retaining molasses for its characteristic colour and flavour.
caster also known as superfine or finely granulated table sugar.
icing sugar also known as confectioners' sugar or powdered sugar; granulated sugar crushed together with a small amount of added cornflour.
raw natural light-brown coloured granulated sugar with a honey-like taste.

SUMAC a purple-red, astringent spice ground from Mediterranean berries; adds a tart, lemony flavour. Can be found in Middle Eastern food stores.

TOMATOES
canned whole peeled tomatoes in natural juices; available diced or crushed. Use undrained.
paste triple-concentrated tomato puree used to flavour soups, stews and sauces.

TREACLE thick, dark syrup not unlike molasses; a by-product of sugar refining.

TUNA reddish, firm flesh; slightly dry. Varieties include bluefin, yellowfin, skipjack or albacore; substitute with swordfish.

TURMERIC also called kamin; a rhizome related to galangal and ginger. Must be grated or pounded to release its acrid aroma and pungent flavour. Known for the golden colour it imparts.

VANILLA BEAN dried long, thin pod from a tropical golden orchid; the minuscule black seeds inside the bean impart a luscious vanilla flavour to cakes and desserts.

VINEGAR, CIDER made from fermented apples.

WHITE FISH FILLETS means non-oily fish; includes bream, flathead, whiting, snapper, dhufish, redfish and ling.

YOGURT we used unflavoured plain yogurt unless specified.

ZUCCHINI also called courgette; harvested when young, its flowers are edible.

conversion chart

MEASURES

One Australian metric measuring cup holds approximately 250ml; one Australian metric tablespoon holds 20ml; one Australian metric teaspoon holds 5ml.

The difference between one country's measuring cups and another's is within a two- or three-teaspoon variance, and will not affect your cooking results. North America, New Zealand and the United Kingdom use a 15ml tablespoon.

All cup and spoon measurements are level. The most accurate way of measuring dry ingredients is to weigh them. When measuring liquids, use a clear glass or plastic jug with the metric markings.

We use large eggs with an average weight of 60g.

DRY MEASURES

METRIC	IMPERIAL
15g	½oz
30g	1oz
60g	2oz
90g	3oz
125g	4oz (¼lb)
155g	5oz
185g	6oz
220g	7oz
250g	8oz (½lb)
280g	9oz
315g	10oz
345g	11oz
375g	12oz (¾lb)
410g	13oz
440g	14oz
470g	15oz
500g	16oz (1lb)
750g	24oz (1½lb)
1kg	32oz (2lb)

LIQUID MEASURES

METRIC	IMPERIAL
30ml	1 fluid oz
60ml	2 fluid oz
100ml	3 fluid oz
125ml	4 fluid oz
150ml	5 fluid oz
190ml	6 fluid oz
250ml	8 fluid oz
300ml	10 fluid oz
500ml	16 fluid oz
600ml	20 fluid oz
1000ml (1 litre)	1¾ pints

LENGTH MEASURES

METRIC	IMPERIAL
3mm	⅛in
6mm	¼in
1cm	½in
2cm	¾in
2.5cm	1in
5cm	2in
6cm	2½in
8cm	3in
10cm	4in
13cm	5in
15cm	6in
18cm	7in
20cm	8in
23cm	9in
25cm	10in
28cm	11in
30cm	12in (1ft)

OVEN TEMPERATURES

The oven temperatures in this book are for conventional ovens; if you have a fan-forced oven, decrease the temperature by 10-20 degrees.

	°C (CELSIUS)	°F (FAHRENHEIT)
Very slow	120	250
Slow	150	300
Moderately slow	160	325
Moderate	180	350
Moderately hot	200	400
Hot	220	425
Very hot	240	475

index

A
apple
  and marmalade freeform pie 153
  pie 127
apricot and plum pie, spiced 132
B
baby rocket quiche 113
bacon
  gluten-free egg, bacon and parmesan pies 107
  liver, mushroom and bacon pies 56
  roast potato and bacon quiche 85
banoffee tart 130
beef
  beef bourguignon and potato pie 78
  beef carbonade pies 86
  beef pies with polenta tops 68
  chunky, and vegetable pie 60
  cottage pie 83
  gluten-free mini meat pies 80
  meat pies 75
  mini beef and guinness pies 72
  steak and kidney pie 84
  sumac beef and pine nut tarts 79
beetroot tart, spinach and 102
berries
  and rhubarb pies 149
  berry frangipane tart 139
  mini berry pies 155
  mixed berry coulis cheese tart 150
C
capsicum, roasted, quiches, prosciutto and 70
caramel meringue pies 141
caramelised fennel tarts 122
caramelised onion tarts 101
celeriac
  crab and celeriac remoulade cups 40
  fish pie with potato and celeriac mash 44
  tuna spinach potato pie 36

cheese
  caramelised leek and brie tartlets 115
  cheese pastries 109
  chicken, spinach and cheese gözleme 18
  fetta and spinach fillo bundles 104
  gluten-free egg, bacon and parmesan pies 107
  goat's cheese and zucchini flower quiches 103
  mixed berry coulis cheese tart 150
  tomato, leek and marinated fetta tartlets 119
chicken
  and fennel pies 13
  and leek pie 9
  and olive empanadas 17
  and vegetable pasties 23
  and vegetable pie 16
  chicken, leek and mushroom pies 22
  chicken, raisin and pine nut empanadas 21
  chicken, spinach and cheese gözleme 18
  mini chicken, celery and thyme pies 24
  pie with parsnip mash 10
  thai chicken curry pies 14
chocolate tart 164
coconut and passionfruit custard pie 154
corn, mushroom, capsicum and potato puddings 121
cottage pie 83
  italian 55
  lentil 120
coulibiac 32
crab see seafood
crème brûlée praline tarts 142
custard pie, coconut and passionfruit 154
custard tarts, portuguese 131

E
egg, bacon and parmesan pies, gluten-free 107
empanadas
  chicken and olive 17
  chicken, raisin and pine nut 21
  pork and olive 71
F
fennel
  caramelised fennel tarts 122
  chicken and fennel pies 13
  crab, fennel and herb quiche 45
fetta and spinach fillo bundles 104
fish see seafood
freeform caramelised leek tarts 108
fruit mince tarts 168
G
gluten-free
  egg, bacon and parmesan pies 107
  mini meat pies 80
goat's cheese and zucchini flower quiches 103
gözleme, chicken, spinach and cheese 18
guinness pies, mini beef and 72
I
impossible pie 140
italian cottage pie 55
L
lamb
  and pine nut little boats 89
  and rosemary pies 59
  italian cottage pie 55
  lamb korma pies 67
  lamb spanakopita 76
  moroccan lamb party pies 64
  moroccan-spiced chunky lamb pies 90
  shepherd's pie 52
leek
  caramelised leek and brie tartlets 115
  chicken and leek pie 9
  chicken, leek and mushroom pies 22

index

(leek continued)
   creamy leek, mushroom and baby pea pies 96
   freeform caramelised leek tarts 108
   tomato, leek and marinated fetta tartlets 119
lemon meringue pie 145
lemon tart 146
lentil cottage pie 120
lime chiffon pie 167
liver, mushroom and bacon pies 56

M
meat pies 75
moroccan lamb party pies 64
moroccan-spiced chunky lamb pies 90
moroccan tart 63
mushrooms
   chicken, leek and mushroom pies 22
   corn, mushroom, capsicum and potato puddings 121
   creamy leek, mushroom and baby pea pies 96
   liver, mushroom and bacon pies 56

N
nectarine tart, roasted 160

O
olives
   chicken and olive empanadas 17
   pork and olive empanadas 71
   tomato, pesto and olive tart 97
onion tarts, caramelised 101

P
pasties, chicken and vegetable 23
pastry 7, 21, 60, 113, 127, 128, 135, 142, 145, 149, 156, 160
   gluten-free 80, 107
   hot water 51
pear cranberry pie 136
pear tarts, roasted 166
pecan, macadamia and walnut tartlets 163
pecan pie 128
pistachio orange pie 135

pork
   pork and olive empanadas 71
   pork pie 51
portuguese custard tarts 131
potatoes
   beef bourguignon and potato pie 78
   corn, mushroom, capsicum and potato puddings 121
   fish pie with potato and celeriac mash 44
   fish pies with cheesy mash 46
   potato and tuna bake 38
   potato samosa 110
   roast potato and bacon quiche 85
   tuna spinach potato pie 36
   veal goulash and potato pies 62
prawn fillo tarts 35
prosciutto and roasted capsicum quiches 70
pumpkin
   pumpkin pie 159
   spinach and pumpkin fillo pie 94

Q
quiche
   baby rocket 113
   crab, fennel and herb 45
   goat's cheese and zucchini flower 103
   lorraine 98
   prosciutto and roasted capsicum 70
   roast potato and bacon 85
   salmon and herb 31
quince tart tatin 156

R
rhubarb pies, berry and 149
rocket quiche, baby 113

S
salmon and herb quiche 31
samosa, potato 110
seafood
   coulibiac 32
   crab and celeriac remoulade cups 40
   crab, fennel and herb quiche 45

(seafood continued)
   creamy fish pie 28
   fish chowder pies 43
   fish pie with potato and celeriac mash 44
   fish pies 27
   fish pies with cheesy mash 46
   macaroni tuna bake 34
   potato and tuna bake 38
   salmon and herb quiche 31
   smoked fish pot pies 49
   smoked salmon pie 39
   smoked trout tarts 30
   tuna spinach potato pie 36
shepherd's pie 52
spanakopita, lamb 76
spinach
   and beetroot tart 102
   and pumpkin fillo pie 94
   chicken, spinach and cheese gözleme 18
   fetta and spinach fillo bundles 104
   pies 93
   tuna spinach potato pie 36
steak and kidney pie 84
sumac beef and pine nut tarts 79

T
thai chicken curry pies 14
tomatoes
   tomato, leek and marinated fetta tartlets 119
   tomato, pesto and olive tart 97
   tomato tarts 114
trout *see* seafood
tuna *see* seafood

V
veal goulash and potato pies 62
vegetable
   chicken and vegetable pasties 23
   chicken and vegetable pie 16
   chunky beef and vegetable pie 60
   roasted vegetable tarts 116
vegetarian tarts 125

Z
zucchini flower quiches, goat's cheese and 103

175

Published in 2011 by ACP Books, Sydney
ACP Books are published by ACP Magazines
a division of Nine Entertainment Co.

ACP BOOKS

General manager Christine Whiston
Associate publisher Seymour Cohen
Editor-in-chief Susan Tomnay
Creative director Hieu Chi Nguyen
Art director Hannah Blackmore
Senior editor Stephanie Kistner
Junior designer Josh Yarbrough
Food director Pamela Clark
Sales & rights director Brian Cearnes
Marketing manager Bridget Cody
Senior business analyst Rebecca Varela
Operations manager David Scotto
Production manager Victoria Jefferys

Published by ACP Books, a division of ACP Magazines Ltd,
54 Park St, Sydney; GPO Box 4088, Sydney, NSW 2001.
phone (02) 9282 8618; fax (02) 9267 9438.
acpbooks@acpmagazines.com.au;
www.acpbooks.com.au
Printed in China by Toppan Leefung Printing Ltd.

Australia Distributed by Network Services,
phone +61 2 9282 8777; fax +61 2 9264 3278;
networkweb@networkservicescompany.com.au
New Zealand Distributed by Southern Publishers Group,
phone +64 9 360 0692; fax +64 9 360 0695 hub@spg.co.nz
South Africa Distributed by PSD Promotions,
phone +27 11 392 6065/6/7; fax +27 11 392 6079/80; orders@psdprom.co.za

Title: The Australian Women's Weekly pie favourites / food director – Pamela Clark.
ISBN: 978-1-74245-072-8 (pbk.)
Notes: Includes index.
Subjects: Pies. Baking. Baked products.
Other Authors/Contributors: Clark, Pamela.
Dewey Number: 641.815

©ACP Magazines Ltd 2011
ABN 18 053 273 546
This publication is copyright. No part of it may be reproduced or transmitted
in any form without the written permission of the publishers.

Additional photography Vanessa Levis
Additional styling Paul Hopper
Photochef Emma McCaskill
Cover Meat pies, page 75

To order books
phone 136 116 (within Australia) or
order online at www.acpbooks.com.au

Send recipe enquiries to:
recipeenquiries@acpmagazines.com.au